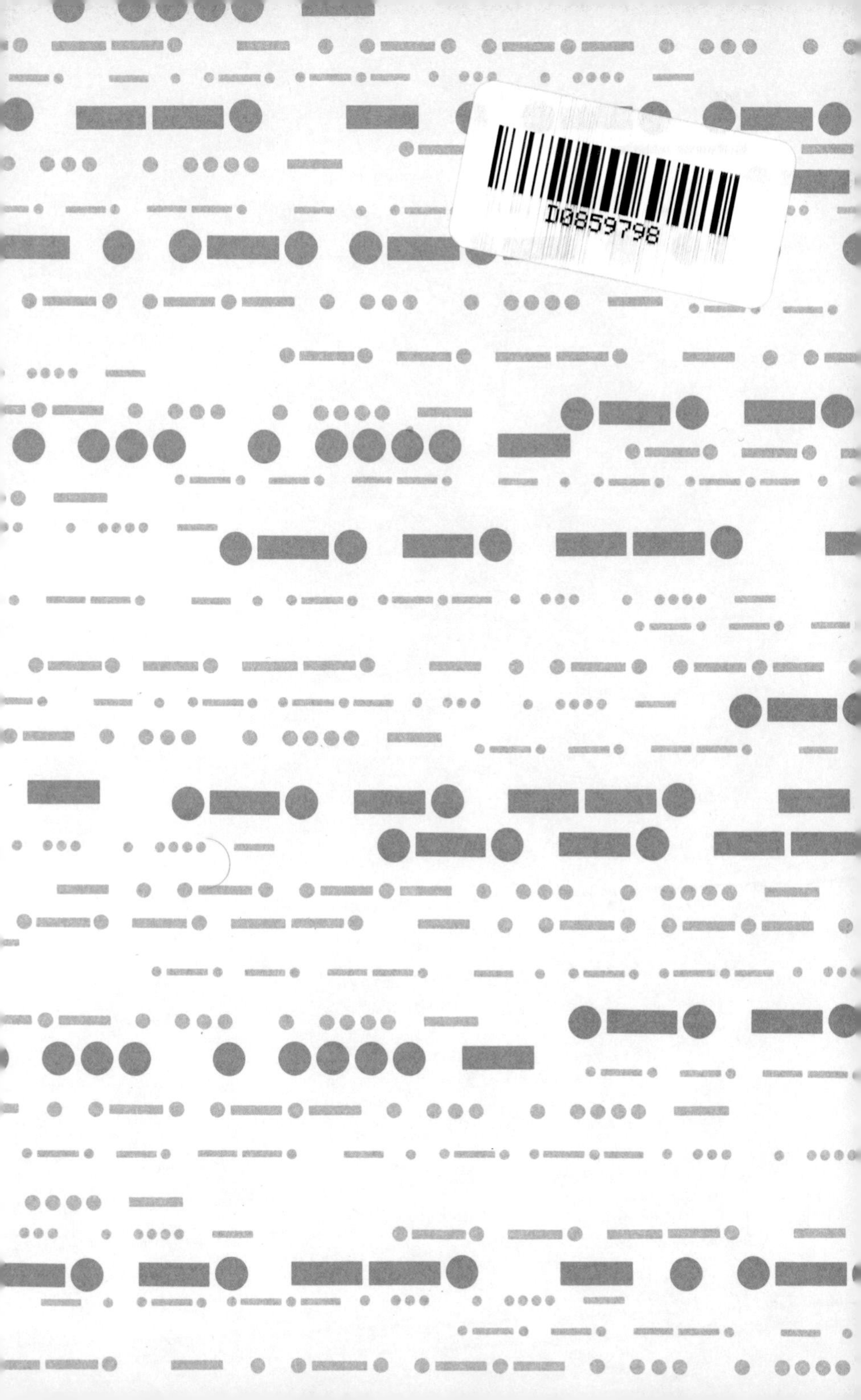
D0859798

CODENAME
DORA

Reprinted 1990 from the 1977 edition.

Library of Congress Cataloging-in-Publication Data

Radó, Sándor, 1899-
[Dóra jelenti. English]
Codename Dora / Sándor Radó.
p. cm. — (The secret war)
Translation of: Dóra jelenti.
Reprint. Originally published: London : Abelard, 1977.
Includes bibliographical references.
ISBN 0-8094-8566-4
ISBN 0-8094-8567-2 (lib. bdg.)
1. Rádo, Sándor. 2. World War—Secret Service—Soviet Union. 3. World War, 1939-1945—Switzerland. 4. Spies—Europe—Biography.
I. Title. II. Series: Classics of World War II. The secret war.
D810.S8R3213 1990 940.54'8647'092—dc20 90-44442 CIP

Sándor Radó

Translated from the authorized German edition
by J.A. Underwood

Abelard . London

The Hungarian edition was published
under the title: DORA JELENTI

First English publication 1977

ISBN 0 200 72339 1

Abelard-Schuman Limited
450 Edgware Road
London W2 1EG
A Member of the Blackie Group

Phototypesetting by Print Origination
Bootle, Merseyside L20 6NS

Printed in Great Britain by
Robert MacLehose & Co. Ltd, Printers to the University of Glasgow

Contents

Sándor Radó—a biographical note

Sándor (Alexander) Radó, the internationally-known geographer and cartographer and a key figure in the Soviet Union's European intelligence network during the Second World War, was born in Budapest on 5 November 1899.

Poor at first, the family soon prospered as the father's small timber business was carried along on the turn-of-the-century boom, and Sándor's younger sister and brother suffered none of the privations that marred his early childhood. His best friend was a foundling whom a market woman had adopted from the orphanage; Laci delivered the family's groceries—and when Sándor's mother found out that he was half-starved he became a permanent guest at the family's table. Through his friend and through his schoolfellows in the working-class suburb of Ujpest Sándor made an early acquaintance with the life of the poor: 'I remember how in May 1912 Laci and I watched endless columns of Ujpest workers marching down the main street into Budapest to take part in the great demonstration. And I remember what a deep impression it made on me when I read in the paper next day that many of those I had seen singing as they marched had died as the demonstration was brutally dispersed. Although not yet consciously sympathising—I was only thirteen at the time—I too, like Laci, sported a red neckerchief at school that day, which prompted a warning letter from the headmaster to my parents.'

His parents were simple, hardworking folk who delighted in their son's rapid progress at school: 'I recall the wonderment, almost the awe with which my mother sometimes bent over my equations or my Latin exercises. I think perhaps it was because they had not been able to study in their own youth but yet had recognized the importance of knowledge that they strove to give their children every possible educational opportunity.' Another landmark in his early life had occurred at the age of six, when he read his first book—an account of a journey to Japan on the Trans-

Siberian railway at the time of the Russo-Japanese War. The endpapers were a map of the then Russian Empire that, Radó tells us, 'stamped itself indelibly on my mind. I would go so far as to say that it determined the whole course of my life. At any rate it marked the beginning of a passionate interest in maps, foreign countries, and geography and history in general.'

As the boy became a youth and Austria ushered Europe into the first of the century's nightmares that interest was fed by the detailed maps with which the newspapers kept a nervous populace informed of the progress of front-line operations. Then, at the age of seventeen, having just completed his school-leaving examination, young Sándor was called up. His parents, anxious to keep him away from the front, managed to get him placed in a fortress-artillery regiment.

'In 1918 I was detached to my regiment's secret staff office in Budapest. It was a turning-point in my life, the beginning of a complete transformation of my scale of values, my political coming-of-age. Staff office received all the secret directives of the Austro-Hungarian war ministry, and one of the war ministry's biggest worries was the rampant demoralization affecting all branches of the armed services. From the Ukraine, part of which was occupied by Austro-Hungarian troops, more and more soldiers were returning either on leave or wounded who, following the October Revolution in Russia, had fraternized with the Soviet troops at the front. Furthermore, with the signature of the Treaty of Brest-Litovsk large numbers of prisoners-of-war returned from Russia already "infected" with Bolshevism. The government in Vienna, blaming the returning soldiers for the fact that the whole Empire was palpably falling apart, did not let them go straight home but kept them in camps to get these dangerous ideas out of their heads. Many things I had not previously understood or even known about now became clear to me. Added to which my commanding officer at the regimental staff office, Major Kunfi, was the brother of one of the leaders of the Hungarian Social-Democratic party; from him I heard for the first time about Marxism and what it meant.'

Enrolling at the law and political-science faculty of Budapest University, where he studied in parallel with his military service, Radó deepened his knowledge of the works of Marx and Engels and found in them, like so many of his generation, convincing answers to the burning questions of the day, a way out of the widespread dissatisfaction felt by many sectors of the population and the hunger and hopelessness that were all the war had brought. Defeat robbed the Austro-Hungarian Empire of any remaining pretence to being the sum of its parts, Hungary lost two-thirds of its 'historic' territory to Czechoslovakia, Rumania, and Yugoslavia, and the popular land-reformer Count Mihály Károlyi was appointed prime minister at the head of a strongly left-wing National Council.

'For me the revolution began with a surprise. I was on my way to barracks early in the morning of 31 October when a soldier came up to me at the tram stop, ripped the badge bearing the king's monogram from my uniform, and stuck a flower in its place; the stars indicating my rank went the way of the badge. At the barracks chaos reigned. . . .' Two weeks later Hungary was proclaimed an independent republic, and at the height of the mammoth demonstration that marked that day an aeroplane swooped over the heads of the crowd filling Parliament Square and scattered pamphlets advocating a socialist republic. 'It was one of the first public appearances of Hungary's revolutionary socialists. Together with the PoWs who had returned from Soviet Russia they formed the core of the new Communist party. It was also the first revolutionary pamphlet I had ever read, and it told me that there existed a movement dedicated to changing the social order radically and establishing it on an entirely new basis.' Before 1918 was out Radó had joined the new party, and on 21 March 1919 its leader, Béla Kun, on conclusion of a pact with a section of the Social-Democratic party, was released from gaol to become the driving force of the government of the so-called Hungarian Soviet Republic.

Only weeks after its foundation the new state's bourgeois neighbours mobilized against it, with the Rumanians advancing from the east, the French intervening from Yugoslavia to occupy the towns along the southern frontier, and the Czechoslovak army attacking under French and Italian leadership from the north. The situation rapidly became critical, and on 2 May, following a colossal and unforgettable demonstration the day before, 'every self-aware worker, Socialist, Communist, and Young Communist' was called upon to join the Hungarian Red Army and defend the soviet republic. Radó volunteered immediately. The fact that the new army had virtually no maps—these having always been supplied from Vienna—encouraged him to turn his beloved hobby to advantage by offering his services as a cartographer, and he was duly assigned as such to the staff of the 6th division.

'I reported to Comrade Ferencz Münnich,* the division's political commissar, and told him my orders, whereupon he in his jovial way said, "We Communists haven't got time to be drawing maps now. I'm appointing you political commissar to the 51st infantry regiment." Dreadfully embarrassed because at nineteen I felt quite unfit for so exalted a post, I objected that I was not an infantryman but an artilleryman. "Splendid!" replied Münnich. "In that case consider yourself appointed political commissar to the divisional artillery battalion." I dared not open my mouth again for fear he would promote me even higher.'

The Hungarian Red Army moved into action and, although driven back by the Rumanians in the east, on the northern front it had soon recovered most of Slovakia, where the Slovak Soviet Republic was proclaimed. The situation was dramatically changed, however, by Clemenceau's suggestion that Hungary should give up its gains in Slovakia and receive back in turn the area east of the Tisza that had been occupied by the advancing Royal Rumanian Army, which was already threatening Budapest. 'Many of us were against accepting this dubious proposal. In a telegram to the Hungarian government Lenin himself drew attention to the underhand character of the imperialist offer, but unfortunately the government, in which Social Democrats were in the majority, decided to accept the Entente's compromise. I shall never forget that mass meeting in Košice where the entire population turned out in the main square and pleaded with us not to abandon them to the interventionists.'

But the Hungarian Soviet Republic was itself on its last legs. Kun resigned, the Rumanians entered Budapest, and the counter-revolutionaries under Miklós Horthy assumed power, beginning their long reign with a wave of arrests and executions. For a Communist, flight was the only course, and Radó ran the gauntlet of the 'White Terror' on a difficult and dangerous journey to the Austrian border where, poker-faced, he presented his Budapest Tramways season ticket and was allowed across; the Austrian

*Later (1958-61) prime minister of Hungary.

frontier guard, seeing a photograph and a rubber stamp, did not bother about what the Hungarian text underneath might say.

'That was on 1 September 1919, and I little thought it was to be the first day of a thirty-six year exile. At the time we Hungarian emigrants believed that our enforced stay abroad was for a few months at most—just until the soviet republic should be re-established; after all Soviet Russia, on which we all pinned our hopes, was still there to carry them.'

Horthy's 'White Terror' continued to spread, however, and Russia itself was torn by civil war. The mood of the Hungarian emigrants sobered somewhat and they began to resign themselves to a lengthy stay in Vienna. But not to inaction: within a few months of their arrival they were bringing out a German-language monthly entitled *Kommunismus*, the first serious Communist review to appear outside the soviet republics. Radó contributed articles analyzing the military situation in Russia.

He also had another idea. Learning that Radio Vienna received and recorded for the information of the Austrian government the 'To everyone, everyone!' telegrams that were sent out daily from Moscow and were the only source of news from the Soviet capital, he decided to bring those telegrams to the attention of a wider public by setting up a news agency and distributing them to the Western press. Friends put him in touch with the left-wing socialist press chief at the Austrian foreign ministry, a man called Schwartz, who got the head of Radio Vienna and his telegraph operators to agree to a 'consideration' of fifty dollars a month. ('In starving post-war Vienna you could have had the entire radio station complete with staff for this paltry sum'). The only problem was to bring this possibility to the attention of the Soviet government, which had no diplomatic representation abroad. Their only representative in Europe was Maksim Litvinov, who at that time was promoting Soviet Russia's foreign trade from an office in Stockholm. Radó got in touch with Litvinov and told him of his plan.

'Months passed, and still no news from Litvinov. Then, one day in July, I received an invitation from the chairman of Austria's largest bank, the Viennese Bank Corporation, to a business consultation. Intrigued, I made my way to the bank's palatial head office where a secretary graciously ushered me into the mighty banker's presence. The chairman was clearly taken aback by my youthful appearance, asking several times whether I was really the person to whom his invitation had been addressed. He then proceeded to expatiate on the long tradition of Austro-Russian trade, on the extensive commercial relations that had once existed between the two countries, and on the fact that his bank had always played an important part in cultivating those relations. "It is my hope," he concluded, "that our bank can continue to serve as the intermediary of economic exchange in the future." I was still staring at him in utter bewilderment when he handed me a cheque for 10,000 Swedish *Kronor*, made out in my name by the Stockholm office of Litvinov's "Centrosoyus".'

In a matter of days the 'Russian Telegraph Agency'—it became known as 'Rosta Vienna'—had an office and the beginnings of a staff. Radó's team eventually included such famous names as Georg Lukács, the great Marxist philosopher and an ex-member of the Hungarian soviet government, Béla Fogarasi, another philosopher who after the Second World War became rector of the Karl Marx Institute of Political Economy in Budapest, Charles Reber of *L'Humanité*, Frederic Kuh of the *Daily Herald*, Gerhard Eisler, later head of radio and television in the German Democratic Republic, Count Xaver Schaffgotsch, scion of a long line of German aristocrats, who had returned from a Russian PoW camp a dedicated Communist ('Schaffgotsch was listed the "responsible editor" of the Agency, which did not prevent him from disappearing from time to time to go hunting on his family's vast estates in Silesia'), and Konstantin Umanski, who later became head of Tass and then Soviet ambassador to the United States. At twenty it is not surprising that Radó occasionally felt uncomfortable in his position as boss.

For the next two years Radó called daily at the building that housed the foreign ministry (and had housed the Congress of Vienna a century before) to collect the Moscow telegrams in person from the head of Radio Vienna. Schwartz had told the doorman to admit him as the diplomatic representative of Ethiopia (a country with which Austria entertained no relations whatever) and this fiction was reinforced from time to time by means of a further small 'consideration'. The system worked perfectly, and ' "Rosta Vienna" played an inestimable part in the effort to tell the world the truth about Soviet Russia. Clemenceau's *"cordon sanitaire"* against the "Bolshevist epidemic" was still in existence at that time and it was vitally important that official Soviet information about the reality of the revolutionary struggle in Russia appeared daily in a major Western capital. . . . The telegrams we published in daily bulletins in German, French, and English which we sent all over the world, mainly to left-wing publications and organizations. . . . Apart from the telegrams "Rosta Vienna" also received magazines and copies of *Pravda* and *Isvestia.* These reached us by a very roundabout route: fishing boats took them from Murmansk to Vardø, a port on the easternmost tip of Norway. From there they went by steamer to Trondheim and on by train via Oslo (then still called Kristiania) across Europe to Vienna. We copied them and sent fascimiles to the libraries, because already then these papers were of outstanding bibliophilic value. We even received a gramophone record of Lenin's speeches, whereupon we hired the Dreher Hall in Vienna and played it to an enormous audience. . . . And then there was another important aspect of our work. The same route by which information about the soviet republics reached left-wing organizations in the capitalist world began to carry a second stream of information in the opposite direction. At a time when the international working-class movement was having to establish its contacts by illegal means and in conditions of the greatest difficulty, we at "Rosta Vienna" found ourselves in a position legally to collect information about that movement from all over the world and pass it on to Moscow in the form of press telegrams. Eventually we were handling so much of this material that we had to set up a separate agency, the "International Telegraph Agency" or "Intel".'

In 1920 Radó, as head of 'Rosta Vienna', was invited to attend the Third Congress of the Communist International in Moscow. After a complicated journey via Berlin, and a bewildering episode at the German-Lithuanian frontier where German police took him off to a bathroom, stripped him, sat him in the tub, and rubbed his back down with something out of a bottle (looking, he learned later, for secret messages written on his back), he reached Riga in Latvia.

'From Riga we continued along the only stretch of railway track connecting Soviet Russia and the capitalist world at that time. At the tiny frontier station of Sebezh, as our ancient locomotive chugged up to a simple wooden arch bearing, in several languages, the legend "Long Live Soviet Power", I experienced a moment of deep emotion. For the first time since the fall of the Hungarian Soviet Republic I felt at home. I was entering the Promised Land, and I was filled with limitless confidence.

'I must confess that my first impressions were not exactly overwhelming, with the train stopping repeatedly in order that the driver and fireman could go and chop fresh supplies of wood in the nearby forests, there being no coal with which to fire the engine.

'I arrived in Moscow in mid-May, when the long Russian winter gives way without transition to the hot summer. My first impressions of the city I had so yearned to see and news of which I daily despatched all over the world were downright depressing. There was a major famine in the Volga region at the time, and the country was in the grip of a typhoid epidemic. There were a number of cases in the National Hotel, where we were put up several to a room. The water was off, the sewage system was not working, and there were no trams. The daily ration per person was one herring, ten cigarettes, and a lump of some indefinable dark substance that went by the name of bread. . . . At the same time I was deeply impressed by the sight—in what otherwise struck one as an enormous village—of the Kremlin, the medieval cathedral, and the vast rectangle of Red Square. But more than all this I was overwhelmed by the atmosphere of unbelievable enthusiasm and confidence, the feeling of looking forward to the world revolution as to a Messiah, the burning hope that filled people in the midst of the most appalling deprivation. On the other hand it was impossible to ignore the old women kneeling before the almost black picture of the Iberian Madonna at the entrance to Red Square, while opposite the revolutionary slogan proclaimed against a red background: "Religion is the opium of the people."

'Every single person I had dealings with was bursting with this enthusiasm. People were pervaded through and through with belief in the future. The mood of revolutionary ecstacy reached its seething climax in the Georgy Hall of the Kremlin, where the Congress of the Communist International sat. The words of the revolutionary speakers were in piquant contrast to the Czarist coats of arms and the lists of knights of the Order of St George that were engraved in gold all round the walls of that enormous hall crowded with delegates from all over the world. We pressmen sat in tiered rows to one side of the platform with the presidium. One day the little door beside me opened and Lenin slipped in. He sat down on the step below me, turned to look at me, and placed a finger to his lips, obviously asking me to keep quiet about his being there. He stayed for some time, making copious notes.

'I and indeed the whole hall were deeply moved when he stepped up to the rostrum. The mere fact that he spoke for several hours, first in Russian, then in German, French, and English, captivated his audience. One sensed that this man, with his rapid pacing to and fro, his shrewd glance, and his animated gestures, possessed abilities altogether out of the ordinary. On another occasion I heard him speaking in Red Square from an improvised rostrum, his manner impassioned, his sentences clipped and decisive. And then at last came a chance to talk to him personally.

'I wanted while I was in Moscow to get hold of as many Russian maps as I could, since I was already thinking in terms of publishing the first map of the soviet republics in the West. Bumping into one of the deputy people's commissars for military affairs in a corridor of the Kremlin one day, I put my request to him. But my Russian vocabulary was simply not up to the task; try as I might I could not make the man understand what I was after. At that point Lenin happened to come past and, seeing that we were in difficulties, offered his services as interpreter. Not content with just interpreting, however, he soon chimed in himself with a question as to why I wanted the maps. Hearing of my scientific interest in geography and cartography, he talked a little about how the problems of imperialism called for special forms of cartographical representation and then asked casually whether I would not like to pursue the question in Russia, where there was a great shortage of Communist geographers. At the time I could not accept because I first wanted to complete my studies. But from then on I resolved to devote myself particularly to the geography and cartography of the Soviet Union and in particular to follow up Lenin's ideas. This I sought to do in my first major geographical work, *The Atlas of Imperialism,* which was published in Berlin in 1929 and Tokyo in 1930. Needless to say, with Lenin's help I got hold of all the maps I wanted.

'During my stay in Moscow I had an opportunity of meeting a number of leading Soviet politicians. Possibly the most interesting of them was the People's Commissar for Foreign Affairs, Georgy Vasilievich Chicherin. He was in fact the first person I called on, because the "To everyone, everyone" telegrams that we published in Vienna came from his press department. Chicherin received me at the Metropol Hotel, where the People's Commissariat for Foreign Affairs was then housed, at two o'clock in the morning—which was well within his normal office hours. Emerging from behind an enormous desk covered with mounds of paper, he strode across the room towards me, looked me up and down with eyes bloodshot from working nights, and smacked his palms together: "So this young fellow is our greatest propagandist abroad. You must do something about your appearance. We can't have our one press representative in the West looking like a mere boy," he boomed, more in jest than in earnest. Most of my nights in Moscow I spent in Chicherin's office, where he personally supervised the drawing up of the telegrams. It was a great experience to observe the extraordinary atmosphere in which this former aristocrat and academically schooled Mozart interpreter and aesthetician directed the Soviet government's foreign policy. When the People's Commissariat for Foreign Affairs moved from the Metropol Hotel to the Kuznetsky Most Chicherin had only one concern: where do I put my desk and where my bed? In the Metropol they stood side by side. The whole staff of the Commissariat enjoyed a friendly, relaxed relationship that took its tone from Chicherin's own remarkable warmth and naturalness. I remember, for example, the following nocturnal scene: Count Brockdorff-Rantznau, the German ambassador, a gaunt Prussian aristocrat of military bearing, arrived for an appointment one night to find the enormous, red-bearded Chicherin in the outer office rocking a baby in his arms. The wife of the soldier on guard duty had arrived with her child; the couple had something to discuss and had asked "Comrade People's Commissar" if he would look after the child for a moment—which he was only too glad to do. One can imagine the count's consternation when Chicherin begged to be excused until his services as nursemaid were no longer required.'

Through Umanski, who had returned to Moscow some months before, Radó also met Mayakovsky, 'then occupied twenty-four hours a day with rehearsals of his play *Misteriya-buff* in the Moscow Circus. I mean that literally; the rehearsals went on until deep in the night and, in the complete absence of public transport, actors, director, author, and author's friends spent the night in the Circus, sleeping in the boxes. It was characteristic of the atmosphere of the period that the female lead was played by the daughter of my Viennese friend, Schwartz, who had just been appointed Austrian ambassador in Moscow. In fact sometimes Schwartz even picked me up outside the Communist International building and drove me to the rehearsals in the embassy car.'

On the return journey, travelling by steamer from Tallinn to Stettin, Radó was spat at by passengers who discovered that he was in possession of a Soviet passport.

Back in Vienna, Radó continued to divide his time between the agency and his geographical studies until in the summer of 1922, the revolutionary role of 'Rosta Vienna' having been superseded by the establishment of official diplomatic relations between Austria and Soviet Russia, he moved to Germany.

With him went Helene Jansen, a young Communist party activist who was soon to become his wife. The daughter of a poor Berlin family (the father had left his wife and three daughters to fend for themselves), she had been involved in the working-class movement since childhood; even before the October Revolution the family's Berlin flat had been a meeting-point for Bolshevik couriers, and throughout the war her mother had offered asylum to deserters from the German army and escaped Russian PoWs. By the time Radó met her in Vienna she was already something of a legend in party circles. She had worked for the first Soviet embassy set up in Berlin in 1918, had accompanied its staff to Moscow when they were expelled later in the year, and had made a dramatic appearance at the founding congress of the German Communist party that December bringing a message from Lenin sewn in the lining of her coat. A month later she had taken a heroic part in the unsuccessful Spartacus uprising of January 1919, being among the last to leave the League's besieged headquarters after providing fire-cover for the others. In December 1920, having been shipped back to Russia by accident with a camp full of PoWs whom she had been converting to Communism, she had fought with the Red Army as they quelled the Kronstadt mutiny.

Radó and Helene spent most of 1923-4 in Leipzig, both of them actively involved in party work and he at the same time continuing his studies at the university. Radó was made provincial organizer of the 'Proletarian Hundreds', the armed brigades of workers that were to spearhead the revolution in Germany and form the core of the future Red Army. The uprising, which was set for the night of 22-23 October 1923, was cancelled at the last minute by the German Communist party leadership, and Radó had the unpleasant task ('That night is one of my bitterest memories') of telling the 15,000 men under his command that the battle they so longed to fight was off and they were to go home. The entire Leipzig leadership of the 'Proletarian Hundreds' was arrested—and immediately released again by a Communist police superintendent. By the autumn of 1924, however, the hunt was on in earnest for 'Weser', Radó's codename on the Leipzig job, and it was time to move again. But not before he had brought out the first political map of the Soviet Union to be published abroad (1924 Westermann, Braunschweig), a work that established his professional reputation as an expert on Soviet geography. (It was Radó, incidentally, who coined the abbreviation 'Soviet Union' as opposed to the official 'Union of Soviet Socialist Republics'.)

There followed a further stay in Moscow, where he was commissioned to write the first travel guide to the Soviet Union, published in 1925. The summer of that year Radó spent in Berlin as a correspondent of the newly founded Tass agency, returning to Moscow in the autumn to become secretary of the World Economic Institute of the Communist Academy, a post that brought him into contact with many leading Soviet academics and political figures and in which he further strengthened his reputation as an authority on the geography of the Soviet Union, contributing maps and articles to a number of internationally-known atlases and encyclopedias. He returned to Berlin at the end of 1926 to set up the foreign branch of Tass's photo agency, 'Press-Cliché', but as soon as the new agency was on its feet he found someone to run it in his stead and, staying on in Berlin, resumed his academic work.

This began to take a new and exciting turn in the autumn of the following year when, returning from a trip to Moscow, he shared the passenger compartment of a small single-engined plane with the chairman of Lufthansa, the German airline company founded the year before. Their conversation, during the course of which Radó outlined his ideas about the geography and cartography of a form of transport that was still very much in its infancy, became the starting-point of a five-year project that culminated in 1932 when he published the world's first international air-travel guide. Radó's pioneering work in aerial cartography was the fruit of several million often hair-raising kilometres flown in the extremely primitive aircraft of the period—when, with no radio, the pilot's chief navigational aid was the names of towns written in huge letters on gasometers or the roofs of churches, and in out-of-the-way areas sometimes the only way of establishing one's whereabouts was to follow a railway line, flying low enough to read the nameboard on the next station.

In Berlin, where as a foreign Communist all academic posts were closed to him, he had the idea of enlivening a somewhat colourless daily press with topical, scientifically-produced maps illustrating world events. It was the beginning of 'Pressegeographie' or 'Pressgeo' as it was known for short, the world's first geographical and cartographical press agency and the firm that was eventually, as 'Geopress Geneva', to provide Radó's cover as a group leader of Soviet Intelligence. But although he devoted most of his time during this period to his cartographical work he did not neglect his political obligations, lecturing in economic geography at the Marxist College in Berlin and occasionally standing in for Helene, who worked nights at Karl Liebknecht House, headquarters of the German Communist party. The job of the night shift was to telephone the latest news from the agencies through to the party's provincial papers all over Germany, and another of Radó's bitter memories dates from Easter 1927 when he had to repeat over and over again to a series of incredulous editors the news that Chiang Kai-shek, until then the leading figure of the Chinese revolution, had turned against the Chinese Communists after taking Shanghai and massacred numbers of his former comrades.

The Berlin years, a fruitful period for Radó since they saw the publication of his first major cartographical work, *The Atlas of Imperialism* (1929; republished a decade later by Victor Gollancz as *The Atlas of Today and Tomorrow*) as well as the air guide, came to an abrupt end at the beginning of 1933 as a result of events that were directly to shape the next eleven years of his life. On 31 January, the day after Hindenburg had appointed Hitler chancellor, Radó received a mysterious telephone call from Berlin police headquarters 'announcing' that he would shortly be required to answer for his political activities. A new, Fascist police superintendent had replaced the old Social Democrat but the staff was still the same, and the call was clearly a warning from someone who realized that his own days were numbered. Sending his wife off to Austria and his two sons with their grandmother to his parents in Hungary, Radó decided to wait out the six weeks until the elections on the slim chance that political good sense would prevail. The working-class movement was split down the middle, with the Social Democrats refusing flatly to enter a coalition with the Communists, and in the middle of February Radó and Frederic Kuh, now Berlin correspondent of the United Press Agency, offered their services as relative outsiders in a last-minute attempt to mediate a compromise. The attempt failed, and a terrorized electorate continued to slide towards the debacle of 15 March.

Helene returned from Austria on the evening of 27 February; the Reichstag was in flames, bands of Nazis roamed the streets howling vengeance on the Communists, and Radó and his wife, knowing that it would be suicide to return to their flat, went straight from the station to her sister's and then, when the maid there turned out to have an SA boyfriend, to the house of a friend in Leipzig to await the election results. On the evening of 15 March, sitting in the crowded buffet of Leipzig's main station with Kurt Rosenfeld, leader of the left-wing Socialist Labour party, they heard the radio announcement of the Nazi's overwhelming victory at the polls. 'No Communist was in any doubt about the fact that the worst forces of reaction had launched their merciless campaign against the progressive, revolutionary organizations of Europe. Duty and conscience bade my wife and myself return to the front. The only possibility of openly combating Fascism was to get out of Germany and find somewhere to set up a militant political newspaper or press agency.'

The Radós and Rosenfeld went to Paris and set up the international anti-Fascist news agency 'Inpress'; with a team of editors that included Vladimir Posner, Maximilian Scheer, and Arthur Koestler, Inpress bombarded the world with news of what was really going on inside Nazi Germany—to such effect that Hitler is said on one occasion to have anathemized the agency and its chief editor, Radó, as the Third Reich's public enemy number one.

Valuable though its work was, however, Inpress was not in fact the 'only possibility', as Radó was soon to discover. But over to him. . . .

J.A.U.

Foreword

In recent years a number of articles and books have appeared in various countries dealing with my activities during the Second World War. The motive behind many of them was sensation-seeking, and the culmination of this series of lies and distortions was the publication in 1966 of a book by two French journalists entitled *La Guerre a été gagné en Suisse*—'The War Was Won in Switzerland'. The authors of this book set out to prove that the Soviet Union owed its victory in the Second World War not to the military successes of the Red Army but to the Swiss group of Soviet Intelligence. This far-fetched thesis prompted a fresh wave of books and articles, principally in the German Federal Republic, where reactionary circles refuse to this day to admit that they suffered military defeat,as a result of the strategic superiority of the Soviet Union. Some see the cause in Hitler's dilettantish military leadership; others in the hardness of the 'Russian winter' or in the brutal treatment administered to the populations of the occupied areas. Now they have found a new and absolutely fantastic explanation: the war was lost because individual officers of the German general staff allegedly betrayed all the Nazi leadership's plans to Soviet intelligence agents. (The 'stab in the back' legend is nothing new of course; German nationalists sought to account for their defeat in the First World War not by the military victory of the Entente powers but by the anti-war movement propagated by Germany's socialists.)

To tell the truth, my first reaction was one of utter amazement when twenty to twenty-five years after the war the work of the Swiss group suddenly created such a sensation and so much importance was attached to the person of its leader. Among other things I was amazed at the German reactionaries' refusal, given their exalted opinion of the impact of intelligence work, to face the fact that the intelligence services of the Third Reich failed to chalk up the slightest success in the Red Army's rear. Probably they do not ask themselves because the answer is only too clear: German Intelligence was doomed to ineffectiveness by the iron determination of the Soviet people to defend its country and its freedom on the one hand and the watchfulness of Soviet Counter-intelligence on the other, which between them thwarted the enemy's efforts in this field. Neither do they ask themselves why so many German workers, peasants, and intellectuals were prepared to risk their lives to help the Soviet Union fight the Fascist threat, a threat to humanity as a whole. Hardly any of the members of my group were Communists, but they were united by the conviction that in the struggle against Nazism all forces must join hands, whether Communist, socialist, liberal-bourgeois, Swiss, German, Austrian, Italian, French, British, or Hungarian. This united front against Fascism is still a living reality today and is the key to a better future. I recently received a letter from a complete stranger, an architect in Switzerland. I quote: 'I have just read in the *Gazette de Lausanne* what you and your group did for humanity. I realize that you saved me too from the horror of Fascism, and I shall feel indebted to you my whole life long.' His debt is of course to all who fought the fight against Fascism, and in the first place to the Soviet people and the Soviet army, on whose shoulders the appalling burden of the war primarily rested. Or as Major Hans Hausamann, a Swiss Intelligence officer who had very little time for Communism, put it: 'For me the question was a simple one: if Germany wins the war the Nazis will stay in power and we Swiss will have had it. Ergo, Germany must lose the war.' The same logic guided all those who in Germany and throughout Europe deliberately took upon themselves to smash Hitler's power and bring down the Nazi regime.

It never occurred to me before 1935 to become an intelligence agent. It is a skilled profession and calls for intensive preparation; its members attend special training establishments where they receive instruction in many fields. I had no such training, and what is more I never received any, regardless of what my many 'biographers' claim to a man.

I have always inclined towards academic work, and I am happy that despite countless obstacles I have been able eventually to realize this ambition. Moreover my whole life has been governed by another great goal. From my youth on I have belonged to the revolutionary working-class movement, spending years, indeed decades in exile doing party work of a conspiratorial nature. This was my training; it was this that enabled me to graduate to the more complex and difficult task of running an intelligence group.

I hesitated for a long time whether I should write my memoirs. As I saw it I had simply done my duty, and I had no wish to be exposed to the glare of publicity. But the recent tidal wave of more or less mythological publications concerning the Swiss group and my part in it (in a number of them, to take a relatively innocent example, I feature as 'Radolfi', and in one even as 'Radomski') has forced me to break my silence, and I want to try at last to give a true version of what happened. All the more so since, thanks to the Moscow journalist W.G. Alexandrov, I have had an opportunity of consulting large numbers of documents that enable me to substantiate my account. I should like to take this opportunity of thanking him most sincerely for all his help.

Sándor Radó
Budapest, April 1971

PART 1

CHAPTER 1

How I became an Intelligence Agent

In October 1935 I travelled from Paris to Moscow to discuss certain matters in connection with the Great Soviet World Atlas, the non-Russian volumes of which I had been asked to edit.

The international political situation was beginning to look very grim. Storm clouds were gathering threateningly over Europe, and the atmosphere in France in particular had become so tense that it began to look as if Inpress, the anti-Fascist news agency I headed in Paris, would soon be forced to close down. Reluctantly I faced the possibility that my contribution as a journalist to the struggle against Nazism had gone about as far as it could go and that I must confine myself in future to what is actually my first profession: I am a geographer.

My first call in Moscow was at the ancient, almost ramshackle building in Rasin Street that housed the editorial offices of the Great Soviet World Atlas with its brilliant team of young cartographers and geographers. It was a joyful reunion. Among the old friends there to welcome me was Nikolai Nikolayevich Baransky, one of the leading lights of Soviet geography and at that time geographical editor of the Great Soviet Encyclopedia, to which I contributed a number of articles including one on my native Hungary (Bela Kun wrote the political section). I also called on a number of Hungarian and German comrades whom I wished to consult in connection with winding up Inpress.

It was here that my affairs took an unexpected turn.

A few days after my arrival a Hungarian comrade, a journalist whom I had known for a long time, rang me at my hotel and we arranged to meet. He told me that he had certain contacts with the Red Army general staff and that he had informed them of the desperate situation Inpress was in, as I had described it to my Hungarian friends a day or two previously. The Red Army general staff, he said, felt that I could make a more useful contribution to the fight against Fascism by dropping the Inpress agency and moving into another field. If I agreed he would introduce me to the persons concerned.

At the time I had no conception of intelligence work and knew no one who was active in it. A year before, on a similar trip to Moscow in connection with the atlas, I had had a meal with my old Berlin friend Richard Sorge in the Praga Restaurant without having the faintest idea that he was a member of Soviet Intelligence—and a leading member at that. I never saw Sorge again, and it was not until decades later that I learned of his by now legendary achievements as an agent in China and Japan.

After much thought I decided to take my Hungarian friend up on his suggestion. It seemed to me that an organization as powerful as the Red Army must inevitably offer far more possibilities for fighting Fascism than a small press agency. My friend made the necessary arrangements and took me along to a flat where we were received by a man named Artusov, a high-ranking officer in the Red Army intelligence service, who informed me that Semyon Petrovich Urizky, the head of Intelligence, would like a word with me. Urizky, he told me, had been a Party member since before the Revolution, was an experienced underground worker, and during the Civil War had been chief of staff and head of the operations department of the 14th Army on the Zarizyn front. He spoke of him as an outstandingly brave and accomplished officer.

The man who entered the room was a stocky, youthful-looking soldier of some forty years of age with a strongly-boned face and a determined jaw. Two Orders of the Red Flag glittered on his chest. After a brief exchange concerning my journey and whether I was comfortably accommodated, Semyon Petrovich came quickly to the point. He wasted no more time on questions; clearly he was well informed already.

'I hear you're having a bit of trouble with the press agency,' he remarked.

'Yes, it's getting very difficult,' I replied. 'And if war breaks out, Inpress is bound to be closed down.' I gave him a full account of exactly how things stood with the agency.

Urizky looked at me with that penetrating gaze of his. A deep furrow appeared on his brow.

'Right,' he said finally, as if summing up his thoughts. 'I've also been told you'd be prepared to help us, in which case you'd probably have to domicile yourself in a different country. Let's think where you could move to if war did break out.' He lit a cigarette and began to pace up and down the room. 'I want you to be quite clear about our objectives and what they involve. We know you're no novice to conspiratorial work. That's why we asked you here. But a Soviet intelligence agent needs to be more than just a good conspirator. You'll need to be capable of getting your bearings fast in a changing political situation, because intelligence work is political work. Our first job at any given time is to find out who our probable military opponents are. Only then do we bring our intelligence network into play. As you know yourself, the Soviet Union has several potential enemies in Europe. Primarily Germany and Italy. These are the circumstances, and this is what we are basing our intelligence strategy in the capitalist countries on.'

He stopped his pacing and came and sat down beside me.

'That's the general picture,' he went on. 'Now let's decide where you're going to move to. I know you speak several European languages. Where would you like to go, and what would you have in mind as a cover for your intelligence activities?'

'I think the simplest thing would be for me to open a cartographical agency,' I said. 'I ran one successfully when I was in Germany, and I've had one in France too, called Geopress. The best place to move to would be either Belgium or Switzerland. Switzerland in my opinion is hardly likely to join a war, but on the other hand it would be easier to get official permission to set up an agency in Belgium, and from Belgium it would be simpler to move to Switzerland if the need arose.'

One thing that emerged crystal clear from my talk with Artusov and Urizky was their conviction that Nazi Germany and Fascist Italy represented the greatest danger to the future of the Soviet Union. Both countries were arming fast, stirring up revanchist hatred in the minds of their populations, and conducting rabid militaristic and anti-Communist propaganda. It seemed certain that, in the event of war, these two aggressive powers would be the Soviet Union's chief enemies. It was of vital importance to keep a close eye on their activities in the international arena, to find out what plans the Fascist leaders were secretly hatching against the Soviet Union, and to expose those plans in time. This, my two companions stressed, was the goal of Soviet Intelligence.

It was also exactly what they wanted me as an intelligence agent to do. It was a pity I could not be sent to Germany; I knew the country well, having lived there for eleven years, and as they had already pointed out I was no novice when it came to working underground. But Germany was out of the question: the Nazis knew both my wife and myself and would pick us up immediately. The alternative was to move to a country adjoining Germany—Switzerland or Belgium, for example, as I had suggested—and start gathering the necessary information there, looking for sources not only in that country but inside Hitler's Reich itself. In this way I would be able, if Germany and Italy did decide to launch a war, to continue gathering information without having to worry about German counter-intelligence or the Gestapo, since these would not be able to touch me in a neutral country.

We eventually decided that I should try and settle in Belgium, which had the additional advantage of being the cheapest country in Europe at that time—a very considerable advantage as regards the profitability of an international agency. My instructions from the head of Intelligence were accordingly to leave France, resume my scientific activities as a geographer and cartographer, and set up a cartographical agency on a business footing in Belgium. I already had something of a name in scientific circles, and we counted on that to make my task easier. Armed with these instructions and much advice I left Moscow to embark on a brand-new career—and one that was to bring me more than my share of surprises.

Back in Paris, I announced that Inpress was shutting up shop and gave instructions for its liquidation. In December I went to Belgium to make preparations for opening the new firm.

In Brussels I went to see the Belgian chief of police. I introduced myself as a geographer, stated that I wished to set up a cartographical press agency, and asked for a residence permit. He heard me out, never once interrupting, and when I had finished said no. I tried to persuade him that I had chosen Belgium particularly because of its superior facilities for the exchange of scientific information. I argued that the country could only stand to gain by the presence of a firm producing maps for a wide range of topical purposes, since the demand for such maps was everywhere on the increase. My arguments were in vain. There was no budging the man.

I returned to Paris and informed Moscow of my failure, giving the letter to the contact man whom I had been introduced to in Moscow.

The answer came quickly: I was to adopt plan two. In accordance with what we had worked out together in Moscow I was to try and settle in Switzerland, that traditionally neutral country, and set up my scientific agency there.

At that time virtually anyone who had enough money could obtain a Swiss residence permit, and it was almost a daily occurrence for some wealthy foreigner or other to buy a house or a piece of land and with it the right to live—though not to work—in the country. But getting permission to set up and run a business there was another story entirely.

Residence permits were issued by the appropriate cantonal government—in my case the cantonal government of Geneva—but they had to have the approval of the federal authorities in Berne as well. I had chosen Geneva because as the seat of the League of Nations and consequently the centre of international political life it seemed to be the most suitable place to set up a scientific information bureau. The League of Nations also had a magnificent library of political and economic literature, as I knew from having often used it for my scientific researches in the past. Obtaining a residence permit from the socialist cantonal government of Geneva presented no great problems because I could make out a case for wanting to pursue my scientific work with the support of the press department of the League of Nations, for which I possessed a written recommendation. The federal police chief in Berne, however, was a tougher nut to crack. To start with he did not like my wanting to settle in Geneva because, as he put it, 'There'll soon be more foreigners there than Swiss'. On the other hand my point about wanting to be near the League of Nations was pretty convincing. In any event he told me that he would only approve an undertaking that was going to be of advantage to the Swiss economy, which meant primarily that the undertaking concerned must take the legal form of a limited company on the board of which Swiss citizens must under Swiss law be in the majority. In my case, since I was a foreigner, this called for two Swiss citizens—whereupon the police chief went so far as to recommend to me two scientists who lived in Geneva. All I had to do was talk them into it.

The first, a geology professor, reacted coolly and sceptically to my offer and eventually said outright that he had no desire to get involved with foreigners. The second candidate, professor of geography at Geneva University, was more receptive to what I had to say about the scientific potential of my Geopress scheme and the material profits that could be expected to accrue. In fact I made rather too good a job of it: he was so sold on the commercial possibilities of the agency that he began to make impossible demands, asking for a seventy-five per cent holding and a fat salary into the bargain. Otherwise, he said, he was not prepared to give me a recommendation for the federal police, which would mean I should not get my residence permit. The situation became so impossible that I was forced to consider breaking off diplomatic relations. I pointed out that there was in fact nothing to stop me setting up shop just over the French border—in Annemasse, for example—and commuting to the League of Nations, where I had managed to get myself accredited to the press department. I would have my maps printed in Geneva, and the Geneva police could hardly object to an arrangement that was so clearly advantageous to Geneva's printers. The professor saw immediately that he had gone too far and began to moderate his demands—first to fifty per cent, then to twenty-five per cent. By now I had got my heels firmly dug in, however, and my partner was lucky to get away in the end with one per cent of the shares and a hundred Swiss francs a month. Soon after that I managed to find a second partner as well.

Things seemed to be going very smoothly, but then when one month, two months, three months went by without my residence permit coming through, I started to have misgivings. My enquiries at the Swiss embassy in Paris were met with a polite request to be patient a little longer: there were still one or two formalities to be attended to. I was asked about my financial situation and was able to produce evidence of a fairly handsome bank balance. Then they wanted to know whether I was sound politically. In this connection they got in touch with the Hungarian police to find out whether I had a police record. Satisfied on this point, the Swiss authorities sought no further details about my life in Hungary. It was a very good job they did not; the situation might have become delicate.

And at last, in May 1936, I received my permit, entitling me to reside and operate as an independent employer in the canton of

Geneva for the next three years. My wife and my mother-in-law received entry permits too, and in the summer of that year we left Paris for our new home. The family travelled by train; I rode in the enormous removal van with two taciturn drivers who took two-hour shifts at the wheel. We drove overnight and I dozed most of the time, waking up occasionally as we roared through some sleepy French town or village. It was already morning as we left the dark gorges of the Jura behind us and drove into Ferney-Voltaire, the last town before the Swiss frontier and the last home of one of France's greatest writers nearly two hundred years before. Suddenly the luxuriant, sun-drenched panorama of Geneva and its lovely surroundings opened up before me.

A new chapter of my life had begun, a chapter that I well knew would be beset with problems and heavy with responsibilities.

CHAPTER 2

Geopress

The first hurdle was behind me. Now I had to concentrate on building up the Geopress Map Publishing Company into a going concern.

In Geneva I rented a flat in a six-storied house in the rue de Lausanne. The man I dealt with—the owner's agent—called himself a *régisseur*. The owner himself I never met; I never even learned his name. I subsequently discovered that most of the rented accommodation in Geneva is in the hands of such *régisseurs*, who constitute an economically and politically influential stratum of Genevan society. It was a four-roomed flat: one room we allotted to the children and their granny, one to my wife and myself, one we made our living-room, and the fourth became my study. There was also a room for our maid, a girl from the German-speaking part of Switzerland. Of course the flat was hardly large enough to accommodate a family of the size of ours and at the same time serve as the office of an agency, but it had other advantages that to some extent compensated for the squeeze.

I had deliberately chosen a house with no buildings opposite in order to avoid any possibility of myself or the flat being watched. No. 113 rue de Lausanne was exactly what I wanted. It was situated on the edge of town in the lower-middle-class Sécheron quarter. Opposite lay the glorious Mon Repos park, and there was a well-known precision-instruments factory nearby. The huge, multi-storied League of Nations building was only a few minutes' walk away, and the headquarters of the International Labour Organization and the International Committee of the Red Cross were even closer. Consequently, apart from artisans, workers, and small tradesmen, Sécheron was inhabited mainly—and our house exclusively—by people who worked for one of these international organizations. They all enjoyed diplomatic privileges and took precious little interest in the life of the city.

It was in this same quarter of Geneva, in Sécheron, that Vladimir Ilyich Lenin lived during his second enforced exile from Russia.

Before the Geopress agency could begin doing business there

were various formalities to be attended to. Furthermore staff had to be engaged, a bank account opened for the new limited company, and a start made on canvassing subscribers. All these tasks fell to the managing director and editor-in-chief, namely myself. I had two Swiss partners, as I have said, but the majority of the shares—ninety-eight per cent—remained in my possession, and later I had to take care of the whole of the practical work of the agency single-handed.

For conspiratorial reasons, and also because it was a great advantage to be so close to the League of Nations, I decided against having separate premises for Geopress. The whole of the work of the agency was done within the four walls of my study. There the maps were planned and drawn, to be sent immediately to the printer's for block-making, and there I wrote the captions in four languages—English, German, French, and Italian. My staff consisted of two people: the cartographer and my wife. Helene did the typing and attended to the commercial side of the business, and a woman who worked at the League of Nations came regularly to do our book-keeping. Between the four of us we managed, and there was no need for me to take on more staff, which was a good thing from the economic point of view as well. By the end of July 1936 our preparations were complete, and in August the new Swiss press agency, Geopress, started work.

The agency grew rapidly and was soon known all over the world. It was the only one of its kind: we published maps giving information about current political and economic developments as well as changes in physical geography, and later on I brought out a series of coloured maps with the title *The Permanent Atlas.* The capital invested in the firm was quickly recovered and the books began to show a profit. The demand for maps was enormous. Our regular subscribers included newspapers, libraries, university geography departments, various public bodies, ministries, general staffs, and embassies; even ex-Kaiser William II was a Geopress subscriber.

The opening of the agency coincided with the outbreak of the Spanish Civil War and we were flooded with orders for maps of the theatre of operations. These did a lot to make the agency's name better known, especially after one of them had been published in the leading French magazine, *L'Illustration.* The world press wanted maps immediately to illustrate their daily reports from the front, and I often found myself burning the midnight oil.

All the time I was in close touch with the League of Nations, where I was accredited to the press department. I had my own post-office box there, I had a seat reserved for me in the library, I had access to official material, and I was invited to receptions, at which I saw among other guests (if only from a distance) the representative of the Soviet Union, Maxim Litvinov. In fact I saw virtually all the top men in world politics at those League of Nations receptions, including the British 'Minister for League Affairs', Anthony Eden, who also played the part of a leader of fashion, the Rumanian foreign minister Titulescu, a splendid speaker whose impassioned gestures put one in mind of a barrister addressing the court, and the pious Lord Halifax, with whom I once travelled on the same train from Paris to Geneva and saw how, arriving in Geneva station at six in the morning, he made a bee-line for church. A man I got on particularly well with was Dr. Rajchmann, a top League of Nations official and a former member of the Polish government and adviser to Chiang Kai-shek; his daughter was a cartographer and it was in collaboration with her that I brought out my *Atlas of Today and Tomorrow*, published in London by Victor Gollancz. Also through Rajchmann I met the English left-wing politician Konni Zilliacus, who likewise worked at the League of Nations, and the foreign minister of the Spanish republican government, Alvarez del Vayo. These contacts were of course extremely important for me.

Meanwhile the international scene was becoming increasingly tense, with the danger of a new world war looming closer all the time.

In 1935 Fascist Italy occupied Abyssinia. In China the Japanese aggressor had been pursuing an expansionist policy for years. In Spain the republican armies were engaged in a bitter battle with the international forces of reaction that stood behind General Franco. For German and Italian Fascism it was the first trial of strength.

All over Europe there was a strong smell of gunpowder in the air.

In this political situation the Soviet government was forced to take steps to defend the interests of the Soviet Union. It was necessary to keep a sharp eye on the aggressors' activities. A part of this important task fell to me.

CHAPTER 3

Inside Fascist Italy

Towards the end of June 1937 I received a postcard from Paris. Written between the lines in invisible ink was a message to the effect that I should meet in Paris someone who would be sent from Central.* I was told the time and place of the meeting and given a physical description of my contact.

I had been in Paris many times already and met people from Soviet Intelligence there to hand over the information I had collected and the maps I had been specially asked to make. These were maps showing the regional distribution of war industries, which I drew on the basis of German and Italian newspaper and magazine articles as well as legally published specialist reviews in the fields of economics and geography. This material was then passed on to Moscow. In some cases I sent my reports to Paris by post—not of course under my own name. I had two codenames, 'Dora' and 'Albert', which I retained even after I had been appointed head of the Swiss group.

My business affairs in connection with the Geopress agency's many subscribers gave me a pretext for frequent journeys abroad. Nevertheless I felt it advisable not to draw unnecessary attention to myself. An alien living in Geneva at that time was issued with a residence permit but his passport was held by the police; every time he wished to go abroad he had to ask for his passport back and leave his residence permit in return. The peculiar situation of Geneva, however, made it possible for me to get round this irksome procedure. The city is virtually surrounded by French territory, being connected with the rest of Switzerland only by a corridor about four miles wide along the north shore of the lake. Since practically the whole of the city's food supply comes from France, an agreement of 1814 set up a so-called 'free zone' outside the frontier of the canton (and hence of Switzerland) from which,

*The headquarters of Soviet Intelligence.

although it was French territory, goods could be 'exported' to Geneva duty-free. This is why the customs posts are not on the political frontier but between one and four miles beyond—in other words, well into France.

I often took advantage of this fact: I got on the tram or took a local train in Geneva and in twenty minutes I was in France—in Annemasse or Saint-Julien—but still inside the Swiss customs frontier. Occasionally I took the steamer that plied between Lausanne on the Swiss side and the health resorts of Thonon and Evian on the French shore of the Lake of Geneva. There was no customs check on these trains and boats and certainly no passport control, so that it was a simple matter to get from one country to the other. Once in France I ceased to be a resident and became a visitor, and as such I could safely board a French train from, say, Evian to Paris. All this changed, of course, when war broke out and the frontier was hermetically sealed.

The time I received that postcard from Paris I caught the train in Evian and arrived in the French capital on the appointed day.

I went straight to the boulevard mentioned on the postcard and found the place where I had been told to wait. I sat down on a bench, polished my spectacles, opened a German newspaper, and laid a book on the seat beside me. These were the signs by which the contact man was to recognize me. I looked at the advertising pillars for a while and watched the passers-by.

Punctually at the appointed time a tall, well-dressed, middle-aged man appeared. I suddenly became aware of his presence when he was only two paces from the bench I was sitting on.

'Excuse me, do you mind if I sit down?' He spoke French with a foreign accent.

'Not at all,' I replied.

He sat down on the side where the book lay. His bony knees looked as if they were almost coming through the cloth of his trousers. We exchanged the code word. The man called himself 'Kolya', which had also been the signature on the postcard.

'We'd better go in the car,' he said.

We got in his car, which he drove extremely well (he was a tank-driver, as I subsequently discovered), and left Paris in a westerly direction. Suddenly there was a string of racing cyclists coming down the street towards us and I noticed that the pavements were lined with cheering spectators: we had somehow got involved in the finish of the Tour de France. We turned off into a wood and stopped in a small clearing that was highly suitable for a confidential talk.

My new acquaintance was a head taller than I. He was courteous but extremely reserved. One got the impression of a man who had been through the mill, although to judge from his appearance he can hardly have been more than forty-five. His thick black hair was already threaded with grey, his yellowish face was criss-crossed with wrinkles, and there was a cold, determined look in his pale, almost colourless eyes. The bags under the latter suggested that he was not a healthy man.

'One would never think to look at you that you're involved in conspiratorial work,' Kolya said suddenly. 'You look like a solid citizen with a thriving business. That's excellent. That's just how you should look'.

He proceeded to the purpose of our meeting. On instructions from headquarters I was as of now to carry out assignments that he, Kolya, would be giving me. We were to meet in Paris, and we agreed a place and time. If there were any change Kolya would inform me by letter. I was to give my reports to him alone. With that we separated and I returned to Geneva with a concrete assignment that I was to fulfil on my next trip to Italy.

Central were extremely interested in the Italian troops that were being sent to Spain to support General Franco. Covering this assignment involved a number of trips to Fascist Italy. I travelled on business, as the proprietor of a cartographical agency. Fortunately Geopress had a great many subscribers in Italy, even including such extreme right-wing publications as *Il Tempo* in Rome. I had dealings on a number of occasions with the paper's Fascist editor. In between I posed as the tourist in search of rest and relaxation.

I also did business with the Italian air ministry. The maps and handbook of European air routes that I had published in Germany had given me something of a name as an aerial cartographer, and I had often flown in the Italian airline company's planes to Greece, Turkey, the Dodecanese (at that time an Italian colony), and Tunisia. The Fiat company had even invited me on the maiden flight on the Turin-London route. In Rome I made the acquaintance of Teruzzi, marshal of the air force and secretary of state at the air ministry. It was through him that I was invited to a reception given by Mussolini himself (Mussolini was also air minister), which gave me an opportunity of studying the man's incredible smugness at close quarters.

Apropos Fascist self-importance, I had an interesting experience on one trip. I wanted a free ticket for the Rome-Sicily-Tunis flight because I needed to do a map of the route, so I called at the head office of the ALI airline company in Rome. The manager, an extremely friendly count who already knew me from our having corresponded, said this would be all right and gave me the address of the president of the company, whose authorization was necessary. When I arrived at the address in the Corso Vittorio Emmanuele, however, two armed Fascists barred my way.

'Vostro biglietto di partito?' they demanded. 'Your party card?'

Imagine my astonishment at discovering that the building I was trying to get into was the headquarters of the central committee of the Fascist party, of which the president of the airline company turned out to be a high-ranking secretary. It was too late to turn back. My papers were checked, and I was admitted.

There were several people in the waiting-room. The black-bearded gentleman sitting beside me politely introduced himself as the federal secretary of the province of Ferrara and asked me, 'Which province do you represent?' The fellow took me for a Fascist official, and a provincial secretary at that! I talked my way out of that one somehow, but it had been a nasty moment.

At last it was my turn to see the party secretary. I handed him the count's letter of recommendation together with my letter from the secretary of state at the air ministry but was rewarded with an extremely cool reception. At first I could not understand why, but when I looked at one of the envelopes lying on his desk and saw that it bore the inscription '*Alla Vostra Eccellenza*' I realized immediately what a serious mistake I had made in addressing him merely as '*signor direttore*'. There was time to put matters right, however; I quickly switched to 'your Excellency', and in five minutes I had the flight ticket in my hand.

As a result of this experience I felt safe enough in taking a look at one or two naval ports. In La Spezia I found three Italian warships lying at anchor, taking on soldiers and weapons. I strolled along and watched the bustle of the port, with the excursion boats hurrying hither and thither and the silhouettes of the warships standing out against the skyline. A young fisherman, obviously recognizing me as a tourist, came up and offered to take me out in his boat. I jumped at the chance.

'What are those vessels out there?' I asked him as we got under way. 'Could we take a closer look at them?'

'Those, you mean? Two torpedo boats and a cruiser. Been there two days already. Wish they'd fuck off. They churn the water up with their great screws and scare off all the fish. Are you Portuguese or Brazilian, *signor*?'

'What makes you think I'm either?' I asked, somewhat taken aback.

'You look like it,' was the simple lad's answer. 'The way you talk, too—just like the Portuguese.'

I said nothing but let him think I was Portuguese.

We rowed up to one of the ships lying at anchor, the cruiser *Giovanni delle Bande Nere*. Suddenly someone hailed us from on deck: 'Hey, Beppo! Who's that you've got in your boat?' Apparently the inquisitive sailor was a friend of my fisherman. Beppo answered that he had a Portuguese gentleman. To my consternation we were invited to come aboard. It soon become clear, however, that the blackshirts simply wanted a chance to show off to a foreigner. They showed us all over the ship. I talked to some of the sailors and found out that the cruiser would soon be sailing for the Balearic Islands—destination: Palma de Mallorca—to take part in the sea blockade of the republican cities.

On a subsequent trip to La Spezia I had an adventure that might easily have taken a nasty turn. I made a bit of an excursion to the hills around the city, from which one had a splendid view of the whole bay—and of course also of the fleet anchored there. Suddenly I was stopped by a military patrol: 'What are you doing here? This is a restricted area.' I assured them I had not seen a single sign (which was the truth) but it was no good: I was taken to the guard-house and brought before a second lieutenant for interrogation. What was I to say to him? If I failed to produce a good story off the cuff I should be hauled off to the barracks as a suspicious alien and might well find myself being thoroughly searched. I was saved by an inspiration.

'I just wanted to look at the bay near La Spezia where the great English poet Shelley met his death.'

Fortunately the officer was a man of some literary education, and it also appealed to his patriotic feelings that a foreigner should be so interested in the famous poet who had chosen Italy for his home. He was further reassured by my passport, since the Hungarian authorities who had issued it were on friendly terms with Fascist Italy. Thanks to Shelley, the incident was closed without further complications.

Another experience I found typical of Fascist Italy was one I had in a first-class compartment of the Florence-Rome express. As part of my tried and tested method of getting into conversation with my Italian travelling companions I pulled out a copy of the Paris newspaper, *Le Temps.* Invariably someone asked what people abroad thought of the Fascist dictatorship, and the trick worked this time too. I was alone with an elderly gentleman who was sporting a Fascist party badge in his buttonhole. The badge notwithstanding, before many minutes he was furiously laying into Mussolini and his government. I asked how it happened that a member of the Fascist party expressed himself in this way, to which he replied disparagingly that, although there were ten million Italians walking around with the badge in their buttonholes, only a fraction of them were convinced Fascists. In the course of conversation he introduced himself: he was legal adviser to Crown Prince Umberto. In the end we became such buddies that he invited me to visit his ten-roomed flat in an ancient *palazzo* in Rome's Piazza San Silvestro, where he proudly showed me his personally dedicated photographs of Umberto and Umberto's father, the king. Unfortunately I was unable to develop this contact further because war broke out soon afterwards.

All the information I gathered on these Italian trips I passed on to my Paris contact, Kolya, with whom I was in touch for the space of about six months.

CHAPTER 4

'Pakbo'

One fine day in April 1938 I looked up from my desk to find the tall figure of Kolya looming in my study doorway. Helene had shown him in. My bewilderment must have been visible in my face because he quickly assured me that everything was all right and that there was no call for alarm. Something urgent had come up, he said.

In conspiratorial matters Kolya was punctilious to the point of being downright niggling, so I knew that he had had no choice but to make this first visit to my Geneva flat in person. Not that his coming would have been likely to arouse the neighbours' suspicions—I had people coming to see me on business all day and every day—but for safety's sake we had made a point of avoiding this type of contact.

Kolya was silent for a moment. He looked worn out. His face was haggard and he was clearly short of sleep. His voice was firm, however, and his look as cool and deliberate as ever.

'I've had instructions from Central to hand my group over to you,' he said at last. 'They've decided to appoint you head of the Swiss group. That's what I've come about. You'll be working independently from now on.'

'What about you?' I asked, surprised.

One was not even supposed to ask such questions, let alone answer them, but this time, in spite of the rule, Kolya replied.

'You stay—I go.' He shot me a penetrating glance. In his eyes I saw determination—but perhaps also that hint of sadness that I had caught there several times before. 'I can even tell you where I'm going,' he went on. 'To Moscow. . . I've been recalled. But that's enough of that. Tomorrow in Berne I shall introduce you to a man called Otto Pünter. His codename is "Pakbo". He's got some useful people. Pakbo is a reliable and experienced man. He'll be your immediate assistant.'

Since the war several authors have claimed that the codename

'Pakbo' represented an abbreviation of 'Parteikanzlei Bormann', suggesting that Pünter got his information from none other than one of the top men in the Nazi party, namely Martin Bormann himself. This is beyond any doubt a piece of pure invention. In his own memoirs, published in 1967, Pünter claimed that his codename was derived from the initials of the places that he and the members of his dubious group of conspirators had used as contact points before the war (*P*ontresina/*P*oschiavo—*A*rth Goldau—*K*reuzlingen—*B*erne/*B*asel—*O*rselina).* Kolya—and, after all, he should have known—gave a much more prosaic explanation: Pünter's peculiar, rolling gait always put Kolya in mind of a steamer; the French for 'steamer' is *paquebot,* which when transcribed according to Russian pronunciation becomes 'pakbo'.

Kolya told me that Otto Pünter was a journalist and the proprietor and managing director of INSA (International Socialist Agency), an information bureau that was closely associated with the Swiss Social Democratic party. He had extensive connections in the press community, the diplomatic corps, and even Swiss government departments. He had condemned Germany's and Italy's intervention in Spain in sharply anti-Fascist articles, which had of course made him unpopular in extreme conservative circles. As far as his own political convictions were concerned, Pünter was a left-wing socialist and sympathized with the Soviet Union. He had undertaken to help our intelligence service for ideological reasons, seeing it as his duty to his party and his country to combat Fascism.

'You know of INSA, do you?' Kolya asked.

'Yes, indeed. I see pieces from the agency in the press now and then. Pünter strikes me as a talented journalist, but if he wants to help us it seems to me rather irresponsible of him to shout his views from the rooftops the way he does. Isn't that a bit of a liability as far as working with him is concerned?'

'Right,' Kolya nodded. 'Pünter's careless. Sometimes he's positively rash. We may have to pay dearly for his recklessness one day. For goodness' sake bear it in mind. He takes no precautions whatever over choosing his acquaintances. He's often surrounded by all kinds of imposters, some of whom are bound to be from the police and the Fascist secret services. I've warned him over and over

*Otto Pünter, *Der Anschluss fand nicht statt,* ('The *Anschluss* that didn't happen'), Berne, 1967, p. 73.

again to be more careful. He thinks we worry too much. He says that as a journalist he can be interested in all types of information without arousing suspicion. After all, it's in the nature of his profession to be inquisitive, and that gives him good cover.'

'Isn't he watched?'

'Yes, unfortunately he is. He's reported that the Swiss federal police open his post and tap his telephone. Now and then an *agent provocateur* makes a clumsy attempt to catch him out over the phone. We suspect the Gestapo already have their eye on him. At any rate it looks as if the Germans are interested in him: a Swiss fellow by the name of Jabet—he's a secretary at the Japanese embassy and a childhood friend of Pünter's—has already been putting out feelers. Recently we passed Pünter a severe warning from Central to steer clear of such people in future.'

The sun was bright in the room and Kolya closed his eyes for a moment, leaning back into the shade.

'Give a lot of thought,' he went on, 'to how you're going to maintain contact with Pünter in future, because this has got to be kept watertight—it's extremely important for us.'

'How did you do it? Did you meet here in Switzerland or in Paris?'

'Here, to start with. Pünter didn't know where I lived. I used to ring him to set up each rendezvous. We met twice a week, usually in the mountains somewhere. But when Pünter found out that he was being watched Central recommended that I stop travelling to Switzerland and get Pünter to come to Paris instead. It seemed pretty certain that he wouldn't be followed there. Although'—and here Kolya smiled briefly—'nothing's certain in our business. There are only two things we can rely on—our own faculty of observation and the habit of caution.'

'So you don't think it would be advisable for me to meet him in Berne or Geneva?'

'No, I don't. Although your situation is different, of course. You both run press agencies and you could have business connections. Legitimate meetings don't arouse suspicion as long as they aren't too frequent. Anyway, I think Central will soon be sending through instructions as to how best to organize the contact. Your contact with Central will continue to be *via* Paris. Introduce yourself to Pünter in Berne under a codename and don't mention Geopress for the time being.

'Now let's look at Pünter's potential,' Kolya went on. 'His main job is to get military information from Germany and Italy and find out all he can about the intervention in Spain. He has some good sources. He gets some useful stuff from a Yugoslav ex-pilot who is now a diplomat and has the codename "Gabel". And he has some useful people in Italy too. On top of all this, as I said, he knows a lot of people in political, diplomatic, and journalistic circles and occasionally gets information from them. Pünter will tell you all about his people himself.'

Kolya drew a tired hand over his yellowish face and then looked me in the eye.

'Pünter's a good worker—that you can depend on. He's quick at making new contacts and winning their confidence. He's an intelligent, cultivated man and he speaks several languages fluently. You'll work well together, the two of you—of that I'm certain. But don't forget he needs a cold shower occasionally. Pünter is a man who likes to take risks. In his case, I must admit, they often pay, but he wants too much all at once and he dissipates his energies. He gets these hare-brained, unrealistic ideas and just has to be talked out of them. Bear that in mind. Encourage him to develop more contacts with people like Gabel. What matters above all is that we get our information about Germany and Italy.

'Well, I think that's about it.' Kolya forced a smile. 'Tomorrow we go to Berne and we'll be meeting Pakbo at six in the evening at'—and here he mentioned a posh restaurant near the Parliament building. 'Pakbo will be there. And remember—he must know neither your real name nor your line of business.'

Kolya in fact went on to Berne by the evening train, and the next day I set out myself to meet 'Pakbo'.

Kolya had arranged our rendezvous for the evening because in the evening the Swiss capital is virtually dead, and 'the fewer eyes the better' is the first rule of conspiratorial work.

It was perhaps ten past six when I entered the restaurant. Kolya was already seated at a corner table from which he could keep an eye on the rest of the room. The next table by the window was vacant. Beside Kolya sat the man I was to work with in future.

At first glance I put him down as about thirty, but I was wrong. I was already thirty-eight at the time, and he was only a year younger, as emerged in the course of our conversation.

Otto Pünter was a stocky, broad-shouldered man with fair hair. A pair of blue-grey eyes twinkled merrily behind his spectacles. His round face shone with health and energy. He turned out to be a lively and pleasant person to talk to. I decided I liked him. He gave me the impression of a man with a broad and inquiring mind, and we found our views on many subjects coincided.

Kolya took little part in the conversation. He ate and drank, put in the odd word out of politeness, and then fell silent again. But he followed closely everything we said, and it was he that eventually brought the talk round to our immediate problem.

'You must arrange your next meeting,' he said. 'Otto, from now on you come under Albert here.' This was how he had introduced me to Pünter. 'The assignments you'll be getting from him come direct from Central.'

Kolya was the first to leave, and I knew it was to go straight to the station and take the train for Paris. After he had gone, Pünter and I arranged to meet again in the next few days. We parted and I caught the last train back to Geneva.

And from that day on I headed the Swiss group of Soviet Intelligence. I never saw Kolya again, although my wife and I received a First of May greeting from him about a fortnight later, postmarked Moscow. So it was April 1938 when I met Pünter-Pakbo for the first time and not June 1940 as, for reasons of his own, he claims in his memoirs.*

I decided we would not meet in Geneva because it seemed to me better not to let Pakbo know for the time being where I lived. In Berne, on the other hand, besides being very well-known he was also under observation. The safest place to meet was somewhere between the two cities—and Chexbres station suggested itself. At first we saw each other only once or twice a week, arranging the next rendezvous on each occasion. I had still not made up my mind how we should keep in touch subsequently.

The first time, as I say, we met on the platform of the tiny, deserted station of Chexbres. It was a stiflingly hot day. We strolled along a path that ran between two vineyards and I had a good look round.

'Looking to see whether anyone's following us?' asked Pakbo.

*Otto Pünter, *Der Anschluss fand nicht statt,* p. 115.

'You needn't worry—I was the only person who got out.'

'Otto, I must ask you to be more careful. You've been given a highly responsible job to do. Kolya told me you've already had *agents provocateurs* after you, to say nothing of the Swiss police. He even reckons the Gestapo are onto you. You know as well as I do that Switzerland's absolutely crawling with German agents.'

The merry twinkle disappeared from Pakbo's eyes and he became serious.

'Not just agents,' he said. 'There's a whole string of Nazi organizations working underground here, and it's no secret that Hitler is planning to annex the German-speaking part of Switzerland, which as you know is two-thirds of the country. Even in the Swiss army there are officers who are dreaming of something along the lines of the annexation of Austria.'

Pakbo's situation really bothered me and I brought the conversation back to what was uppermost in my mind.

'Yes, and these Swiss Fascists are bound to be hand in glove with German Intelligence. You're undoubtedly being kept under observation—you've got a reputation for being as red as they come. I saw an article in the *Courrier de Genève* headlined "The Comintern in Switzerland". It mentioned your name and your agency and accused you of "dangerous Bolshevist agitation".'

Pakbo chuckled.

'All right, but it was worse than that,' I went on. 'The writer claimed to have information that you were in touch with Comintern agents. It was obviously a piece of provocation, but we must be clear about how dangerous these things can be. After an open insinuation like that it will be tricky for you to go on receiving information from your important contacts.'

Pakbo shook his head.

'That doesn't bother me, Albert. You're new to Switzerland—you don't know our liberal system yet. I told Kolya this and Central too—they'd been ticking me off for taking too many risks. As a journalist I have the right to collect information and pass it on to anyone I please. They can only arrest me if I damage the national interests of Switzerland—which I never have done and never will do. Also I get a certain protection from the fact that I'm a respected member of the Social Democratic party here, which carries a lot of weight in Switzerland. But anyway,' he added with a smile, 'I will be careful—I promise you.'

'All right, Otto, we'll leave it at that. Now let's get down to business. Tell me first how Gabel operates. Who is he, in fact?'

'Who is he?' Pakbo repeated my question and was thoughtful for a moment. 'As far as we're concerned he's an extremely useful and utterly reliable man. He's a consul, and he represents the interests of the Spanish republican government in Yugoslavia. He works from Susak, a port just inside the Yugoslav-Italian frontier. A close acquaintance of his is General Franco's official representative in Yugoslavia. It's from him that Gabel gets his information about Italy and Spain.'

We had left the station far behind us. There was not a soul in sight.

'My first impression of Gabel,' Pakbo went on, 'and this was reinforced at subsequent meetings, is that he is weak on politics. He's incapable of judging the present political situation or probably any other. He's anti-Fascist, but his sympathies are more emotional than rationally worked out. He hates the Italian blackshirts far more than the German Nazis. He's a man of violent and unstable moods, which is of course a big disadvantage in our work. I'm trying to work on him, though. I think we can rule out any possibility of his betraying us. He's a thoroughly open, honest character.'

'When and where do you meet?'

'We'll be meeting at the end of this month at a village on the Italian frontier, just inside Switzerland.'

I asked him more about how he maintained contact with Gabel and it emerged that there was a heavy loss of time involved. Pakbo did not want to go to Gabel in Susak because, although as a Swiss citizen he did not need a transit visa to cross Italy, for a notoriously anti-Fascist journalist it would have been a risky journey. Gabel, however, who had a diplomatic passport, could easily get a transit visa to Switzerland without arousing suspicion because Susak was only just across the river from the Italian port of Fiume, where the authorities knew Gabel well. So Gabel brought his information to Pakbo in Switzerland. If for some reason he could not get away from Susak they got in touch by post and agreed the place and time of the next meeting in a coded letter.

'That's a long stretch,' I remarked. 'By the time Gabel has brought his report to you and we've passed it on to Central the information may well be out of date, particularly as regards troop transports to Spain. We'll have to find a better solution. What about contact with your other people—is that simpler?'

'Much simpler,' Pakbo nodded. 'They're in Switzerland and I can meet them any time.'

These were people Pakbo had recruited on Kolya's instructions, many of whom supplied important information. One of them was a German Social Democrat who had served in the League of Nations administration in the Saar before the 1935 plebiscite. He had emigrated from Germany and taken Swiss nationality, and he was widely connected. He hated the Fascists. He had agreed to pass on such information as came into his hands, and he had promised to report soon on Hitler's military plans. In our reports to Central we later dubbed this source 'Poisson'.

Pakbo and I arranged our next meeting and I returned to Geneva.

Rather than arrive at the main Cornavin station in Geneva, which was always crawling with spies, I had decided to leave the train at Pregny, a quiet station not too far from my flat in Sécheron. So I took an omnibus train that stopped at every station and I had plenty of time to think about my talk with Pakbo. Frankly I was disappointed. Everything Pakbo had said struck me as the sort of insignificant stuff that gets hawked about in journalistic circles. It smacked of cheap romanticism. Was it worth maintaining so complicated an organization for the sake of such trifles? Possibly to Kolya, who came from a little village in Bessarabia (as he had told me himself), it had all seemed interesting and important. Knowing the world of journalism as I did, however, I was not particularly impressed. For this reason I always treated Pakbo's reports with a certain amount of caution—as he mentions with some acerbity in his memoirs. The fact is, I did not at that time regard Pakbo as by any means a first-rate intelligence source. He was much better at the 'technology' of intelligence work, at manufacturing micro-cameras and inventing simple secret signs. But it all had rather a romantic flavour as if he had been an admirer of Poe and Jules Verne.

I had no intelligence training myself. Like so much else in their sensation-seeking book, *La Guerre a été gagnée en Suisse* ('The War was won in Switzerland'), the French journalists Accoce and Quet's assertion that I was trained as an agent in an institution I have never even heard of in the vicinity of Moscow is a piece of pure fantasy.* The fact that I was well-versed in underground work did not entirely make up for my lack of professional experience in the field of intelligence. In fact my inexperience became painfully apparent when I took over as head of the Swiss network and was confronted with innumerable questions to which I had to find the right answer fast. I was very grateful during this period for the advice I received from someone at Central who signed himself 'The Director'.

It was clear to me from the start, however, that the scope of the group was inadequate and its way of going about things naive. And all the time the approaching war was casting its shadow more threateningly over Europe: republican Spain was lost, and in Munich the Western powers signed Czechoslovakia over to the Fascists.

In December 1938 I received urgent instructions from Moscow to build up and expand the group, and I discussed with Pakbo how we could not only make better use of our existing sources but also recruit new ones. By early 1939 we had a small team supplying us with a steady stream of interesting information, which we were able to fill out with other reports from various sources. The most valuable intelligence still came from Gabel. Following instructions from Central he reported on the strategic movements of the Italian army and air force and collected information about the state of the Italian munitions industry and about arms consignments to Franco. He supplied detailed material regarding the development of Italy's shipyards and other branches of industry, and his friends kept an eye on naval movements in the ports of Genoa, Naples, and La Spezia. Whenever a ship or submarine sailed out on course for Spain they tried to get word to Gabel as quickly as possible.

Reports on the state of the German armed forces and on troop movements came mainly from Poisson, *via* Pakbo. In the summer of 1939 this source gave us the important information that the Hitler regime was planning to occupy Danzig, at that time a 'free city' under League of Nations administration. It was this act of aggression that, as everyone knows, unleashed the Second World War.

All the information that my group collected I passed on to Central *via* Paris.

*P. Accoce and P. Quet, *La guerre a été gagnée en Suisse,* Paris, 1966, p. 139.

I still had a lot of friends in France, including many Hungarian emigrants, from the time when I had lived and worked there. I was on close terms with Count Mihály Károlyi, the former president of the Hungarian republic, a wonderful man and a holder of some very progressive views. On Horthy's rise to power the exiled Károlyi had lost any chance of returning home and had settled with his family in Paris. There they lived, in severely straitened material circumstances but with wide family connections in the Hungarian legitimist aristocratic circles that stood in opposition to the Horthy regime. The Károlyi family, who knew me as an anti-Fascist journalist from Inpress days, also supplied me with information, primarily in the field of foreign affairs since they had access to certain diplomatic circles.

My contact with Paris was not to last much longer, however, for the world was already on the threshold of its six-year ordeal.

CHAPTER 5

On our own

Already by August 1939, with Hitler increasing his pressure on Poland, the tension in Switzerland was enormous. Tourists and holidaymakers began leaving the country in droves. In the streets and restaurants one heard nothing but talk of whether war was going to break out or not. The Swiss government announced that the shops would close for two months if it did and that people should lay in supplies accordingly. Panic buying set in. People not only hoarded mountains of tinned food but for example bought their children several pairs of shoes in different sizes and put their money into gold and jewellery.

On 27 August Switzerland's neighbours mobilized. Only two days later all postal and telephone connections with France were cut off. International air traffic was suspended. Concerts starring celebrities from abroad were cancelled. Desperate tourists literally stormed trains that were already filled to bursting. The exodus of foreigners caused unbelievable jams on the roads and at the frontier crossing points. Our maid, whom we had come to regard as one of the family, left us from one hour to the next; Geneva was too near the frontier for her liking and she went home to her parents in the German-speaking part of Switzerland.

Otto Köcher, the German ambassador to Switzerland, had assured the Swiss government in an official communiqué that in the event of war Germany would respect Swiss neutrality, but still the tension continued to build up hourly. Hitler's political promises had already lost a lot of their credibility. On the evening of 30 August the lights were still burning as the Swiss went to bed, but the countries on Switzerland's borders already had blackout orders.

In the early hours of 1 September German troops occupied the 'free city' of Danzig and moved into action along the Polish frontier. England and France—Poland's allies—were still trying for a peaceful solution.

The next day, 2 September, Switzerland too decreed general mobilization. It was a beautiful late-summer Saturday and the lake-shore was crowded with Genevans basking in the sun. Only hours later the mobilization order was pasted up on the advertising pillars. Soon trains were rolling out of the stations taking soldiers to their mustering points. Four hundred thousand men took up positions in the forests and mountains; the Swiss were determined to fight for their country.

The government informed the Germans that if they put a foot over the frontier all the centres of Swiss industry would be blown sky-high—by 1942 preparations had been made for the destruction of over a thousand factories in this event*—and that the population would retire with the army to the so-called 'Réduit', a vast natural fortress in the Alps, and fight the invader from there. Stored in the mountains were food supplies for four years.

The gold reserves of the Swiss National Bank, which amounted to three times the face value of the notes in circulation, were already in America, in the cellars of Fort Knox. Through secret channels the Germans were given to understand that it was not worth attacking Switzerland because for one thing the gold was no longer there and for another they would only be exposing their rear to a well-armed and fully-mobilized army in the mountains.

The Germans had no wish to embark on a prolonged campaign in the Alps, especially now that the most tempting prize—the gold reserves—was out of reach. It would have been pointless sacrificing troops to conquer a tiny country that its Fascist neighbours had in any case already cut off from the outside world. Hitler was content for the time being that Switzerland should comply with his military demands. Switzerland's excellent munitions industry started working for the Wehrmacht at full capacity, and between Germany and her Italian allies transports were allowed to pass through the country unhindered and even free of charge: there was talk of settling up after the war—when Hitler, confident of victory, felt he would be able to attend to little Switzerland at his leisure.

Two years later, in August 1942, the German ambassador in Berne stated in answer to a question from the German foreign ministry that 'Switzerland has stock-piled enough food and raw

*Jon Kimche, *Spying for Peace*, Weidenfeld & Nicholson, London, 1961, p. 73.

materials to be able to hold out in the "Réduit" for approximately two years'. The ambassador pointed out that 'this tough mountain people will defend itself fiercely and there is not a chance of the [for the Germans] vitally important traffic arteries falling into the hands of the invader intact'.*

Finally, on 3 September 1939, Great Britain and France declared war on Germany. For millions of men and women all over Europe it was the beginning of a period of trial and affliction, of mourning, of misery, and of heroic struggle against the dark forces of Fascism. Almost the entire continent was sucked into the maelstrom.

The outbreak of war brought our operations to a virtual standstill: our contact with Central *via* Paris was severed. The thing we had most feared—but could not anyhow have avoided—had come about. And with the Swiss-French frontier sealed, all postal, telegraph, and telephone services idle, and military censorship in force, I could not begin to hope to get in touch with Paris again for the time being.

In this state of enforced inactivity all we could do was kick our heels and wait. The weeks stretched into months and still there was no word from Central as to what I should do and how I was to renew contact. I was worried and at the same time completely baffled by the director's continued silence. I was head of an intelligence group, there was a war on, and we had no contact!

*Gert Buchheit, *Der deutsche Geheimdienst,* ('The German Secret Service'), Munich, 1967, pp. 409 f.

CHAPTER 6

The world's largest prison

At last, in December 1939, a message came through: someone passing through Geneva dropped a letter in my box by the front door.

The letter informed me that an agent would be getting in touch with me in a few days to re-establish contact with Central, and a few days later I duly received a visit from a tall, slender, almost fragile-looking woman in a closely-fitting woollen dress. I put her age at about thirty-five. Her movements were smooth and a trifle languid.

I took her into my study and we exchanged the password.

'My codename is Sonya,' said my visitor with a smile. She spoke German. 'The director told me to get in touch with you. I was given your name and address and instructions to call on you and find out how things stand with your group. The director wants to know how the agency is doing and whether you have enough money. Also, what facilities do you have for collecting information, how long will you need to establish radio contact, will you need help running the transmitter, and would it be possible for you to communicate with headquarters *via* Italy? I'm supposed to clarify all these points with you and report back to the director. You'll undoubtedly be receiving further instructions through me.'

Taking her points one by one I told her that Geopress continued to provide a sound cover organization and that the local authorities suspected nothing. The outbreak of war had considerably reduced our income because with the Swiss frontier sealed we had lost a lot of our foreign subscribers. We were a long way from going bankrupt, however, because we still had the Swiss market, where nearly all the big papers were subscribers of ours, and we were still able to supply our subscribers in Italy and Germany, because here communications were still open. As far as our intelligence work was concerned we were still receiving information regularly but it was simply piling up because I had no means of passing it on to

Central. We definitely needed a transmitter, trained radio operators, and a flat or house to operate from. Reliable people could no doubt be found, but would it be possible to let us have a new set, or could the set we had—an ancient and poorly constructed one—be repaired? We needed a code, and transmission and reception times would have to be agreed.

'There are plenty of problems, as you can see,' I said, and they all need solving as a matter of urgency if we are to operate effectively. As regards going to Italy, I don't think that's particularly opportune at the moment. Would I need to, anyway, if we're going to have a direct radio link with Moscow? Contact *via* Italy would be a pretty complicated business.'

Sonya promised to send a coded report to Central next day, and we further agreed that from then on she should call me 'Albert'.

From early January 1940, at first through Sonya, we had a stable radio link with headquarters in Moscow.

During the time we worked together I knew precious little about Sonya. I had no idea where she lived, for example, or whom she worked with, or what type of intelligence she collected. The rules of conspiracy forbade me to ask her and her to volunteer the information. I assumed she was a confidential agent sent from Central and that she would be appropriately experienced.

The Englishman Alexander Foote, who as 'Jim' was a member of Sonya's group and subsequently of mine, writes in his *Handbook for Spies* that on orders from headquarters he contacted Sonya in Geneva in 1938.* Apart from him Sonya had another associate, also English, a young man with the codename 'John'. Both of them had fought in the International Brigade in Spain, and when offered a secret and dangerous assignment they had both jumped at the chance. They had been sent to Switzerland and Sonya became their instructress. She taught them the rules of conspiracy, how to use secret codes and operate a radio, and in fact everything an intelligence agent needs to know. Their training lasted several months, and during this period Jim and John made occasional trips to Germany, completing simple assignments, collecting military information, and incidentally perfecting their German, a grounding in which Sonya had also given them. Our two groups—Sonya's and mine—operated independently and in

*Alexander Foote, *Handbook for Spies,* Museum Press, London, 1949, p. 25.

complete isolation until circumstances forced us to contact each other.

In March 1940 I received through Sonya a radio telegram from Central. The director informed me that someone called 'Kent' would be visiting me from Brussels. Kent would bring me the necessary documents for organizing our own radio link with headquarters, instructions regarding certain details of our work, and money for Sonya and her associates as well as a reserve fund for my group.

I was delighted to hear that we should soon be in direct contact with Central and no longer be a burden on Sonya's transmitter, which she needed to have fully available for her own work. All we had to do now was to repair our reserve set or instal a new one. Having an independent radio link with Central was extremely important as far as future operations were concerned, and it also meant that in the event of an arrest—something we had to reckon with all the time—one set would remain in service.

The contact man's visit was unavoidable. Nevertheless it bothered me that Central had given Kent (and before him Sonya) my name and address. To my mind this was extremely imprudent. Granted that the outbreak of war had made travel difficult and that there was no other way of getting word to me, arrangements should still have been made for me to meet Kent somewhere other than at my flat. I got in touch with Central immediately and protested at this gratuitous revelation of my identity and where I lived. The director evidently found my protest justified because nothing of the kind ever happened again.

Kent appeared before the end of March, turning up at my flat one day without so much as a telephone call to announce his arrival. He was a lean, fair-haired, elegant-looking fellow with an easy, even somewhat condescending manner and an air of enormous self-confidence. One had the impression of a man of the world.

'I've had instructions from the director to look up Dora,' he announced. It was what the telegram had said he would say.

'Are you Kent?'

'Yes, that's the name I operate under,' he replied. 'Did you get the director's radio message?

I nodded. We had identified each other and we proceeded to get down to business.

'My instructions were to bring you the material you need for your work,' Kent went on. 'I also have to discuss with you certain organizational questions arising out of the war situation. I've come from Brussels, and I must say it wasn't easy crossing two frontiers. But I have to go back the same way—orders are orders.'

He spoke French, but very badly and with a strong accent. He had been rummaging in a large, crocodile-leather briefcase as he talked.

'Here is the material. This is the code book for encoding your telegrams, and this other one contains the transmission and reception schedule.'

I decided the man was arrogant: there was no other word for it. His long, narrow face bore a strong resemblance to that of a horse, and it occurred to me that anyone who had once seen it would never forget it, which for an intelligence agent is hardly an advantage.

'You're to write your messages in German,' he continued. 'It's vital that you install your set and train your operators as soon as possible. Central stress that this must be given priority. Have you got operators? No? That's bad. You must concentrate all your efforts on finding and training some fast. Don't think that what the papers call the "phoney war" along the Siegfried and Maginot Lines will last for ever. I have information to the effect that the Germans will attack in the spring. I'm afraid the Allies don't stand a chance, and in that situation it will remain to be seen whether a man like Hitler is going to respect the German-Soviet non-aggression pact. You're no doubt aware that there are large concentrations of German armed forces on the Soviet Union's new frontier in Poland.'

Sober fellow, I thought to myself. Of course anything was possible. But the man's schoolmasterly tone got on my wick. He was so obviously full of himself, and I have never been able to stand people like that.

'Thank you for the free political instruction,' I told him.

Kent swung round towards me and for a moment his long face wore an ironic smile. But he remained serious.

'Let's not waste any time,' he said evenly. 'Just listen carefully to everything I tell you. When I've done what I've been sent here to do I'm quite prepared to talk about things you want to talk about.'

I said nothing, and Kent launched into an explanation of the complicated ins and outs of the encoding process. Afterwards he dictated me a few telegrams for practice and I encoded them with the help of the book. He also explained how I was to use the transmission programme.

'Later on, when you have your own sets, Central will tell you your call signs, wave-lengths, and transmission times. A transmitter must never operate according to a system. On the contrary, the number of transmissions and the times of transmission must be changed as often as possible; it's the best protection against being located. It would be a good thing if your operators had a number of flats or houses to work from rather than just one. It would reduce the danger. Keep changing them if you can—but again, avoiding any kind of system. The thicker the fog the better.'

Kent's instructions were detailed and sensible. He certainly knew what he was talking about. We were at it for several hours, and by the end we were both pretty tired. When the last encoding exercise was finished Kent asked me how much money I could let him have. I stared at him in some confusion because my message had said that he would be bringing me money. He explained that he had not dared to take much cash with him on such a risky trip and that he was relying on me to finance his journey back. I gave him what I could—it was not a great deal—and next day he returned to Brussels.

I never saw Kent again, just as I had never seen him before, notwithstanding what the German counter-intelligence officer W.F. Flicke maintains in a book that is in any case riddled with unfounded assertions.* A year later, in March/April 1941, he was again instructed to contact me on some urgent matter, but before he could do so Central cancelled the directive. I read in the Western literature after the war that German Counter-intelligence uncovered and smashed Kent's Brussels group towards the end of 1941; Kent himself went into hiding and managed to get away to France, but the Gestapo caught up with him in the end and he was arrested. His arrest was later to prove a severe blow to the Swiss group because Kent knew a lot about us and told the Gestapo quite a bit of it. But I anticipate. . . .

In May 1940 the Germans bürst through the Allied defences and occupied Belgium and Holland. In June, with the capitulation of

*W.F. Flicke, *Agenten funken nach Moskau* ('Agents are radioing Moscow'), Kreuzlingen, 1954, pp. 34 f.

France, Switzerland was completely encircled by enemy powers, only a narrow corridor near Geneva remaining open to car and bicycle traffic through to Pétain's unoccupied zone. The thunder of guns was audible in Geneva; it came from Fort d'Ecluse on the Rhône, where remnants of the French army continued to put up a fierce resistance until the armistice. And about the same time Italy joined the war.

Showing conspicuous respect for international usage, Mussolini declared war twenty-four hours before opening hostilities—in contrast to Hitler, who had attacked without any formal declaration of war at all.

Twenty-four hours later large numbers of British aircraft took off to bomb Italy. Their route lay over Geneva, and the Swiss crowded the balconies of their houses to feast their eyes on the sight of the bombers flying past in battle formation thousands of feet above. Suddenly they heard explosions—and realized to their horror that bombs were falling on Geneva. Numbers of the curious died on their balconies that night. What had happened? The British pilots, most of whom were Australians, had instructions to bomb Como, a railway junction in northern Italy of great importance to German-Italian collaboration. Both Como and Geneva lie at the south-western tip of long lakes, and the Australian pilots, unfamiliar with the geography of Europe, had mistaken their target.

For me that night had important consequences. All the people living in the six-storied house where my flat was were League of Nations officials of foreign nationality. They moved out or I should say fled before morning—not merely from Geneva but from Switzerland as well—leaving me the sole occupant of the house. Later this was to make conspiratorial work very much simpler.

Switzerland's situation—caught between two powerful enemy blocs, or rather forming an island in the middle of Fascist-dominated Europe—became more and more difficult. It involved much tacking about to preserve the country's neutrality and meant carefully avoiding anything that might have been used to justify an attack on Swiss territory. The mere fact that seventy per cent of the population spoke a German dialect would have been pretext enough in the Nazis' eyes for incorporating the country in the Great German Reich.

One saw evidence of the pressure being put on the country

everywhere one went. German deliveries of military equipment and coal to Italy were all sent *via* Switzerland, and Jon Kimche writes that some hundred and fifty trains, each with up to fifty to sixty trucks, passed through the country daily on their way to Hitler's southern ally.* I was in Chiasso on one occasion and saw German goods trains crossing the frontier into Italy at the rate of one every ten minutes.

The British bombers too flew over neutral Switzerland on their way to German and Italian targets, and every night we heard the muffled drone of their engines. Switzerland was the only neutral country in Europe that continued to light its streets at night, so that the Germans referred to it bitterly as the 'lighthouse' of the RAF. Eventually they made the Swiss introduce the blackout, and after that the only light in Geneva at night came from the German searchlights on Mont Salève, just across the frontier in occupied France.

The economic situation worsened daily. In peacetime, with stock-raising more profitable than growing cereals, the available farmland had been used for grazing and cereals imported from abroad. Now, with imports cut off, the Swiss had to decide which came first—man or his cattle? In the spring of 1941 virtually all the stock was slaughtered and the grazing land ploughed up for planting. Rationing was introduced and one was restricted to half a pound of bread a day.

Surrounded as they were by enemies and under constant threat of invasion, the Swiss, particularly the German-speaking section of the population, showed astonishing courage. The bitter joke made the rounds that Switzerland was now the world's largest prison: Hitler and Mussolini had cut off completely four million people. They made no secret of their hatred of Fascist Germany, and in the eastern part of the country the people deliberately spoke nothing but their dialect, which is very different from proper or High German. On trips to Berne or Zurich I noticed that I was the object of hostile glances in the tram because I asked for my ticked in High German. Having no opportunity to learn the Swiss dialect, I eventually stuck to French even when I was in Zurich, especially as one could get by there with French very well.

But it was not only Switzerland's situation that was critical: our

*Jon Kimche, *Spying for Peace*, p. 42.

own position was becoming increasingly precarious. Sonya had known all about Kent's visit because it was she who received and decoded the telegrams from Central, and she was depressed that he had brought no money. Evidently her funds were running low. She left her villa near Montreux—I discovered after the war that this was where she had lived—and moved to Geneva with her children and John, whom she had recently married. She took a flat very close to my own, which annoyed me because in a small town like Geneva the fact that everyone in the quarter knows everyone else made it dangerous to meet. It was to be expected that even the narrow corridor through to Vichy France—and hence *via* Spain or Portugal to England or the United States—would one day be closed, and Sonya, in fear of the Germans and worried about her children, started making serious preparations to leave the country with them and John.

CHAPTER 7

A trip to Yugoslavia

The outbreak of war meant, as I have said, a serious loss of income for Geopress, so that soon the agency was only bringing in enough for my own family requirements; there was nothing left over for collecting intelligence. What made matters worse, however, was that the same circumstance—namely the war—made it an extremely complicated business for Central to finance us. They had tried with Kent, but not even that enterprising man had dared to bring the money over the frontier: the customs might have arrested him as a currency smuggler, and it would have been ridiculous to risk having the head of an important intelligence group put behind bars for such a trifle. The money could of course have been sent to my bank, but it would have aroused suspicion to have large sums credited to my account all of a sudden. Another way had to be found, but this took time.

Foote maintains in his book that I lived off the Swiss Communist party, which is a complete and utter lie; I was not even in touch with the Swiss Communist party, as my latest 'biographer', Drago Arsenijevič', would have it.* It is a basic rule of Soviet intelligence that any kind of contact with the party is to be avoided. In any case the tiny Swiss Communist party, obliged to operate underground, can hardly have had any money to speak of.

Central were aware of our predicament and proposed the only possible solution under the circumstances: the director announced over the radio that he was sending us some money by special courier. Since it was inconceivable that the courier could get into Switzerland, however, encircled as it was by German and Italian troops, I was to meet him somewhere outside the country. Headquarters had in mind Vichy, but when I went along to the French consulate in Geneva and saw the kind of questionnaires I

*Alexander Foote, *Handbook for Spies*, p. 78; Drago Arsenijevič', *Genève appelle Moscou* ('Geneva calling Moscow'), Paris, 1969.

was required to fill in, it became clear to me that the consulate was in fact a branch of the Gestapo. I passed this information back to Central, adding that the journey would be extremely risky and I would almost certainly be caught. The next proposal was that we should organize a rendezvous in Yugoslavia or Bulgaria, neither of which was as yet occupied by the Germans.

After looking into the possibilities I reported to the director that I could probably manage to reach Yugoslavia. Central gave me a rendezvous in Belgrade, told me the password, and described how I would recognize the courier. He would be giving me money, a microcamera, new chemicals for secret documents, and instructions as to how to use them.

At that time travelling from Switzerland to Yugoslavia was a formidable undertaking. It meant taking the train through either Austria or Italy. Austria was clearly out of the question, being a mere annex of Nazi Germany, so my only chance was to get hold of a transit visa for Italy—no easy matter, since Mussolini's government was already at war with the Western Allies and was not inclined to issue visas to aliens.

I managed it, however. I wrote to a man called Suvich, secretary of state at the Italian foreign ministry and a man whom my agency regularly supplied with maps, stating that my wife and I had to travel to Hungary for family reasons. Suvich issued a special permit. The process was additionally simplified by the fact that both my wife and myself were citizens of a country that was in alliance with Italy.

Leaving the children in the care of their grandmother, Helene and I set out in October 1940 on a trip as perilous as Kent's to visit me. There was a direct connection from Lausanne to Belgrade—the comfortable Simplon Express—and we boarded the train one midnight, trying unsuccessfully not to think about all the things that might happen to us before we arrived.

This particular Simplon Express consisted in its entirety of a sleeping-car, a restaurant-car, and the mail-van. To our astonishment we found that we were the only passengers. Apparently the Italians issued transit visas only in exceptional cases and on this day the privilege was ours alone.

We duly took possession of the sleeping-car, congratulating ourselves on our good fortune. The cook enquired politely what we would like to eat and when; he also recommended that we order coffee before passing the frontier since in Italy the Allied blockade had made coffee a scarce commodity (which, given the Italians' notorious partiality for coffee, was a source of terrible temptation to them: the joke went that for a kilo of coffee even the king was for sale).

This comfortable state of affairs did not last long, however, for when the train emerged from the then longest tunnel in the world—the Simplon—and drew into the Italian frontier station of Domodossola a detachment of Fascist militia climbed aboard and took up residence in the next compartment. The blackshirts accompanied us right across northern Italy. When I left the train in Milan to buy a newspaper they all leapt out after me. Yet never once did they address a word to us, escorting us in tactful silence all the way to the Yugoslav border. If they had known who their subject was!

We arrived safely in Belgrade and of course had no intention of continuing our journey to Hungary. The director's telegram had said that I was to go to the square where the Wrangel Chapel stood. The Wrangel Chapel had been built by a White Guard admiral of that name who had lived in Belgrade as an emigrant during the twenties. I was to meet the contact man by the chapel. I was to have a copy of the *Journal de Genève* in my hand and the courier would be carrying the Bulgarian newspaper *Dnes*.

There had evidently been some misunderstanding because I found that the Wrangel Chapel had been pulled down long ago; there was only the square where it had stood. The time agreed for our rendezvous came and went and the contact man from Central failed to appear. Naturally I stayed in Belgrade: it would have been too aggravating to return empty-handed after such a complicated journey, and in any case we needed the money badly.

We put up at the Hotel Srbski Kral ('King of Serbia'; the hotel was flattened by the first bomb to fall in the first German air raid on Yugoslavia in April of the following year) and took a walk through the city. On our return we saw with some alarm that the Hungarian flag was flying from the hotel flagpole. I asked the waiter about this and was told that the Hungarian foreign minister, Count Csáky, was staying at the hotel, having come to Belgrade to sign the treaty of 'perpetual friendship' with Yugoslavia. (This particular 'perpetual friendship' lasted exactly six months—until April 1941, when Fascist Hungary was among those who helped the Germans to throw their yoke over Yugoslavia.)

There was another occasion in Belgrade when a flag gave us a nasty turn. The morning after our arrival we were woken by the sun streaming into the room, and the first thing we saw when we looked out was an enormous German swastika flag. What on earth had happened? Had the Germans occupied Yugoslavia overnight? It turned out that our hotel, being situated on the steep east bank of the River Sava, overlooked the flatter Zemun on the other side where the Bessarabian Germans, then on their way to be resettled in Germany, had set up camp. They had arrived with their possessions piled on enormous carts and the German reception committee in Belgrade was sending them on by ship up the Danube to Germany. With typical Nazi insolence—and the permission of the right-wing Stojadinovič government—the committee had immediately hoisted the swastika over the camp, giving us at least a terrible shock. Moreover the lorries and cars of the German authorities roared about the city provoking the population by ostentatiously displaying the Fascist emblem.

Day after day I went to the appointed place at the appointed time, but the courier from Central still did not appear. I was beginning to lose hope. To reduce the agony of waiting my wife and I enrolled in a lending library and read from morning till night, trying to calm our nerves and telling ourselves that it was all right, the man had been delayed, he would turn up in the end. And one day, after about two weeks, my daily vigil was rewarded by the appearance of a man who was evidently looking for someone. It soon emerged that he was the man sent from Central.

He handed over a large sum of money, a microcamera, a new powder for secret documents, and the instructions for its use. I gave him the camera back because I could never have smuggled it past the frontier and we did not particularly need it in any case. The customs might have found the powder and the instructions too, but there my wife had an idea: she concealed the material in her mass of blonde hair.

We went back the way we had come—again escorted by the detachment of Italian blackshirts—knowing that we had taken a big risk but glad to be returning with the means to pursue and expand our work.

CHAPTER 8

'Edouard', 'Maude', and 'Jim'

An intelligence agent is useless as a combatant without a well-organized link with headquarters; he is no good to his own country and represents no particular danger to the enemy, even if he knows all the latter's secrets.

In the summer of 1940, before my Belgrade trip, I managed to find the ideal person to establish such a link. He was a radio engineer by trade, trained in Paris, and he had a small radio business in Geneva, complete with repair shop.

After careful consideration I decided that Edmond Hamel—that was his name—was a man who could be entrusted with something as important as a radio link of this kind. Shared ideological convictions had brought us together: Edmond was anti-Fascist and held left-wing socialist views. He immediately agreed to help us, although I made no secret of the fact that his decision might have dangerous consequences for him. A small, thin, inconspicuous-looking man, he would never have been described as daring by someone who did not know him, but he turned out to be a disciplined and reliable associate as well as being an outstanding engineer.

Olga, his wife, was outwardly the exact opposite: tall, well-proportioned, and energetic. She came of a poor peasant family and her powerful hands showed that she had been used to heavy physical work from girlhood on. Olga was a straightforward, likable person. It was really she who was the head of the family: the entire household rested on her broad shoulders as well as the commercial side of the business. Her parents had given her the name Olga out of sympathy for the Russian emigrants who had fled to Switzerland after the 1905 Revolution and whom they had befriended. She had grown up in simple, homely circumstances and shared her husband's political convictions, seeing the Soviet Union as the ideal of working humanity. I asked Olga too if she would help us, and she courageously agreed. By about six months later the flow of information to be transmitted had swollen to such a flood that she had to learn Morse signalling too. Her thirst for knowledge and her ingenuity made her an outstanding radio operator. Her signalling was fast and faultless—in fact, surprising as it may seem, she was better at it than her radio-engineer husband.

The Hamels lived in the rue de Carouge, the main street of Geneva's working-class quarter of Plainpalais, at number 26. The shop and the repair shop occupied the ground floor, and from there a wooden staircase led up to the flat on the first floor. On my visits I generally used the shop entrance, but when working there at night the other members of the group used the rear entrance, identifying themselves with the password: 'Greetings to the Hamel family from Mr. Weber.'

Edmond and Olga knew me as 'Albert'. My second codename, 'Dora', was known only to Central and was the one I used in my communications with the director. My radio operators did not know that, and of course I told no one my real name or my address. In my telegrams to Central I referred to Edmond as 'Edouard' and Olga as 'Maude'.

Edmond started learning the Morse alphabet and how to operate the key in August 1940. Olga, as I have said, began later. Sonya instructed them, on the director's orders, and she also brought her own set and installed it in Edmond's shop; they found a good hiding-place where it could be stowed away when not in use. John and Jim, who were already skilled radio operators, gave Sonya a hand. In between practising with Edmond and Olga, at the appointed times, which were mostly at night, they listened in to Central. When Sonya left Switzerland John stayed on at Central's request to complete Edmond's and Olga's training.

Shortly before she left Sonya introduced me—as Albert—to Alexander Foote (codename 'Jim'). The director decided that Jim should stay in Switzerland and join my group as a radio operator. Before this meeting Jim knew nothing about me, and even afterwards he knew neither my name, nor my address, nor what I did for a living. I, on the other hand, thanks to what Sonya had told me, was able to form a pretty clear picture of the Englishman.

We met at Sonya's flat in Geneva. The impression of him I received was a rather mixed one. Foote was undoubtedly an intelligent and determined man. He had a sense of humour, even inclining towards irony on occasion. Tall, broad-shouldered, and powerfully-built, he had blue eyes set in a permanently clean-shaven face; the pallor of his complexion, however, hinted at some latent illness. His schooling was only moderate and he had never learned a trade. He could speak a bit of German; his French was better, but he drawled his words like someone mastering a stutter.

What most surprised me about him was his total lack of political education. Resourceful and ingenious when it came to tackling problems of a technical or economic nature, the man had trouble finding his bearings in the complicated international situation and probably had only a vaguest notion of the working-class movement. I remember turning up at his flat with a bottle of champagne on the twenty-fifth anniversary of the October Revolution and being greeted with a puzzled stare: he had no idea of the significance of the date.

Not long after Sonya's departure I received the following instructions from the director: Jim was to move to Lausanne and operate Sonya's set from there; John was to stay and maintain radio contact with Central from Geneva.

It was a sensible and timely decision.

As a first-class radio engineer Edmond had no trouble in getting hold of the necessary parts and building a new transmitter (you could not buy them, of course; in wartime the sale of such articles was strictly forbidden). He made us a really efficient set, and with it John kept up our link with Moscow.

We now had two sets, and in view of the danger of being located it would have been inexpedient to have both of them operating from Geneva. So Jim moved to Lausanne, found a suitable flat, and obtained a residence permit for the canton of Vaud, in which Lausanne is situated. He installed his set and by March 1941 had established a stable link with Central. This I learned through John, whom I met occasionally at the Hamels'. (Jim, remember, did not have my address.) He also gave me Jim's Lausanne address and telephone number.

Jim was a talented pupil of Sonya's and became an outstanding radio operator. He had an extraordinary capacity for work and could transmit large numbers of telegrams in a night. I sent him the encoded texts through John until the latter left Switzerland.

After that I contacted him personally or sent my wife with the texts to Lausanne. On these occasions she used the codename 'Maria'.

By the spring of 1941 Edmond and Olga, who learned keenly and quickly, had completed their training and John was able to leave the country. This meant that before the Nazi attack on the Soviet Union I had at my disposal two transmitters and three trained radio operators.

CHAPTER 9

'Sissy'

Life is full of surprises.

One day Helene came home in a state of high excitement.

'Guess what, Alex,' she burst out. 'I've just bumped into the girl I used to work with in Germany—Rachel Dübendorfer.' My wife seemed worried and confused. 'I'm not sure whether this is a good thing or a bad thing as far as we're concerned. Bad, I should think. She knows me very well—she was a shorthand typist in the Agitprop department.' (Before the Hitler *putsch* my wife had worked in the Agitation and Propaganda Department of the Central Committee of the German Communist Party in Berlin.)

She shot me an uncertain look.

'You can imagine what it was like bumping into her again after all these years. She emigrated from Germany too and settled here in Geneva. She got married at some stage but I gather she's now divorced. I couldn't quite work it out. In my opinion it's a pity we've met again. What do you think?'

'It's most unfortunate. Rachel knows me as well. She could easily get us into trouble. You should have ignored her.'

'I couldn't. You know how careful I am, but there was nothing I could do about it. I was just buying something at the confectioner's and Rachel walked into the shop. Of course she recognized me immediately and threw her arms round my neck. What could I do?'

'Well, it would have been better if it hadn't happened. I hope at least you haven't invited her here.'

'No, but do you know what was funny—she didn't invite me to her place either. That's to say, she invited me, but only very vaguely, and then she forgot to give me her address. She was in a tearing hurry, too.'

'Well, we'd better think about how you'd better behave towards her in future, because the two of you could bump into each other again any time.'

But we did not need to rack our brains for long. We were in for a surprise.

One day in May a telegram came through from Central instructing me to contact immediately one Rachel Dübendorfer, who lived in Geneva. I was to call on her, identify myself by means of a password, and take over the intelligence group she headed.

It was an order, if an astonishing one, and it had to be carried out whether I liked it or not. My opinion was that it was not good policy to expand our group by adding new groups to it. Keeping the individual groups strictly separate would have been much more in line with the rules of conspiratorial work. I also saw it as a disadvantage that Rachel Dübendorfer knew so much about my wife and myself. Furthermore, I was to let her have my address, which meant we should have to invite her round from time to time. After all, we were old party comrades. Up until then, however, no one except Kolya, Sonya, and Kent had known where I lived.

I found the number in the telephone book, rang up, and one evening my wife and I went round there. It was a spacious flat on the first floor of an old apartment house. The door was opened by a plump and stately woman who, on seeing my wife, gave her a joyful hug and led her by the hand into the hall.

'Come in, come in, both of you! That time in the confectioner's I quite forgot to give you my address. And this, if I'm not mistaken, is your husband Alex.'

She showed us into one of the rooms.

'Have I got a surprise for you!' she announced. 'Your eyes will pop out of your heads.'

They nearly did; the ways of providence are strange indeed.

Out of the drawing-room came a tall, fair-haired man of about fifty. His imposing figure, pale-blue eyes, and combed-back hair were somehow familiar. He said nothing but looked smilingly from my wife to myself and back. It's Paul Böttcher, I thought.

'Paul Böttcher!' I said. 'The man who helped us get married!'

Over supper we relived the old story. It took us back to the early twenties: Helene and I were living in Leipzig and had decided to get married. This was not without its problems because under Hungarian law at that time a man only reached his majority at the age of twenty-four. I was only just past my twenty-third birthday, so as a Hungarian citizen I could not marry without parental or official permission. Since we were living in Germany, however, the local authorities were empowered to grant such a special dispensation to marry. Paul Böttcher was at that time *Kanzleichef* (home secretary, more or less) in the Labour government of Saxony in Dresden. I went to see him with a letter of recommendation, he promptly issued us with a *Dispens,* as it was called, and along we went to the registrar.

Paul Böttcher had joined the German Communist Party at the beginning of the twenties. He was a compositor by trade. Up until the First World War he had been a social democrat and had been persecuted for revolutionary propaganda activities. As a Communist he had been an active party worker, a member of the central committee and a member and later chairman of the parliamentary Communist party in the state legislature, though he had later resigned from the German Communist Party. When the Fascists had come to power he had left the country.

In Switzerland he had met Rachel Dübendorfer, whom he had known in Germany. They had become friends and set up house together. Actually Böttcher was living 'underground' because he could not find a job anywhere. He earned a little money writing newspaper articles under an assumed name.

During the conversation it emerged that Paul Böttcher had long known that I had moved to Geneva with my family and was running Geopress, and of course Rachel had known too. I must say I was a little disturbed to hear this, but fortunately these were people of my own stamp and reliable comrades who were even involved in the same work as myself. That made things rather different.

Rachel was born in Poland but her parents had moved to Germany when she was a child and she had lived there until Hitler's coming to power. Now a Swiss citizen, she had managed to get into the International Labour Organization headquarters in Geneva, where her knowledge of French and German secured her a job as a typist.

Rachel Dübendorfer's intelligence work thus took place in the context of her official work, as it were. Her codename at headquarters was 'Sissy' and she headed a small group that collected information about the German armaments industry. With the outbreak of war they had lost contact with Central and the group's activities had been temporarily suspended.

I should like to remind the reader at this point that if he is to have a faithful picture of the work of the Swiss group of the Soviet intelligence service he should bear in mind the particular circumstances under which we operated there. I have already touched on this subject in reporting my conversation with Urizky in Moscow in 1935. I feel I must stress the point once again, however, and refute once and for all the distortions and perversions of the truth that self-styled 'historians' continue to publish in the Western press to this day with the aim of sullying my own and my associates' names and misrepresenting the purely conspiratorial and anti-Fascist nature of our activities. My group as well as those of Sonya and Sissy were organized in Switzerland rather than in Germany in the interests of our own safety and because of the importance of the job we had to do. Our operations began even before the war and were directed exclusively at the aggressors. We collected no material about other European countries, nor were we ever asked to. This applies particularly to neutral Switzerland, with the obvious exception of such information as had some bearing on the Fascist onslaught.

Purely as regards collecting intelligence it would probably have been more useful to have set up these groups on German soil, and indeed there were Soviet intelligence agents in Germany who passed valuable information on to Moscow from there, but this was something that could be done only by people who were absolutely 'clean' as far as the Nazi secret service was concerned. Helene, Sonya, Sissy, Böttcher, and myself were all well-known to the Gestapo as members of the German Communist party. We could hardly have held out for long working underground, so that the only way in which we could be of any use was by operating outside Germany in an adjoining country. I imagine Kent's group was set up in Brussels for the same reasons. It goes without saying that the purpose was not to collect intelligence against Belgium because such a tiny country clearly represented no danger whatever to the Soviet Union.

Central's purpose in putting Sissy and her people under me was twofold: on the one hand I was to reactivate her group and on the other hand my group was to be strengthened by the addition of some new and experienced members.

We subsequently managed through Sissy to tap an intelligence source that had access to information of the very greatest importance. In fact we became almost incredibly well-informed—a circumstance that was to cost us dearly later when German

Counter-intelligence, aghast at this incomprehensible leakage of top-secret information, finally began to sniff around to such effect that they picked up a trail leading to Switzerland.

CHAPTER 10

When will Hitler attack?

In 1940–41 this was the most important question to which Soviet Intelligence had to provide a clear answer.

Was Fascist Germany going to attack the Soviet Union in the near future or did it mean to wait until it had carried the fight against Britain to a victorious conclusion? If it did not mean to wait, the Red Army high command must know in time what forces the enemy intended to throw against the Soviet Union and when.

It would be naive to assume that the Soviet government was in ignorance of the direction in which Hitler, that latter-day prophet of a crusade against Communism, was bound to turn his hordes sooner or later. War was of course inevitable and had in fact been imminent ever since Germany had begun its campaign of slaughter in Europe. But it was desperately important that the attack should be put off as long as possible and also that the Anglo-French bloc should be prevented from trying to set Germany and the Soviet Union at each other's throats. It was a promising situation for the capitalist countries and they could well have exploited it by organizing a new and even more powerful Entente with which to destroy the world's first socialist state. As we know from documents that have now been published, the British and French governments had in fact woven such plans.

The Soviet-German non-aggression pact upset the calculations of all those who had been scheming to push others into war. For the Soviet Union, on the other hand, it meant above all time—time to complete the fitting-out and modernizing of its army. There is no doubt that the non-aggression pact, which at the time shocked and disheartened so many sincere supporters of the Soviet Union, was a triumph of Soviet diplomacy.

The political sky was darkening steadily and the military information passing through my hands was disturbing in the extreme.

Particularly noteworthy were the reports that Pakbo brought

me. In January 1940, with our link with headquarters re-established, Pakbo resumed contact with one of his best sources—the man we called 'Gabel', who had by then advanced to a diplomatic post in Berne. Making use of his old Italian contacts, Gabel primarily furnished us with information about Mussolini's army.

Pakbo also continued to meet the German emigrant we had dubbed 'Poisson', who on the basis of his extensive pre-war contacts (he had once, as I have said, been a high-up League of Nations official) still moved in League of Nations diplomatic circles and had access to oral information of a military and political nature concerning the German government's intentions. And in addition Pakbo got information from his journalist colleagues and from diplomats he met at embassy and government receptions.

From about the summer of 1940 onwards we started receiving extremely alarming reports from a variety of sources. One of my telegrams ran:

6 June 1940. To the director.

According to the Japanese attaché Hitler has been saying that after the now imminent victory in the West the German-Italian attack on Russia will begin.

Albert.

This was something the Japanese embassy secretary had divulged in conversation with Pakbo. (Up until the end of 1940, incidentally, I signed all my telegrams with the codename 'Albert'.)

I myself sometimes made trips to the nearby frontier of occupied France, where often no more than a country road lay between neutral Switzerland and the Nazi occupier. Only a few steps away stood soldiers of the German army; I could even talk with them. It was a queer feeling, I must admit, to have this immediate contact with the Wehrmacht.

In December 1940 we received instructions from Central that Pakbo should find out through Gabel what the current strength of the Wehrmacht was and where its various units were stationed. Moscow was worried—not only as a result of our reports but also because of the reports coming in from other agents. A few days later

I radioed what information we had collected through to Moscow, and it subsequently transpired that our findings were a help to the Red Army general staff in making its plans.

Outwardly there was no indication that Germany would soon attack the Soviet Union. At first the attack was concentrated on England, and a fierce battle raged at sea and in the air. The Germans tried to blockade the British Isles, which engaged too many Wehrmacht forces. Their allies the Italians spent the winter of 1940-41 fighting unsuccessfully in Greece and being smashed by the British in North and East Africa. Although German jackboots covered most of Europe—and with the exception of Greece and Yugoslavia most of the Balkans as well—Hitler still had plenty of problems in the West. He seemed little inclined to embark on a fresh military adventure in the East and instead seemed prepared to respect the spirit of the Soviet-German pact.

It would have been the logical thing to do. This time, however, the world had to do with conquerors of a special stamp, whose highest political principle was total irresponsibility, faithlessness, and effrontery.

In the winter of the same year Pakbo managed to make contact with a Swiss secret-service officer. He turned up at our next rendezvous in a state of great excitement. Glancing through his report I could see why. Only hours later we were sending Central the following encoded telegram:

21 February 1941. To the director.

According to information provided by a Swiss officer Germany currently has 150 divisions in the East. In his opinion Germany will attack at the end of May.

Dora.

And in April we sent this one:

6 April 1941. To the director.

From Louise.

All Germany's mobile divisions are in the East. The German troops formerly stationed on the Swiss frontier have been transferred to the south-east.

Dora.

'Louise' was the codename I had given to the Swiss secret-service officer who was the source of both the above reports. We continued to receive information from him through Pakbo. Central thought very highly of this source and recommended that we activate it further.

Moscow was clearly disturbed by such reports and undoubtedly drew the consequences as regards military operations. The director asked us to continue to pass on everything we could find out about Germany's and Italy's preparations for war against the Soviet Union. Moscow's receivers scanned the ether for the alarming reports beamed in by its watchful agents, and today it is common knowledge—although they never officially told us—that Central knew how close the war was and made what preparations it could in the complicated circumstances obtaining at the time.

A week later Gabel and Poisson started to come up with some concrete facts and we sent the following telegrams to Central:

12 April 1941. To the director.

From Gabel.

Distribution of the Wehrmacht in mid-March: 50 divisions in France, 15 in Belgium and Holland, 10 in Denmark and Norway, 17 in East Prussia, 44 in the Generalgouvernement [the Nazis' name for occupied Poland], *including 12 mobile and armoured divisions; 30 in Rumania, 22 in Bulgaria, 20 in Slovakia, Bohemia, and Austria, 8 in the Munich-Ulm region, 5 in Italy, and 5 in Africa. 226 altogether. A further 25 new divisions are currently being organized in Germany.*

Dora.

22 April 1941. To the director.

Poisson has heard from a Swiss member of parliament that government circles in Berlin are giving 15 June as the date of the attack on the Ukraine. They reckon with only feeble resistance.

Dora.

It was evident from this intelligence that the plans of the German military leadership had undergone a change. According to the reports we had sent Moscow in February 1941, Germany had wanted to attack the Soviet Union at the end of May. Such indeed was Hitler's original intention, because he hoped to wipe out the Red Army in a *blitzkrieg* before winter set in. We know today, however, that the German general staff was forced to postpone the attack on the Soviet Union for four to five months by the fact that their troops had run into unexpectedly fierce resistance in Yugoslavia and Greece. The fighting there meant that the Germans had to concentrate large forces in the Balkans.

Poisson was well-informed, which was why we were able to give the date—15 June. A few days after I had sent the telegram off, however (and I quote from the Nuremberg Trials archives), 'the German supreme command adopted provisionally a decision to begin the attack on the Soviet Union on 22 June 1941'.

Around the same time my partner in the Geopress agency (the geography professor) told me on one of the few occasions we ever met that he had been on a study trip to Germany and had paid a visit, at the invitation of an officer friend of his, to the Zossen army camp south of Berlin. General Rommel, recently back from Africa, had been there and had mentioned in the course of conversation that the day of the attack on the Soviet Union was not far off. In his opinion they need not reckon with much resistance and could expect a quick victory. The professor's report tended to confirm what we already knew about the attack Germany was preparing.

In May and June we received further confirmation of our earlier intelligence that German armed forces were being massed in areas adjoining the Soviet frontier. I quote from one of our telegrams at that time:

From a conversation with a German officer at the beginning of June it emerges that the mobile units on the Soviet frontier are on permanent alert, although the tension is lower than in late April/early May. Preparations on the Russian frontier are less conspicuous than in the April-May period but much more intensive.

On the morning of 17 June an excited Sissy rang me at my flat and asked me to come round immediately: she had something important. I did so, and I found she had received some information from one of her people who had been in Germany on business for his company and had just come back. We passed it on that same night:

17 June 1941. To the director.

There are now about 100 infantry divisions on the Soviet-German frontier, a third of them mobile. Also 10 armoured divisions. In Rumania troops are concentrating near Galatz [Galati].

Currently being organized are the élite divisions reserved for special operations. They include the 5th and 10th divisions stationed in the Generalgouvernement.

Dora.

There was no longer any doubt about it: the German army was ranged on full alert along the frontier of the Soviet Union and was just waiting for the signal to attack.

Soon after that I learned from another source of Sissy's—one that was new to me—the exact date of the attack: 22 June. I immediately informed Central, although of course we were adding little of importance to what we had already reported.

According to W.F. Flicke I gave 'Taylor' (alias Christian Schneider; see chapter 17) as the source for this date.* At that time I did not even know of Taylor's existence. It was only much later that I learned that the report had come from him.

Jim, on the other hand, states in his book that I delayed putting this ominous report through to Central.† This is untrue. He further claims that I told him the report came from 'Lucy' and 'Werther', although I knew nothing of either at the time. And in any case Jim received all telegrams from me in coded form; he had no means of knowing what information he was transmitting.

After the war I learned that Richard Sorge, who was operating in Japan, had also provided the Soviet general staff with very early information about the Germans' preparations for war on the Soviet Union.

On 22 June I switched on the radio and heard Hitler making his declaration, screeching hysterically about the historical mission of the German *Volk,* about the last great campaign, and about how the ruthless offensive against Bolshevism had begun. . . .

German troops crossed the frontier of the Soviet Union and opened what was to be the decisive battle of the war. I and my

*W.F. Flicke, *Agenten Funken nach Moskau,* p. 108.

†Alexander Foote, *Handbook for Spies,* p. 114.

group could only wait for fresh instructions from Central, knowing that the job in store for us would be an arduous and responsible one.

PART 2

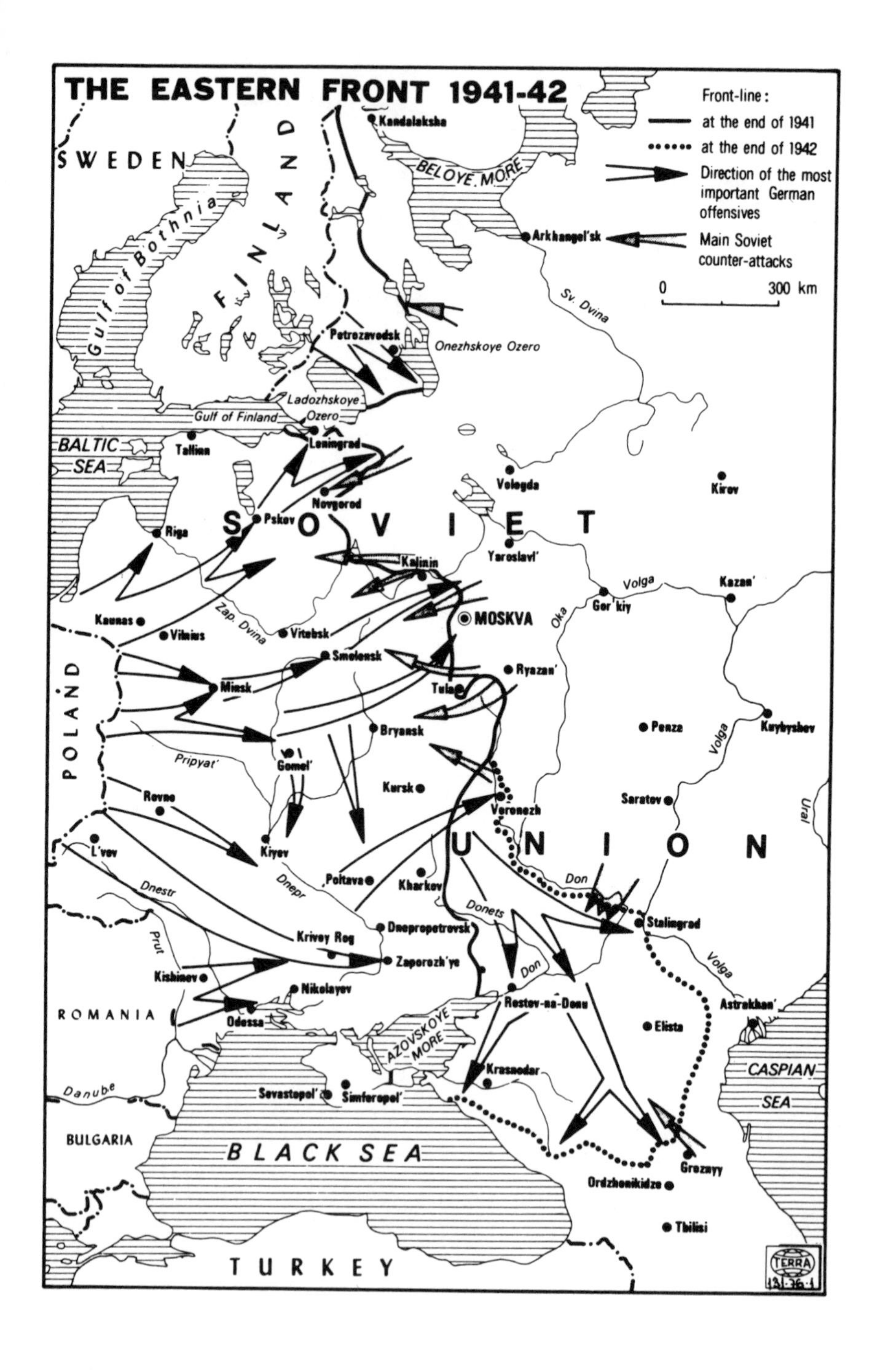
THE EASTERN FRONT 1941-42
Front-line:
at the end of 1941
at the end of 1942
Direction of the most important German offensives
Main Soviet counter-attacks
0
300 km
SWEDEN
FINLAND
Gulf of Bothnia
Kandalaksha
BELOYE MORE
Arkhangel'sk
Sv. Dvina
Petrozavodsk
Onezhskoye Ozero
Ladozhskoye Ozero
Gulf of Finland
BALTIC SEA
Tallinn
Leningrad
Novgorod
Vologda
Kirov
Riga
Pskov
SOVIET
Yaroslavl'
Kalinin
Volga
Kazan'
Gor'kiy
Oka
MOSKVA
Kaunas
Vilnius
Zap. Dvina
Vitebsk
Smolensk
Ryazan'
POLAND
Minsk
Tula
Bryansk
Penza
Kuybyshev
Pripyat'
Gomel'
Kursk
Volga
Revno
Voronezh
Saratov
Ural
L'vov
Kiyev
UNION
Dnepr
Poltava
Kharkov
Don
Dnestr
Donets
Stalingrad
Prut
Krivoy Rog
Dnepropetrovsk
Zaporozh'ye
Volga
Kishinev
Nikolayev
Don
Rostov-na-Donu
ROMANIA
Odessa
Astrakhan'
Elista
AZOVSKOYE MORE
Krasnodar
CASPIAN SEA
Danube
Sevastopol'
Simferopol'
BULGARIA
BLACK SEA
Groznyy
Ordzhonikidze
Tbilisi
TURKEY
TERRA

CHAPTER 11

The Barbarossa Plan

23 June 1941. To the director.

In this historic hour we solemnly and with unshakable loyalty vow that we shall fight with redoubled energy at our forward outposts.

Having spoken with my people I sent Central this telegram in all our names in the early hours of 23 June.

I had rung Jim, Sissy, and Pakbo on the morning of the day before. It was clear to all of us what we must do from now on and what was expected of us in this situation, but we decided nevertheless to get together and have a thorough talk about our problems. With Pakbo, who lived in Berne, I made an appointment for the next day. My wife and I wanted to visit Sissy and Böttcher that evening, so my first port of call was Lausanne, to see Jim and Edouard and Maude.

Jim lived in the upper part of the town. We usually met in Geneva or Lausanne at busy places such as cafés or stations, but sometimes circumstances were such that I had to go to his flat, in which case I would give him a ring first.

He had taken a furnished flat on the fourth and top floor of a large apartment house. As a place for conspiratorial work it had a lot to be said for it. At the end of a long landing a double door fitted with heavy bolts offered protection against eavesdroppers as well as representing a serious obstacle to any unwanted visitors who might seek to invade Jim's privacy: by the time the police got both doors open Jim would have had plenty of time to destroy the transmitter and burn his secret papers.

The flat consisted of living-room, one bedroom with recess, kitchen, bathroom, and offices. A marvellous flat for a single person, but expensive: it cost 200 francs a month, and the landlord demanded payment six months in advance.

The furniture was old and shabby. Jim's exceptionally powerful receiver stood on a table in the corner of the living-room and the aerial ran diagonally across the room. There was no need for concealment because listening to the radio was perfectly legal. The rest of his apparatus—the secret part—fitted into a secret compartment at the top of the wardrobe. Jim had very skilfully built the transmitter into the body of a typewriter, and the secret compartment was so cunningly constructed that you would have had to smash the wardrobe to pieces to find it.

The police inspector from the Aliens Department had already visited Foote once to issue his residence permit for Lausanne. The visit had gone off well. The inspector had asked about Foote's financial situation, because aliens without work permits were only allowed to rent flats if they had a bank account large enough to support them for at least four years or were in regular receipt of money from abroad. There was a regulation according to which aliens of insufficient means were put up in special boarding-houses or refugee camps.

Foote had a very respectable bank account—a part of the money that the courier from Central had handed over to me in Belgrade and that was now proving its usefulness.

Foote told the inspector that with the Germans surrounding Switzerland he could not return to England but that his livelihood was assured because he received 750 francs a month through Thomas Cook, the travel agents. He also told him that he was disinclined to live in a hotel because as a rich man not in the best of health he found a flat of his own more comfortable. He had a doctor's certificate relating to a complaint he had picked up in Spain during the Civil War. The courteous inspector duly made a note of this fact and did not even ask to see Foote's cheque book. After that the police never bothered him again. He was issued with a provisional residence permit, and this was extended every six months without any trouble.

On 22 June I stepped from the train in Lausanne's main station and walked the short distance to Jim's flat. It was a Sunday and the streets were almost empty. Here and there people stood in doorways anxiously discussing the news that had come through on the radio that morning.

The bolts of the inner door grated in answer to my ring. There followed a few seconds' silence as the master of the house took a look through the peep-hole in the outer door. Then another bolt grated and there was Jim. He ushered me quickly into the hall and carefully locked the door behind us.

As always, Jim had a pipe in his mouth and looked as if he had just that minute shaved. He tried to appear calm but his face betrayed his agitation. The ironic twinkle was gone from his eye. In his excitement he drawled his French vowels even more than usual and I switched to English to make it easier for him.

We talked about how the military situation might develop. We shared the conviction that the Soviets would repulse the attack and start a counter-attack—a conviction based on our faith in the strength, heroism, and readiness of the Red Army.

I asked Jim how his set was working and whether his contact with Central was reliable. He assured me everything was fine. We agreed that we should meet twice a week in future and that in urgent cases I should give him a ring.

'You must meet my wife—I'll bring her next time,' I told him. 'She'll be the courier and bring the information if for any reason I can't make it to the rendezvous. Don't worry—my wife has a lot of experience and she's extremely careful.'

A few days later I introduced Jim to my wife, using her codename 'Maria'.

Back in Geneva, I looked up the Hamels. It was a Sunday, as I have said, so the shop was closed. I found them both at home, waiting impatiently for my arrival.

The news of the German attack had taken Edouard and Maude by surprise. They were very upset—particularly Maude. A simple soul, she was furiously abusing the Germans, Germany, and Hitler for having broken his word. It was as much as I could do to calm her. We sat down at table and spent half an hour discussing things. I was basically concerned to find out whether their radio contact was all right and what their morale was like.

Edouard and Maude made a good impression on me and I left their place satisfied. They would fight. They even felt we were not doing enough. They begged for more work and said they would gladly take turns to man the transmitter right round the clock if it would help the Red Army.

Late that evening my wife and I went to see Sissy and Böttcher. Sooner or later we should be receiving instructions from Central about our new operating conditions. In order to be in a position to make suggestions to the director we first had to get together and examine our facilities and our potential. We already had our eye on some competent people whom we wanted to bring in, and this was basically what we talked about. Sissy too was on the look-out for ways of approaching useful people. We agreed that she should let me know as soon as she made contact with any new sources; we could then give them clearly-defined jobs to do.

While we were at Sissy's we heard the BBC broadcast of Churchill's speech. Although the British prime minister had long nursed an antipathy against the Soviet Union he was now obliged to announce in the name of his government that in the struggle against Germany the goals of Britain and the Soviet Union were henceforth identical and that the two countries would fight together against the common enemy. This political decision on the part of the British government was of the very first importance, confirming as it did that Hitler's diplomats had failed in their attempts to organize a united capitalist front against the Soviet Union. Germany was now in the difficult position of having to fight a war on two fronts. Although the second front was some time in coming, it boded well for the future.

A few days after this I received the following order:

1 July 1941. To Dora.

Concentrate your whole attention on procuring information about the German army. Watch and report regularly on the regrouping of German troops from France and other western zones towards the east.

Director

From then on our group devoted its activities to gathering intelligence about Hitler's Germany and Fascist Italy.

Later on Central was to set us wider-ranging and more complicated tasks, and it was in order to be in a position to fulfil these that we were now concerned to build up fresh contacts leading directly to sources of information.

Apart from gathering intelligence, an important part of our work during the first month of the war against the Soviet Union was recruiting new people and establishing direct contact with valuable informants. We had been doing this before, of course, and it remained a major concern of ours subsequently, during the period 1942-3. But in that phase of the war, with the Red Army suffering reverses and occasionally being forced to give ground, the search for new intelligence sources was of particular importance.

Pakbo was the first to strike lucky. At our next meeting he told me delightedly that in a café in Berne a journalist had introduced him to a man who had until recently been press attaché at the French Embassy. He had been sacked for his Gaullist leanings, Pétain's government having issued instructions that all supporters of the general were to be removed from government employ.

'So your unemployed diplomat is a supporter of the French Resistance?' I said, summing up what Pakbo had told me.

'Right. He's an army officer and has undoubtedly done his bit for France. Naturally he hates the Pétain crowd, not so much for what they have done to him but because they have betrayed France. Judging by a few hints he dropped, he's very widely connected. He even has contacts in Berlin because he used to work there as a journalist, and coming from Alsace he speaks perfect German.'

'A man who is prepared to fight for the liberation of France would be very welcome as regards our work. I'll ask Central what they think.'

Central gave their approval, and the Frenchman, as soon as he learned who Pakbo was, enthusiastically agreed to work with us. In his view the Red Army represented the only force in Europe at that time capable of crushing the German army and so helping to bring about the liberation of France. To achieve this goal as soon as possible, our friend was prepared to do anything. Working under the codename 'Salter', he really gave us of his best. I never met him myself; Pakbo was the contact-man.

The situation on the Soviet-German front was becoming critical. The Red Army had not been able to mobilize in time and was retreating eastwards under pressure of superior strength. In a series of heavy engagements during July and August the enemy occupied Moldavia, Byelorussia, the Baltic states, large areas of the Ukraine, and a part of the Karelian-Finnish Soviet Republic. There was fierce fighting along the roads leading to Leningrad and around Smolensk, Bryansk, Dnepropetrovsk, and Kherson. Odessa, surrounded from the mainland, put up a heroic defence, drawing practically the entire Rumanian army. The enemy, holding as he did the strategic initiative, had visions of being able to wind up the 'eastern campaign' within a matter of weeks, as foreseen by the Barbarossa Plan.

The Barbarossa Plan has received thorough coverage in the post-war literature. Elaborated in Hitler's 'Directive No. 21', it laid down that the German armed forces must 'stand ready to conquer Soviet Russia in rapid relay operations before termination of the war against England'. The strategic concept was as follows: 'The Russian troops stationed in western Russia are to be wiped out in bold operations by the armoured units penetrating deep into Russian territory. No effective units must be allowed to withdraw. . . . The ultimate goal of the campaign: to seal off the Asian part of Russia along the general line Archangelsk-Volga.'*

For the execution of his ambitious plans, which extended as far as the Urals, the Führer was counting heavily on the help of his powerful ally, Japan. Japan could have pinned down a great many Soviet troops in the Far East, which would have made it very much easier for the German army to achieve its goal in the West. The Kwantung Army stationed in Manchuria along the Soviet border represented a serious threat.

Although there was a non-aggression pact between the Soviet Union and Japan it was extremely important to the former to find out what a warlike Japanese government had in mind. Through diplomatic circles in Berne we did in fact manage to find out a certain amount. In August 1941 Central received the following telegram:

7 August 1941. To the director.

The Japanese ambassador in Berne has said that there can be no question of a Japanese attack on the Soviet Union as long as Germany has secured no decisive victory at the front.

Dora.

More detailed information was of course provided by Richard Sorge, the Soviet intelligence agent operating in Japan at the time. His reliable reports meant that the Red Army high command need have no misgivings about throwing several divisions from the Far East into the western theatre, divisions that in the critical days to

**Hitlers Weisungen für die Kriegführung* ('Hitler's instructions for the conduct of the war') *1939-1945*, Frankfurt-am-Main, 1962, pp. 183-8.

come were to play a large part in repulsing the German attack on Moscow.

During this difficult first phase of the war the Red Army general staff needed various pieces of strategic intelligence particularly urgently. Central bombarded us with questions almost daily. The transmitters in Geneva and Lausanne were kept busy all night and sometimes even for part of the day sending the information our group had collected:

2 July 1941. To the director.

The Germans currently have Operational Plan no. 1 in force. The target is Moscow. The operations that have been started on the flanks are merely diversionary manoeuvres. The accent is on the central sector of the front.

Dora.

23 August 1941. To the director.

28 new divisions are being organized in Germany. They are to be organized by September.

Dora.

20 September 1941. To the director.

The Germans reckon that by taking Murmansk they can sever the Soviet Union's transport links with England and America and that with the help of Japanese pressure they can cut off deliveries from America via Vladivostok.

Dora.

The above is only a tiny fraction of the intelligence that we collected during the first months of the war against the Soviet Union and passed on to Moscow.

Despite the enormous distance separating Switzerland and Moscow, contact with Central was good. They had a very powerful transmitter that we could pick up easily, and their experienced operators, used by now to Jim's, Edouard's and Maude's 'handwriting', quickly identified the call-sign in the babble of voices filling the ether.

For a while everything went smoothly. In July 1941, however, the thing that we expected to happen and that we feared more than anything else happened without our being aware of it.

The German Abwehr—their military counter-intelligence service—was building up its monitoring network. With the help of both long-range and short-range radio direction finders Abwehr experts located large numbers of the illegal transmitters being operated in cities throughout Europe by various intelligence services, resistance and partisan movements, and underground Communist organizations.

We know today that around the middle of 1941 the long-range radio direction finders stationed at Cranz (now Selenogradsk, near Kaliningrad) on the Baltic coast to monitor intelligence transmissions beamed at Moscow discovered a powerful transmitter maintaining an intensive interchange with the transmitters in the West. It was situated in the Moscow region, and the Germans assumed that this was the radio station of the headquarters of Soviet Intelligence. After the attack on the Soviet Union they monitored illegal transmitters in Berlin and Brussels that were sending coded messages to Moscow. The Abwehr's radio communications department informed the Gestapo, and the whole German counter-intelligence apparatus mounted a search for these Soviet agents' transmitters.

In early July the Cranz unit also monitored our group's Geneva transmitter. At first they could only get an approximate position for Edouard and Maude's set, but within a year the Germans had established that it was in Geneva. In 1954 a leading officer in the Abwehr's radio communications department, W.F. Flicke, published a book—to which I have already had occasion to refer—giving details of how the search was narrowed down.*

Flicke, who served for thirteen years with the Abwehr and knew all the secrets of its radio communications department, confirms that the Germans were monitoring our Geneva transmitter continually at this period, and that before long they located Jim's transmitter in Lausanne as well.

An invisible threat hung over our group, while we, blissfully unaware that the enemy already knew of our existence and was even 'listening in', calmly went on with our work.

The fact that the Germans were already picking up our

*W.F. Flicke, *Agenten funken nach Moskau,* pp. 8-18.

transmissions did not of course mean that they were in a position to wipe out our organization then and there. Flicke's contention that certain of my telegrams were already being deciphered at that time is a piece of pure invention. When he talks about 'cracking' my code system, which is supposed to have enabled them to decipher some of my telegrams or at least parts of them, he is talking about something that with the double-transposition method is a sheer impossibility. Only a person who knows the secret key can decipher a double-transposed text—and then of course he can read the whole thing, not just parts of it. The telegrams Flicke quotes as having been monitored during the autumn and winter cannot possibly have been deciphered by the Germans until two years later, when they got their hands on the code-key.

Nevertheless, a thousand miles away on the Baltic coast lurked a danger for us all.

CHAPTER 12

The Battle of Moscow

The situation on the Soviet-German front deteriorated further. The German army, still as regards its principal arms the superior force, held onto the initiative.

On 10 August I was able to report from a reliable source that the German high command was throwing forces *via* Bryansk against Moscow.

As Paul Schmidt, Ribbentrop's former press chief, wrote (under the pseudonym Paul Carell) in his 1966 book on 'Operation Barbarossa', my information was undoubtedly correct: that is exactly what the German general staff was planning to do.* Operations in the field, however, developed very differently from the way Hitler's staff strategists had planned. In a series of fierce defensive engagements the Soviet troops thwarted the enemy's *blitzkrieg* calculations, and by August 1941 it was obvious that the plan that German propaganda had sold so hard had not in fact succeeded. All major sectors of the front were provisionally stabilized.

In consequence of the Red Army's defeats that summer, however, the enemy penetrated pretty deeply into Soviet territory. By the beginning of September the Fascists had taken the naval bases on the Baltic and laid siege to Leningrad, whose only remaining links with Moscow were by air and by ship over Lake Ladoga. To the south, Hitler's forces had amost reached Smolensk, only two hundred miles from Moscow. The enemy was in possession of almost the entire Ukraine left of the Dnepr and was threatening the Kharkov industrial region, the Donets Basin, the Crimean peninsula, and the military bases on the Black Sea.

In the Geneva cinemas my wife and I watched heavy-hearted as the weekly German war newsreel showed pictures of Leningrad.

*P. Carell, *Unternehmen Barbarossa* ('Operation Barbarossa'), fourth edition, Frankfurt-am-Main, 1966, p. 97.

They had filmed the city through a telephoto lens from the Pulkovo Hills and the spire of the Admiralty tower was clearly recognizable.

On 6 September Hitler ordered the Wehrmacht high command to launch a general attack along the entire Soviet-German front. The northern army group received orders to take Leningrad and link up with the Finnish troops advancing southwards between Lakes Ladoga and Onega. The southern army group's target was to conquer the Crimea and the Donets Basin. The main thrust was to be made by the central army group, which was to encircle and destroy the Soviet units stationed east of Smolensk and then advance on Moscow.

So began the gigantic struggle that, according to Hitler's reckoning, was to decide not only the campaign against the Soviet Union but the entire war.

From our posts in Switzerland we anxiously followed the heroic resistance put up by the Soviet capital. The German radio stations announced with bragging self-assurance that Moscow's fate was sealed: if the Führer's valiant troops did not enter the city in triumph today they would do so tomorrow. The voice of the Soviet Information Bureau's Moscow announcer remained calm, however, and we clung to our conviction that the defenders would win the day, although the situation was undoubtedly very grave.

Meanwhile our own operations continued. The transmitters in Geneva and Lausanne maintained firm contact with Central, and Jim, Edouard, and Maude had as much work as they could handle.

The principal direction of thrust pursued by the German armed forces emerged clearly from the intelligence I was getting from my sources. What we had to do now was collect fresh information about the enemy's strategic plans, his available reserves, his regrouping of troops, and the losses he was suffering in the heavy fighting before Moscow. Central wanted reliable data—cost what it might.

I told my people through Pakbo and Sissy that they must get hold of information faster and that they must ferret out some fresh sources. Soon Pakbo informed me that an old acquaintance of our man Salter was prepared to come in with us.

Like Salter, the new man, to whom I gave the codename 'Long' in my telegrams to headquarters, was a professional intelligence agent. Where Salter had used the diplomatic service, Long used journalism as a cover for his underground activities. An officer of the Legion of Honour and an important agent of the Deuxiéme Bureau of the French general staff, Long had been Berlin correspondent of several major French newspapers before the war. After the defeat of France in 1940, not prepared to collaborate with the Pétain crowd he had emigrated to Switzerland and thrown in his lot with the supporters of General de Gaulle. He was now living in Berne and working for the intelligence service of the National Free French Committee based in London.

The government of the Soviet Union had contacted the Free French Committee immediately after the speech made by its chairman, General de Gaulle, on 24 June 1941, in which he had stated: 'The French people stand beside the Russian people in their fight against Germany. . . .' Subsequently, on 27 September 1941, the Soviet Union concluded a military alliance with the Free French Committee.

In view of this military alliance, a stable and lasting pact during those years, it is not surprising that this experienced French intelligence agent was keen to work with us. It made him a 'double agent'—but it did not make him a traitor. On the contrary, it was a meritorious gesture, contributing as it did towards crushing the forces of Fascism.

Long joined my group in October 1941. He was a shrewd and proficient collector of information. He already had excellent and extensive contacts, presumably dating from the pre-war period, in a wide variety of social circles, and now he proceeded to build up new ones. He had access to a lot of important sources of intelligence. He set up a contact with the Swiss intelligence service, and he had close connections with German bourgeois emigrant elements and with certain people in Berlin. He also received some valuable intelligence from secret Gaullists in Vichy government jobs.

Our contact with Long was through Pakbo. They met in Berne, where they both lived. As a professional agent Long took care of the evaluation and distribution of his information between the Soviet and Gaullist intelligence services. He told Pakbo on several occasions that he gave Soviet Intelligence priority because the Red Army high command on the Soviet-German front could make the best use of the information he got hold of.

One night in October Central's call-sign disappeared from the ether.

My operators informed me straightaway that they were no longer getting through to their colleagues in Moscow. Up until then the powerful voice of the Moscow transmitter had always come through beautifully. Jim, Edouard, and Maude spent whole nights at their sets, combing through the peeps and taps of other stations for Moscow's call-sign. It was not there.

What could have happened? If the director had introduced a new call-sign and new transmission times we would have been informed in advance. Perhaps Central's radio station had been hit by a bomb?

Deeply disturbed, we tapped out question after question. No reply. The besieged capital continued to resist, but Central was silent.

29 October 1941. To the director.

For several days now we have not been receiving you. How is your reception of our transmissions? Shall we continue transmitting or wait till we have contact again? Request reply.

Dora.

But again there was no reply. Previously Central had acknowledged everything, saying that radio telegram number such and such had duly been received. Now nothing at all came back. It was as if their transmitter had never existed. Clearly something out of the ordinary must be up.

In fact we guessed the cause. Probably, we thought, in view of the dangerous situation obtaining in the Moscow region, Central had taken the precaution of evacuating their transmitter further eastwards. It would take time before the radio station could be made operational in its new position and contact restored. Our assumption was based on the news broadcasts from Moscow and Berlin and on Western reports published in the Swiss papers to the effect that certain Soviet government departments and all diplomatic missions had been transferred from Moscow to Kuybyshev. The evacuation theory was the only explanation we could find of Central's breaking contact in such a precarious situation.

General S.M. Shtemenko, then a young colonel in the

operations department of the Soviet general staff, provided the answer to the riddle in his memoirs published in Budapest in 1969; 'In the interests of guaranteeing proper direction of the troops under any circumstances, HQ decided to split the general staff into two levels. The first remained in Moscow; the second was evacuated. . . . On the morning of 17 October we began loading the safes onto railway trucks. . . . We reached our destination on 18 October.'*

These dates coincide exactly with the interruption of our radio contact.

At the end of November or the beginning of December, with the Germans still putting terrible pressure on Moscow despite their enormous losses, headquarters resumed contact with us. (Shtemenko writes that the section of the general staff that had been evacuated returned to Moscow in December.) Once more we picked up their powerful beam. The operators at Central calmly tapped out the call-sign, asked questions, gave instructions—but never said a word about the interruption, just as if nothing had happened. Everything slipped straight back into the old pattern. Reassured, we started transmitting at top speed the mass of material that had accumulated at our end. Most of it was from Long's sources, and it included information of the very first importance.

Here are some of the reports that, with a delay of about a month owing to the interruption, we sent through at that time.

27 October 1941. To the director.

A member of Ribbentrop's staff (I shall be calling this source 'Agnes') rang the editor of the Neue Zürcher Zeitung *from Berlin to say:*

1. The tanks of the propaganda companies are stationed in Bryansk, waiting for the entry into Moscow. The date of the entry was to have been 14 October, then 20 October.

2. On 17 October orders were issued for the eventuality that the siege of Moscow takes some time. Heavy coast artillery and artillery from the Maginot Line and Königsberg has been en route for the Moscow front for several days.

*S.M. Shtemenko, *Where Victory was Forged* (Hungarian), Budapest, 1969.

The German press has been forbidden to report on the battle of Moscow.

Dora.

Long's informant was none other than the well-known journalist Ernst Lemmer, who often wrote as Berlin correspondent for the *Pester Lloyd,* the German-language daily that was published in Budapest and was the semi-official organ of the Horthy government. Long had got to know him in Berlin before the war. Lemmer was editor of the German foreign affairs bulletin; since 1940 he had also been Berlin correspondent of the *Neue Zürcher Zeitung.* 'Agnes' later furnished Long with some important information from Ribbentrop's ministry. After the war Lemmer was for a long time a member of the West German government.

Another well-informed source of Long's was, as I have said, an officer in the intelligence service of the Swiss general staff. We called this source 'Louise'. Here is some of the information he collected for us:

28 October 1941. To the director.

According to information received from Hungarian government circles, the Hungarian expeditionary force on the eastern front comprises 40,000 men.

Dora.

26 October 1941. To the director.

From Berlin, via Louise.

At the end of June the Germans had 22 armoured divisions and 10 reserve armoured divisions. By the end of September 9 of these 32 divisions had been completely wiped out; 6 divisions had lost 60 per cent of their personnel, half of whom were replaced. Four divisions suffered 30 per cent machinery losses, which were also made good.

Dora.

Another report of Long's is worth mentioning; despite the delay of several weeks it could still have been useful:

Hitler's order to take Murmansk and advance to the Caucasus was based on the assumption that Leningrad and Odessa would be taken by 15 September. Both plans have now been abandoned.

There are currently 20 to 22 divisions in France, mainly veteran reserves. Their present strength varies greatly owing to the constant losses. At the beginning of October the troops stationed in Bordeaux and further south were transferred to the eastern front.

During December our Geneva and Lausanne transmitters maintained intensive contact with Central. We needed to pass on the information flowing in from various sources as quickly as possible. Jim, Edouard, and Maude really stretched themselves, working all night and occasionally even in the daytime, tapping out the telegrams, I quote two telegrams from December:

9 December 1941. To the director.

From Berlin, via Louise.

The new attack on Moscow was not provided for in the strategic plans but was launched because there is widespread dissatisfaction in the German army at the fact that since 22 June none of the original targets has been achieved. The resistance put up by the Soviet troops has forced the Germans to give up plans no. 1, Urals, no. 2, Archangelsk-Astrakhan, and no. 3, Caucasus.

Dora.

12 December 1941. To the director.

From officers in Munich, via Louise.

At the beginning of November plans were made for the German army to winter along the line Rostov-Smolensk/Vyasma-Leningrad.

The German army has thrown its entire reserves of men and materials into the fighting around Moscow and in the Crimea. The barracks and camps in Germany are practically empty. The infantry training period has been cut to eight weeks.

For the attack on Moscow and Sebastopol the Germans have ordered to the eastern front heavy howitzers and long-range cannon with special tractors and armoured cars from strongholds inside Germany.

The German high command feared as early as the beginning of November that these operations would fail, because it emerged that the retreating Soviet troops had taken up fortified positions in front of Moscow.

Dora.

The tide had turned. The information passing through our hands confirmed that in the ranks of the enemy fear and panic had set in.

The observations of Lieutenant General Dr Eugen Bircher of Zurich were typical in this respect. Bircher headed the special medical delegation that the Germans had invited to visit the area behind the eastern front. One of our people succeeded in getting into Bircher's confidence, and in the course of their private conversations Bircher came up with some highly interesting information.

Just back from Smolensk, the doctor considered that the situation on the eastern front was no longer in the German's favour. Up until his last trip Bircher had expected the Germans to win, but now he acknowledged that victory was out of the question. Before the November attack was launched he had been in Berlin and spoken with Göring, an old acquaintance of his. Göring had told him: 'We're launching a fresh attack on Moscow soon, putting everything we've got into it, and we hope to mop things up in a couple of weeks if the snowdrifts don't hold up our heavy artillery.' 'And if they do?' Bircher had asked, but Göring had merely shrugged his shoulders. The German generals Bircher had talked to on the subject had said more or less: 'If Moscow falls we go on; if it doesn't we pull the troops back to Smolensk and dig ourselves in.'

Bircher had many opportunities of talking to German officers. An army doctor attached to the German general staff told him that they had lost 1,250,000 dead and wounded on the Russian front up to the beginning of October. Losing two million would plunge the army into a crisis. According to German general staff calculations, this could be reckoned with by the end of the winter.

Depressed by the failure of the Moscow operation, many Germans seemed to feel a need to pour their hearts out to Bircher. There was also the fact—at which Bircher hinted—that these officers belonged to a group that stood in opposition to Hitler. They disagreed with certain of the Führer's political and strategic ideas and dreamed of setting up a dictatorship of the military élite in Germany. Many staff officers, we learned, held the view that

Hitler's irresponsibility had manoeuvred the army into an impasse. The generals, the officers of the general staff, and allegedly Göring himself already considered victory impossible. Among the officer corps the first signs of doubt were beginning to appear. The aide-de-camp to Field Marshal von Brauchitsch, commander-in-chief of land forces, apparently confessed to Bircher that in the field marshal's opinion the war was lost. The troops were exhausted and their fighting spirit draining away. As for the Wehrmacht's strike power, sixteen armoured divisions had been smashed on the Russian front by the end of October. Judging from what this 'neutral' Swiss observer had to say, the morale of the German army was badly shaken.

Everything we got out of Bircher we immediately passed on to Central.

Another telegram from this period complemented Bircher's information:

6 January 1942. To the director.

Via Long, from a Swiss general staff colonel who spoke with von Brauchitsch's aide-de-camp on 11 December 1941. The aide said:

In the last four weeks the Germans have been losing about 32,000 dead daily. The German crack units were not up to the situation and have been smashed or destroyed. Half the air force and half the available motorized transport have been destroyed. The Russians have only just thrown in their crack troops and these are superior to the German troops.

Dora.

And in the same period Pakbo brought me a report from Long that indirectly backed up what we had learned from Dr Bircher:

21 December 1941. To the director.

A liaison officer in the German high command has told Long:

1. In Germany plans are being made to train between 650 and 700,000 nineteen and twenty-year-old soldiers.

2. We are not so much worried by the size of the losses we are suffering on the eastern front as by the quality of those losses. The units that have been demolished were the best and most experienced in the German army; they had always won their battles before. The rest is just a shapeless mass.

3. We need a breathing-space of two to three months if we are to be in a position to deliver the decisive blow in the spring. There is a danger that the Russians will not allow us such a pause.

Dora.

Finally, further confirmation came ten years later, when General Guderian published his memoirs: 'Owing to the resistance of the Soviet troops before Moscow,' he wrote, 'the strength of the fighting units diminished sharply, which had a badly demoralizing effect on the troops that were still fit for action.'*

The 13 December was a red-letter day for us. Not for a long while had Helene and I been as cheerful as when we heard the Soviet Information Bureau announce over Radio Moscow that the Germans' plans to encircle and capture Moscow had met with failure. His voice ringing with triumph, the announcer read out the war bulletin that said the Soviet troops had repulsed the enemy's second attack on Moscow and on 6 December launched a counter-attack that had resulted in a heavy defeat for the enemy.

At the same time the fronts had extended. On 7 December the Japanese attacked Pearl Harbour and the United States entered the war against the Fascist bloc.

In the first few days of 1942 we received information to the effect that Hitler had been forced to resort to exceptional measures to make good his enormous losses of men and materials. He had summoned his country to total war, which meant mobilizing the entire human and industrial resources of the Third Reich. Some two million men received their call-up papers.

There were changes in the German general staff, with new commanders replacing the 'guilty'. An infuriated Führer sacked Field Marshal von Brauchitsch and assumed command of the land forces himself. This we were told by Agnes, our Berlin source. At the same time I informed Central:

Agnes warns against placing our hopes on a quick German defeat. Despite enormous losses of men and materials the German army and German industry have sufficient reserves.

*Heinz Guderian, *Erinnerungen eines Soldaten* ('Memoirs of a soldier'), Heidelberg, 1951.

The warning was justified. It would have been fatal to underestimate the strength of the Wehrmacht. But it was also important to take advantage of the enemy's state of shock and not leave him time to recover. The Red Army high command was aware of this, and in January the Soviet troops switched to the attack along the whole length of the front.

CHAPTER 13

'Rosa'—and some new sources

During the course of 1942 our group expanded as a number of new people, eager to dedicate themselves to the fight against Fascism, came in with us.

The flow of intelligence had been increasing steadily and our three radio operators and their two transmitters were working almost to capacity. Nevertheless the Red Army general staff kept requesting more and more information about the enemy, so Central recommended that we look around for another radio operator to hold in reserve. Finding a suitable person, building him a set, and training him to use it was by no means a simple matter, but there was no other solution.

In the end we found a girl. Her name was Margarete Bolli. The daughter of an office-worker living in the Basel region, she was descended on her father's side from members of the heretical Waldensian sect who had been driven out of Italy centuries ago for their anti-clerical persuasions. Father and daughter were both convinced anti-Fascists, and Margarete had already done one or two 'runs' under her father's orders. She hated the Nazis. To begin with we simply let her know that there was a possibility of introducing her to some competent comrades if she wished to take part in the fight against Fascism. The girl enthusiastically agreed.

The slim, dark-haired, Southern-looking Margarete operated as a courier at first. She did her work well, she was cautious and circumspect, and at rendezvous she was punctual to the minute.

Later we offered to initiate her into the secrets of radio transmission. The task of training her fell to Jim, because he was the best with the Morse key and knew a lot about radio transmission technique. Jim had to be in constant contact with Central, however, and was unable to travel to Basel, so we decided that his pupil should come and see him at intervals in Lausanne. The girl's parents thought she was visiting relatives who lived there. As for Jim's neighbours, they could hardly be suspicious if the unmarried foreigner occasionally received visits from a girl.

The winter and spring of 1942 were spent in training. As soon as the girl was familiar with the set and could operate the Morse key well, I arranged with her parents—we had to let them into the secret now—that we should instal the set in their flat. Although they had no illusions about the kind of risk they and their daughter were running they agreed without any hesitation, prompted by a passionate desire to do their bit to beat Nazism.

Edouard got hold of the necessary parts and built a powerful transmitter—he had no idea for whom—and Jim installed it in the Bolli's flat. Margarete went on practising her Morse and her key-work at home. Whenever Jim had a few free hours he visited the Bollis and instructed the girl further in the reception and transmission of coded telegrams.

By the end of the summer Margarete's key-work was really quick, she no longer made any mistakes, and I began to involve her in the work of the group, giving her the codename 'Rosa'. To start with it was the short, simple reports that she transmitted to Central, but as time went on we gave her longer ones. I either brought her the coded texts myself or sent my wife.

Unfortunately Rosa soon had to move out of her parents' flat because her father, fearing a search, was becoming increasingly nervous. In fact he finally demanded that we stop transmitting from his flat, and Rosa determined to leave Basel. He was very worried about what might happen to his daughter, but he put up no resistance.

We managed to find a comfortable, one-room flat in the rue Henri-Mussard in Geneva, and in August 1942 Rosa moved in. Edouard helped to instal the set. Rosa was registered as a student from the German-speaking part of Switzerland who had come to learn French.

Like Edouard, Maude, and Jim, she worked mainly during the night and slept during the day. Rosa was in contact only with myself, Helene, Pakbo, and Jim, and the last two saw her only when there was an urgent message to be taken or collected and neither my wife nor I had the time. The other members of the group did not know her, which kept our security watertight. Rosa's address in the rue Henri-Mussard was known only to Helene, myself, and Edouard, who had installed the set there.

So by the autumn of 1942 we had three transmitters in

operation—Jim's in Lausanne, Edouard and Maude's in Geneva, and now Rosa's in Geneva as well.

While we were training our fourth radio operator we continued our efforts to recruit new informants. This job fell to my four principal associates, Pakbo, Sissy, Long, and Salter. Again in the interests of conspiratorial security, my contact with Long and Salter remained indirect, *via* Pakbo..

Long was extraordinarily successful at tracking down sources that were important for us. This shrewd and careful man won the sympathy and subsequently the active support of highly-placed German civil servants whom one would have thought far beyond the reach of an intelligence agent. I cannot say in detail how he managed it, but this much is certain: his new acquaintances really went out of their way to help the Allies, passing on to Long everything they learned about their country's plans and military preparations.

Another interesting new contact of Long's was an officer in the Lyon branch of Pétain's military Intelligence. When Long let drop that he was working for the Gaullists the officer let him have even more information than before.

Long also concluded a deal with an Austrian aristocrat who was apparently fiercely anti-Fascist. He had emigrated to Switzerland after Hitler swallowed Austria in the *Anschluss* of March 1938, and he was prepared to do anything in his power to damage the Fascist cause. His dream was the restoration of the Austrian monarchy. He lived in Berne and worked, as far as we knew, for the intelligence service of the Polish government-in-exile in England. Being an aristocrat, he had excellent connections abroad and in diplomatic, industrial, and financial circles inside Switzerland.

The officer from Lyon we called 'Minnie of Lyon'; the Austrian aristocrat received the codename 'Grey'.

Salter, too, found some well-informed people. He made friends with the military attaché at the Vichy government's embassy in Berne. Salter thought that the attaché in fact suspected he had to do with a Gaullist agent, but their relationship was extremely friendly. He promised Salter any help he could give him. Probably he was taking out reinsurance against an Allied victory. In our telegrams we referred to the attache as 'Lilly'.

Another compatriot whom Salter managed to approach was

diplomatic courier to the Vichy foreign ministry with access to Pétain's military Intelligence in the capital of occupied France. We dubbed the courier 'Minnie of Vichy'.

A word about some other sources that turned out to be useful. For example there was a French businessman, a former colonel and divisional chief of staff, who lived in occupied France but often came to Switzerland on business. Long met him on several occasions. Then there was a German businessman, a director of the Bosch works in Stuttgart, who also visited Switzerland frequently on business. In Long's view he was closely connected with a number of German generals. Long coaxed some important information out of him, principally concerning the munitions industry. In our telegrams he appeared as 'Peter'.

Switzerland offered many opportunities for meeting German officers, industrialists, and civil servants—all of course extremely interesting as far as we were concerned. Many of them Long had known since before the war, when he worked in Berlin as a correspondent for the French papers. Over supper or a drink, Long sometimes picked up something really useful.

Pakbo, too, as leader of a group of informants, did not confine himself to collecting reports and passing them on to me but himself took an active part in roping in new contacts.

In the early part of 1942 Sissy also came up with some new helpers. She told us that 'Marius'—who represented France at the International Labour Office in Geneva—made frequent official trips to Vichy, where he met a friend of his who was well in with the prime minister, Pierre Laval, and had access to Otto Abetz, the German ambassador to France. We called Marius' friend 'Diemen'.

But one of Sissy's most useful people was 'Taylor'. This was the codename I gave (he did not even know it himself) to the lawyer and former German citizen Christian Schneider. Schneider was a translator at the International Labour Office. When the Nazis had come to power in Germany he had turned his back on his home and stayed on in Geneva. A dedicated anti-Fascist, Schneider worked with us knowingly and out of conviction. At the end of 1942 he was to render our group a great service by putting Sissy into contact with Rudolf Roessler, with whose help we actually penetrated the 'holy of holies'—namely the Wehrmacht high command. But more about that later.

Sissy further managed to extract secret information from the office of the German military purchasing commission in Geneva, which was in contact with the Swiss munitions industry.

These new sources tapped by Pakbo, Long, Salter, and Sissy supplied vital additional material to that already flowing in from our old team. In this way we learned a great deal about the German general staff's plans for the summer of 1942, plans that were to turn the Caucasus and the Volga steppes into one enormous theatre of operations.

CHAPTER 14

The enemy gathers his strength

The first offensive action by the Red Army in the winter of 1942 changed the situation radically. During this period the Soviet troops inflicted some heavy defeats on the Wehrmacht; on some sectors of the front they threw the enemy back hundreds of miles in the space of four months. The losses suffered by the Wehrmacht between December 1941 and April 1942 were enormous. Even the German high command, whose figures tended to be on the low side, admitted to the loss of more than a million men.*

Fascist Germany had received its first serious wounds. Staff officers up and down the front counted their dead and wounded. In the Reich and its satellites fresh reserves were called up. And all the time our group was gathering material about the extent of those losses and the mobilization of those reserves.

A director of the Junkers aircraft factory, visiting Switzerland on business, told Long that Germany's hospitals were full to overflowing with soldiers suffering from frostbite; he put the figure at more than 100,000.

According to information provided by the Swiss Intelligence officer we called 'Louise', the German armoured units had lost three-quarters of their tanks and were being re-equipped. He also told us that by the end of March not only all the reserve officers in Germany but even the officers on the retired list would have been called up. They were to replace men who were fit for front-line duty but were currently serving with troops stationed in the occupied countries. Both Louise and Sissy also received reports of a shortage of technical personnel, well-trained pilots, and U-boat officers.

Yet in spite of its enormous losses the Fascist bloc still commanded tremendous reserves of men and materials, and Germany's military leaders, obsessed with the thought of revenge,

*Walter Görlitz, *Der Zweite Weltkrieg 1939-1945*, vol. 1, Stuttgart, 1951, p. 292.

were planning a general offensive for the spring of 1942. The reports flowing in from the Soviet intelligence network showed that the enemy was gathering his strength in massive preparations for the next phase of the war. Germany started brutally putting the screws on its allies, demanding more and more cannon-fodder for the eastern front.

In February and March 1942 Long and Salter passed me the following information:

Rumania has agreed to provide a further six divisions for the spring offensive.

Ribbentrop has asked Hungary for 800,000 soldiers for the eastern front. In Hungary eight divisions have been mobilized.

During his visit to Rome Göring demanded that Il Duce *send at least fifty divisions to the eastern front.*

In Germany a total of six million men are supposed to have been called up for the spring offensive.

In the early part of 1942 the Red Army, strengthened by the success of its winter offensive, took up defensive positions. For a while the front was stable, but it was a case of the calm before the storm: the military leaders of both sides were busy making their preparations for the summer campaign.

Useful information came in through Long in January, February, and March 1942. According to a report he handed Pakbo on 14 January he had recently spoken with a National Socialist party lawyer from Leipzig (the man, incidentally, who had defended Hitler after the attempted *putsch* of 1923). This dyed-in-the-wool Nazi had volunteered the information that Hitler wanted to wind up the war against Russia by the autumn of 1942. By that time Moscow was to have been taken and German troops to have reached the Volga, if not the Urals. There was a campaign planned for the Caucasus as well.

In the remaining telegrams that we sent Central in March we were able to report the approximate date of the Germans' spring offensive and a number of concrete objectives of the German high command. I quote two of these telegrams:

8 March 1942. To the director.

Via Long, from a Catholic lawyer in the Saar Territory, an anti-Fascist with good connections on the staff of Army District XII in Wiesbaden.

1. The operation against Turkey will be launched simultaneously with the thrust on the southern sector of the eastern front towards the Caucasus and Teheran. Preparedness to attack has been ordered for the third Sunday in April.

2. The planning authorities for economy and industry in the Caucasus and Persia are to have been set up in Dresden by 1 April.

Dora.

17 March 1942. To the director.

Via Long, from the counsellor at the Swiss embassy in Berlin.

1. The Germans have put off the military operation against Sweden for the time being. Most of the relevant measures have been revoked.

2. The military operation against Turkey is not yet definite but is probably on.

3. The German high command regards its projected attack against the Don line towards the Caucasus as decisive. If they can get their hands on the Baku oilfields and Germany can hold out until the end of 1943, the German high command reckons the war can be won.

Dora.

These telegrams touch on German plans to attack Turkey and Sweden. In fact, as is well known, Germany did not violate the sovereignty of either country, which might suggest that here was a case of our having been deliberately put on the wrong track. The German secret service did of course make heavy use of the 'plant' to conceal the high command's real intentions and lead enemy agents astray. In this case, however, the reports were correct. Such plans did exist; they were just never carried out.

Actually in the case of neutral Sweden it was more a piece of blackmail than a serious project. Hitler wanted to scare the Swedes in order to keep them docile and stop them going over to England and the Allies. This northern neighbour was important to Hitler not only because of its strategic position but also because it was one of Germany's major steel and iron-ore suppliers.

As for Turkey, an Axis ally, the threat of a German invasion was probably very real at that time. The Turkish government had not declared war on the Soviet Union, but on the frontier of Soviet Armenia a large Turkish army was waiting only for the order to advance. It is now known that this threat from the south forced the Soviet high command to station substantial forces in the Caucasus. In that difficult autumn of 1941 the Turks were expected to attack at any time. But the way the Wehrmacht was thrown back from Moscow cooled the Turkish generals' enthusiasm and made them more cautious; they had to give up their plans to conquer Trans-Caucasia. Japan's reaction was similar, and Germany found that no amount of diplomatic pressure would budge its Far-Eastern ally.

So the Nazis worked out the following alternative: they would push through Turkey to the Soviet Union's Trans-Caucasian frontier and from there launch a thrust towards Baku on the Caspian Sea and into Persia, which was already occupied by Soviet and British troops. Strategically this would mean killing several important birds with one stone: the southern approaches to the Soviet Union (British and American aid arrived *via* Persia) would be cut off, Turkey would be involved in the war, and Germany would get its hands on the vitally important Caucasian oilfields while at the same time striking a telling blow at the Soviet army and Soviet industry.

The plan admittedly made a great deal of sense and constituted a fresh danger to the Soviet Union. But the Germans failed to carry it out in time, and by the spring of 1942 it was probably already too late. The Turks would surely not have let German troops march through their country unhindered because of their fear of Soviet retaliation: the Soviet Union would have been forced to defend its southern frontier and would not have confined that defence to its own territory.

Towards the end of March a number of new reports came in to the effect that the Germans were preparing to attack on the southern sector of the front. We urgently transmitted the following message to Moscow:

25 March 1942. To the director.

From General Hamann.

a) The final date for completing preparations for the spring offensive is 22 May. The attack is to be launched between 31 May and 7 June.

b) The Germans calculate that if only they can conquer the North-Caucasian oilfields they can remedy their petrol shortage and exploit the natural resources of the Ukraine. Parachute regiments are being held in readiness to prevent destruction of the oilfields. According to their calculations any oil-wells that are destroyed can be made operational again within six months. The necessary machinery and crews are standing by. They are the same crews as were organized in July 1941.

Dora.

General Hamann was a highly-placed German officer with whom Long had managed to make contact. The reason why he was so well-informed was that he was attached to the staff of the German high command.

Other sources confirmed that the Wehrmacht would be throwing its main thrust against the Caucasus in late May at the earliest. We also found out that the Germans now had thirty per cent more tanks than in 1941, which in terms of mobile units give them a clear advantage.

Today we can say with authority that the above information, as radioed to Moscow by the Swiss group, tallied almost exactly with the strategic plans contained in the documents that Soviet troops later seized from German staff headquarters. This emerges from—among other sources—Order No. 41 of the German high command, dated 5 April 1942, which outlined the plan and the principal operations of the summer offensive for the German troops on the eastern front. The order says in part: 'As soon as weather and terrain conditions are favourable the German army must take advantage of its superior strength to seize the initiative once more and impose its will on the enemy. The target is the total destruction of the human reserves still at the Soviets' disposal; we must capture as many important centres of the Russian munitions industry as possible. To this end we shall employ the entirety of the armed forces at our and our allies' disposal.' The order pointed out that 'the original objective of the eastern campaign' still held good, namely to 'crush the Soviet armed forces and conquer the Soviet Union up to the Archangelsk-Volga line'.*

General Zeitzler, formerly chief of staff of Germany's land forces, wrote of Hitler's intentions: 'When Hitler planned the summer offensive of 1942 his main object was to take Stalingrad and the

**Hitlers Weisungen fur die Kriegführung, 1939-1945, op. cit.,* pp. 183-8.

Caucasus. The consequences of this plan, had it been carried out, would undoubtedly have been enormous. If the German army on the lower Volga had managed to cross the river and so sever this main traffic artery between north and south and if we had managed to divert the Caucasian oil to cover Germany's military requirements, the situation in the east would have been altered radically and our hopes of a favourable outcome of the war multiplied.'*

Finally, a passage in the memoirs of Field Marshal Friedrich Paulus confirms that 'the 1942 summer offensive was an attempt to put into operation the plans that had been foiled in the late autumn of 1941, namely to carry the war in the east to a victorious conclusion'.†

While forging their plans for the summer offensive the leaders of the Third Reich launched a major diplomatic ploy involving Great Britain and the United States. Realizing that after the beating they had taken before Moscow their projected *blitzkrieg* against the Soviet Union was not going to work, they started weaving political intrigues in the hope of cracking the united anti-Fascist front and forcing the Soviet Union into a position of economic and military isolation.

The negotiations for a separate peace were conducted at the Vatican in conditions of the strictest secrecy. We got wind of them none the less, and I quote in full a telegram that still has its relevance today as regards the struggle of the forces of peace against aggression and war:

1 January 1942. To the director.

From Rome, via Long.

Report by the General of the Jesuit Order, Ledochowski, of his conversation with Cardinal Maglione, secretary of state at the Vatican.

1. At American ambassador Myron Taylor's last audience with the Pope the latter asked for clarification of the US position regarding the Soviet Union. The Pope warned Roosevelt against concluding any political agreements with the Soviet Union over and above his military assistance on the grounds that it would

*See *The Fatal Decisions,* New York, 1956, p. 132.

†See *Der Zweite Weltkrieg: Dokumente und Materialien* ('The Second World War: Documents and Source Material'), Berlin, 1961.

H

probably not be long before a choice must be made between Germany and Bolshevism.

In this event the Pope would opt for Germany, and he would be glad if Germany and England concluded a compromise peace.

The new Europe would be made up of authoritarian states co-operating in a corporate basis.

A compromise peace was already favoured by France, Spain, Italy, Japan, Hungary, and Turkey.

If the United States and England fell in with the Pope's plan—which Germany was not expecting—and concluded a separate peace with the aforementioned countries, Hitler would be isolated and his replacement by representatives of the army or their friends expedited.

2. The principal conditions for a compromise peace:

a) Germany should not need to be demobilized, the reason being that it provides a barrier between the Red Army and Europe. Italy should get back Libya and Eritrea and receive Dalmatia, Albania, and part of Tunisia.

[In this connection] *Mussolini indicated that no treaty exists between him and Hitler regarding joint peace aims and a joint peace agreement.*

b) Spain should be given economic advantages and receive compensation in China. France, Belgium, Holland, and Norway should recover their territorial integrity; likewise Yugoslavia, in the form of a federation, and Poland in a form subsequently to be agreed on. Czechoslovakia and Austria were not mentioned.

3. The standpoint of the Vatican is basically pro-Fascist and anti-Russian.

Behind the Pope's action are Mussolini, Pétain, the British envoy in Madrid, and Myron Taylor himself, who in the United States is an adherent of the big corporations of the world economy.

4. In an interview given to the American press Pétain has said he is ready to support any initiative of Roosevelt's in order to win his support for these plans, but this has not succeeded.

5. The Vatican's plan is actually a German-Italian plan with the object of rescuing the Axis.

Dora.

Further comment on this report is, I believe, unnecessary. In it others besides the then leaders of the Roman Catholic church stand plainly exposed, and the reader will not find it difficult to draw the appropriate conclusions.

According to our information the set-back suffered by the German troops on the eastern front had sown confusion among Hitler's satellites. In Italy, Rumania, Finland, Hungary, and Bulgaria people's confidence in the Führer's lucky star and in his 'unbeatable' army was shaken. Political differences began to arise between the members of the Fascist alliance.

The Germans asked Mussolini for fresh troops. Mussolini, however, was in no hurry to send soldiers to the Soviet-German front. He was more concerned about his conquests in the Mediterranean and Africa, where he was under considerable pressure from the British. Italy itself, in the grip of serious economic difficulties, was beginning to show signs of internal unrest. The tension between army and party that I had reported on as early as 21 September 1941 continued to increase.

Our information about the friction between Italy and Germany came through diplomatic channels. In the middle of January 1942 Long heard something new from the Uruguayan envoy who had just arrived from Berlin. We reported:

. . .Hitler accuses the Italians of not helping him enough against the Russians. He is asking for 25 divisions as well as special mountain-infantry units for the eastern front, 30 divisions for Greece, Yugoslavia, Holland, and Belgium for the purpose of maintaining order.

We also received a report of growing dissatisfaction among the population of Finland and concern in Finnish government circles as a result of the unfavourable outcome of the battle of Moscow and the heavy losses around Leningrad and in Karelia. Not even the belligerent Mannerheim crowd still believed in the Germans' promise of a quick decision in the eastern campaign. In early 1942 Germany's northern ally completely abandoned the line it had been holding and even began to consider the possibility of a political and military change of course. We received this information via Louise from Finnish journalists in Berlin:

. . .The Finns are apparently no longer planning any offensive

operations. The Germans and the Finns now always fight separately. The Germans are active on Lake Onega and in the Salla region. There is a movement in Finland in favour of forming a bloc with Sweden and Norway. If this is successful it would be desirable for the English to land in Narvik and lead an attack on the Germans.

The defeat had also demoralized Horthy, the Regent of Fascist Hungary, as we heard from our Austrian source:

2 April 1942. To the director.

Via Grey, from his friend the anti-German son of the Hungarian prime minister Kállay.

1. No Hungarian troop reinforcements were sent to the eastern front in the period 7 December to the beginning of March. Hungarian divisions were withdrawn from the Ukraine at the New Year. At the beginning of March five Hungarian divisions and the 41st mobile brigade were stationed on the right bank of the Dnepr.

2. Keitel requested the mobilization of 300,000 Hungarian soldiers for the eastern front. Horthy has refused in view of the unfavourable atmosphere in Hungary and recommended that the German troops in Yugoslavia be replaced by Hungarian units.

3. In Siebenbürgen [northern Rumania] *there are two Hungarian infantry divisions, one cavalry division, and one mobile brigade. Stationed in Budapest, allegedly to protect the German embassy, are two Waffen-SS regiments. There are German observers in every ministry.*

Dora.

According to information that reached us later, the SS in fact had only one battalion stationed in Budapest at that time.

The mighty counterblow struck by the Red Army before Moscow had similar political and economic repercussions in every one of Hitler's satellites.

Meanwhile preparations for the summer offensive were being pushed ahead at full speed. Germany was determined to strike back and so recover its grip on the political and military situation.

Having sacked and replaced the generals whom he held responsible for the defeats of that winter, Hitler managed to put a fairly swift stop to the rot in the German high command. A very much more difficult task was to accelerate and increase armaments production and the supply of fuel. By mobilizing the economic reserves of virtually the whole of Europe, however, the Nazi leadership succeeded in boosting the military potential of the Reich rapidly in the first half of 1942.

The task that Central set us was to look into these vital questions. Among other things the Red Army general staff wanted us to collect data about aircraft and tank production, output and reserves of mineral oil, construction of airfields and ordnance depots, and the organization of new military units.

We complied to the best of our abilities, and I quote a small selection of the material we transmitted to Moscow during that winter of 1941-2:

The Germans are planning to build 3,100 aircraft in January 1942: 2,400 in Germany and the occupied countries, 300 in Italy, and 400 in unoccupied France. The daily capacity of the aircraft industry in the area controlled by the Vichy government is 15 machines.

The Lorrain works near Paris is turning out Messerschmidts, the Morane works fighter planes. The latter are equipped with two Morane 'Typhon' cannon. The Hispano works near Paris is building a new fighter with an engine of the firm's own construction.

Rumania's mineral-oil output has dropped by 7 per cent. In summer the entire output is transported up the Danube. There are enough ships because the Germans have diverted all tankers from Holland, Belgium, Poland, and France to the Danube.

In the opinion of some generals Germany has large reserves of synthetic petrol.

Germany's fuel resources, including synthetic-petrol production, amount to 5 million tons a year. Not included in this figure are the imports from Rumania.

A new synthetic-petrol plant has been opened in northern France. Its output will be transported to Italy via Switzerland.

Some camouflaged munitions-factories and a synthetic-petrol plant have been built in the Leipzig region.

One synthetic-petrol plant is being built in the Vienna area and another in Kladno, near Prague.

The main supply centres for the eastern front are Dresden and Breslau.

Smolensk is the food and munitions base for 40 to 50 divisions.

In 1942 the German army is to be fed from the Ukraine harvests.

The current strength of the German armed forces and the Todt Organization is 14 million men.*

The Germans currently have 22 armoured divisions in Europe and 2 in Africa. They intend to organize a further 5 armoured divisions before the end of May.

Prenzlau air-force base sixty miles north of Berlin is the base for flying operations on the eastern front. Large numbers of aircraft are housed in underground hangars. There are large repair-shops on the west side of the airfield. The field's anti-aircraft defences are not particularly strong.

Orly airport (south of Paris) has underground hangars. Underground aircraft factories have been built near Hanover and near Suhl (Thuringia).

The chief tank-manufacturing centres are the Auto-Union works in Chemnitz and Zwickau. Zwickau currently has between 2,000 and 3,000 tanks ready for transport to the eastern front.

In the Leipzig region new munitions-factories have been built in the forests between Torgau and Herzberg and between Würzen and Eilenburg.

The above data may appear fragmentary to the layman. The general staff experts in Moscow, however, by carefully analyzing everything we sent them and comparing it with information from other sources, was able to piece together a pretty good picture of the enemy's war industry and military potential.

Our informants also kept an eye on enemy troop movements and the organization of new units in Germany and the occupied countries. During the winter and spring of 1942 it was Long's, Salter's, and Pakbo's sources that were most productive in this respect.

A particularly well-informed source was Louise, our Swiss intelligence officer, because his people in Berlin got their information straight from the German high command. Here, for

*An impressed-labour force building fortifications under the direction of the engineer Fritz Todt.

example, is one of his January reports answering a number of Central's questions:

17 January 1942. To the director. Reply to no. 96.

From Louise.

1. Apart from the SS armoured units Germany currently has 21 armoured divisions. One of these is in Bordeaux and two—the 15th and 21st—in Libya. One division was destroyed by the British on its way to Libya. There are 16 divisions on the eastern front. There are no armoured divisions in Holland and Norway.

One armoured division is being organized in the Paris area and four in Germany. They are to be ready by May 1942.

2. No troop transports from the eastern front towards the west have been observed in recent weeks.

3. According to unconfirmed information there are six German divisions stationed in Bulgaria.

4. On the eastern front there are three fortified lines:

Line 1: Kharkov-Bryansk, then between Vyasma and Smolensk towards Leningrad.

Line 2: Kherson-Smolensk-Leningrad.

Line 3: Odessa-Gomel-Leningrad.

The Todt Organization has 100,000 men employed on defensive works.

The nature of these fortifications puts them in a category between the Somme entrenchments of the First World War and the concrete-bunker type. A similar effort is being invested in the defensive works in the Generalgouvernement [occupied Poland].

5. On top of the air-fleets already known about there are said to be another five in Germany. Germany is trying to boost its aircraft production to 2,800 a month by January. Aircraft production since the beginning of the war has averaged between 2,000 and 2,500 a month.

Dora.

On this last point the information provided by our sources was erroneous. In fact Germany had only five air-fleets in 1941 (four of them employed against the Soviet Union), and no more had been raised by January of the following year. The figures for aircraft production was also inaccurate. Hitler's Germany cannot possibly have been producing 2,000 to 2,500 aircraft a month at that time. As far as we know today Germany produced 11,030 aircraft in 1941 and 14,700 in 1942, which works out at about half as many as we said in our telegram. We appear to have been unintentionally or perhaps deliberately misled here.

We learned that the Germans were concentrating transport in the ports of Bulgaria and Rumania with which to throw troops against the Caucasus. Some 800 craft were assembled in Constanta, Varna, and Burgas alone.

We also learned—this came through Long—that the Germans wanted to mount a major military operation on the Atlantic and in the Barents Sea from 1 April onwards in order to cut off arms deliveries to the Soviet Union. A fleet of 140 U-boats under the command of Admiral Donitz was to attack the Allied convoys.

The archives now reveal that this information was passed on by Central to the People's Commissar for the Navy, to whom it proved useful in assessing the enemy's naval strength and repelling attacks.

As spring approached, Pakbo and Sissy began to receive reports showing that the German high command was suddenly in a great hurry with its preparations for the new plan. Obviously Hitler had told his generals that they must not exceed this extremely tight timetable: summer was the best time for a strategic offensive, and he did not want to miss it.

Details regarding the assembly and regrouping of the German troops were of course top secret, but here and there we managed to pick up something and pass it on to Moscow. Once again Louise's contacts in the German capital proved very useful indeed. I quote two telegrams from this period:

3 and 4 April 1942. To the director.

From Louise.

In early March the troops mustered for the spring offensive took up their positions one after another all over eastern Germany, in the Baltic States, in Poland, and in the occupied areas of the Soviet Union, particularly in the south. In numbers and above all in terms of equipment they are undoubtedly stronger than in June 1941. The artillery also has more fire-power, particularly in the southern sector, than it had in June 1941. All roads in the southern sector are completely inundated with munitions transports.

Changes in the deployment of the German army at the

beginning of March: the staff of the 98th division (possibly the 90th division) in Allenstein; the 197th infantry division transferred from the Baltic to Odessa; the 23rd (Potsdam) division with its reserve was transported to Nikolayev on 23 February; the 3rd mobile division has arrived in Zaporozhye from Frankfurt-an-der-Oder. In Landsberg-an-aer-Warthe are a number of regiments and one staff, probably to fill out the troops for the spring offensive.

Dora.

6 April 1942. To the director.

From Louise.

1. Paratroops, SS units, and armoured units are arriving in Nikolayev daily.

2. Köningsberg [Kaliningrad], *Warsaw, and Insterburg are full of troops waiting for the attack. These areas are being made increasingly secure against air attack.*

3. Large numbers of troop-transport planes have been concentrated in Zaporozhye. The chief assembly area for tanks is Stalino in the Donets Basin. It has been established that Smolensk has a large number of trains and a big camp for engineering units.

Dora.

Our radio operators were transmitting similar messages to Central every night of March and April.

It would be wrong, however, to suppose that the Swiss group was infallible. Sometimes mutually contradictory figures or untrue statements found their way into our reports. With the aid of the mass of documentary material now available it is possible to pinpoint exactly when and in what way we were wrongly informed. I have mentioned one or two cases. Most of them occurred in the early part of the war.

Why did they occur? Were we too gullible, perhaps, regarding all the information we got hold of as equally credible?

The answer is of course that we were not and did not. We sifted everything we received and only passed on to Central what we thought might interest the Red Army high command. Nevertheless certain of our telegrams did contain incorrect information, and there were two reasons for this. One reason was the large-scale campaign conducted by the German secret service to mislead enemy intelligence by, for example, having people posing as enemies of the Nazis 'blab' false information in the guise of state secrets. It may be that some of our sources occasionally took the bait. The other reason, however, was that certain of our informants in the early period of the war, given their rank and position, were simply not able to get hold of the information we asked them for. It was not until after the battle of Stalingrad that we tapped our really valuable sources, though even they were not beyond making the occasional mistake.

It follows that in drawing up their intelligence summaries for the Red Army general staff Central undoubtedly did not rely on the information provided by the Swiss group alone, despite what Flicke, Carell, Accoce and Quet, and so many other Western authors who have published books in this field since the war insist on maintaining. Apart from the Swiss group and its other intelligence groups Central had access to further sources of information: the partisan forces operating behind the enemy lines, Soviet front-line and air reconnaissance, and so on. The final picture of the enemy's intentions was the product of all these sources put together.

These few mistakes aside, we can say with confidence today that the Swiss group was fulfilling its purpose by 1941, and I would stress particularly that the reports we sent in about the preparations for the German summer offensive of 1942 squared completely with reality.

There is an interesting passage in this connection in the Hungarian *History of the Great Patriotic War of the Soviet Union, 1941-1945:* 'Soviet Intelligence found out in good time that the German army was preparing a large-scale summer offensive and concentrating powerful forces in the southern sector of the Soviet-German front. Our intelligence service informed the supreme command and the general staff of the blow that was being prepared in the sector of the south-western front towards the Volga and the Caucasus.

'While accepting the possibility that the German army might launch an attack in the south, army headquarters was of the opinion that the enemy, who was grouping powerful forces in the immediate vicinity of Moscow, would in all probability throw his main thrust not in the direction of Stalingrad and the Caucasus but against the middle sector of the Red Army front with the object of taking Moscow and the central industrial region.

'The fact that the Soviet supreme command had misjudged the direction of the enemy's main thrust meant that the decisions taken in the first phase of the summer campaign were strategically inappropriate. Instead of concentrating its forces in the south-western and southern sectors of the front and building up an impregnable defence in depth on the left wing of the Soviet-German line of battle, army headquarters reinforced the middle sector and the Bryansk front and concentrated the major part of its troops here on the right wing, covering the Tula-Moscow sector.'*

This blundering assessment of the intentions of the German high command smoothed the way for the Germans' operations in the southern sector—with, as everyone knows, disastrous consequences. The German armoured divisions burst through the Soviet defences on the Don and went rolling on towards the Volga and the northern Caucasus. As Marshal Zhukov wrote in his memoirs: 'If the Soviet army headquarters had had some reserve armies stationed behind the south-western theatre of operations the catastrophe suffered by the troops in that sector in the summer of 1942 would have been avoided.' And as he further wrote: 'It must be said that the supreme commander realized that the critical situation that arose in the summer of 1942 was the outcome of his own mistake in approving the plan of action for the operations of that summer.' †

**History of the Great Patriotic War of the Soviet Union, 1941-1945* '(Hungarian), vol. II, Budapest, 1964, cf p. 199 of German edition.

† G.K. Zhukov, *Memoirs and Reflections,* Moscow, 1969, pp. 399 and 407.

CHAPTER 15

The first alarms

Certain events of the spring and summer of 1942 caused Central and myself considerable concern, indicating as they did that the security of our group was threatened.

While we were working at full stretch collecting and transmitting all this information, German secret-service agents, who already knew of our existence, were trying to pin-point our location.

I have mentioned already that the Abwehr monitoring station on the East Prussian coast picked up our two transmitters and Central's transmitter as early as July 1941, the beam of the radio direction finder indicating on the map that the illegal transmitters were being operated from Switzerland. Subsequently, by monitoring from different points, the Germans obtained more precise readings: there was every indication that the transmitters maintaining contact with Moscow were situated in Geneva and Lausanne.

At this point the matter was taken up by radio reconnaissance headquarters in Berlin. On the basis of the intensive radio contact between Moscow and Switzerland they established that there was a high-powered Soviet intelligence unit operating in the latter country. The Abwehr's powerful monitors stayed tuned to our transmissions day and night. All the material was recorded, but that was as far as they got. Their efforts to discover the secret of our code met with failure. All the Germans knew was that a total of three transmitters were operating in Geneva and Lausanne, which is why the Abwehr nicknamed us 'The Red Three' or 'The Red Troika'.

When the report that a trio of Swiss transmitters was in constant contact with Moscow reached the special counter-intelligence department headed by Admiral Canaris it caused tremendous consternation. The Germans were well aware that, at this stage of the war, shortly before the crucial German offensive on the eastern front, the information contained in our radio telegrams could be highly prejudicial to the Wehrmacht. But without knowing the code they had no means of knowing what those telegrams said.

All this emerged a number of years after the war from the German archives and from W.F. Flicke's book about the operation mounted to smash our group,* an operation in which as a leading counter-intelligence officer he was personally involved.

The Germans could not of course openly conduct a search for illegal transmitters in the territory of a neutral country, so they sent in secret agents. One of these agents surfaced in Geneva towards the end of April 1942 and soon came to the notice of our group.

A friend of one of my people received a visit from a man who introduced himself as a French journalist, said his name was Yves Rameau, and started talking about an underground organization that he had set up in France. They had their own transmitters, he said, and they had facilities for getting hold of military information that would undoubtedly be of use to the Russians, but unfortunately they had no means of passing that information on. Much to our friend's surprise the journalist went on to ask him whether he did not have some kind of contact with the Soviet Union or at least facilities for getting information through, adding that the Soviet authorities concerned would know him by the codename 'Aspirant'.

As an experienced operator our friend did not of course take the bait but simply told 'Aspirant' that he had come to the wrong man: he knew nothing about such things. Nevertheless this curious visit suggested caution. Moreover the visitor behaved in a generally suspicious manner in Geneva. In conversation with journalists and diplomats and while visiting White Russian emigrants he loudly proclaimed his anti-Fascist views and gave himself out to be a supporter of de Gaulle, and even a Communist. All this came to our ears, and we also heard whom he got in touch with in Geneva. 'Aspirant' behaved exactly as an *agent provocateur* would have behaved, and I became increasingly convinced that he was not at all what he said he was and that he might well have been sent to Geneva on somebody's payroll. I mentioned my suspicions to Central. In his answering telegram the director said he shared my view and warned us not only to have nothing to do with 'Aspirant'

*W.F. Flicke, *Agenten funken nach Moskau.*

but to be very much on our guard against him.

Soon afterwards we managed to find out whom the codename 'Aspirant' in fact covered. It emerged that Rameau's real name was Zweig (*rameau* is the French and *Zweig* the German for 'branch'), that he had worked for the French Deuxième Bureau before the war, and that following the capitulation of France he had offered his services to the Germans. I vaguely remembered having met a journalist by the name of Ewald Zweig, a tabloid-press scribbler who could be had for any man's money, back in the Paris days. There was every indication that this was the same fellow. My duty, however, was to abide by Central's instructions and avoid all contact with him. I did in fact bump into him subsequently, but I shall be coming back to that. It was more than a year later.

Around the same time I started having trouble with the Swiss police and immigration authorities. My residence permit expired, and it was only with considerable difficulty that I managed to get it renewed. We also received a visit from the treasury department, who wanted to know the amount and origin of Geopress's income. There was nothing wrong with my book-keeping, and the man apologized and went away again. Nevertheless all these complications threatened the existence of the Geopress agency and with it the operations of the entire intelligence network that I had been to so much trouble to build up.

The two things that offered us most protection were the fact that we were working from a neutral and unoccupied country on the one hand and our strict observance of the rules of conspiracy on the other. Furthermore the government and people of Switzerland were strongly anti-Nazi and sympathized with the cause of the League of Nations. All these factors meant that we could operate comparatively undisturbed.

At the same time, however, the Swiss authorities, fearing an invasion, had to keep in with the Germans and pursue a policy of cautious compromise. By blackmailing the country with the threat of attack the Germans did on occasion manage to get their way.

The blatantly pro-Allied attitude of the Swiss government as well as certain of its actions to the detriment of Germany were in any case a source of irritation to the Nazis, so that from time to time troops were concentrated along the frontier, a spanner thrown into the diplomatic works, and rumours put about to the effect that an attack was imminent. Whenever this happened the local Fascists started making feverish preparations for a *putsch*.

The situation became particularly dicey in June 1942 when the world press came out with the Anglo-American-Soviet treaty concerning the opening of a second front in Europe. The Swiss government was afraid that as soon as the Allies landed in France the Germans would march straight into Switzerland, and secret information provided by Swiss Intelligence supported this view.

Our German sources too reported that in the event of a second front being opened up the invasion of Switzerland was not to be ruled out. For us this would have meant having to operate under occupied conditions, which besides being extremely ticklish calls for careful preparation and quite different methods.

The tension continued into August, and the Germans started troop manoeuvres on the Swiss frontier. I told Jim to inform Central immediately and ask for advice. We received instructions to continue our activities underground in the event of German occupation. Clearly very worried, the director asked whether we were ready for this, where we intended to run our transmitter from, how we proposed to go underground, who would be able to continue operating with his own papers under occupied conditions, whom we could use as contact men, and so on and so forth.

This new danger threatening our organization left no time for shilly-shallying. I had to prepare my people, find secret rendezvous points, brief contact men, fix pass-words, teach Pakbo and Sissy encoding, and solve a host of other problems.

Central telegraphed almost daily to find out how we were getting on with our preparations for going underground and to beg of us at the same time to continue collecting information with undiminished intensity: the great German summer offensive was already under way.

CHAPTER 16

The thrust towards the Caucasus

Like that in 1941 before Moscow, the situation in the southern sector of the Soviet-German front in the summer of 1942 was extremely precarious.

The enemy launched his main thrusts in the direction of Stalingrad and the Caucasus, and the troops of the Red Army, unable to hold up under the enormous pressure, were forced to retreat; as they did so the enemy's air force and armoured divisions caused tremendous losses in their ranks. For the time being at least the initiative was back in the hands of the Nazi generals.

How did it happen? Why did the Red Army suffer this fresh defeat after having itself inflicted a heavy defeat on the Germans in the course of the winter campaign? What was it that enabled the Fascist army successfully to continue its advance in accordance with the plans worked out by Hitler's high command? The explanation lies in a combination of circumstances.

One reason was that the promised second front in Europe had failed to materialize. The communiqué issued on 12 June 1942 at the end of a successful round of Anglo-American-Soviet negotiations had said in part, '. . . Complete agreement has been reached to the effect that the opening of a second European front in 1942 is imperative', and Roosevelt had assured the Soviet government on two separate occasions that this commitment would be fulfilled. Furthermore the defeat suffered by the German army before Moscow had, together with the effects of the Red Army's winter offensive, forced the German high command to move large numbers of armoured units to the eastern front, seriously weakening its lines of defence in western Europe. The armed forces of the United States and Great Britain, on the other hand, are considered by Hungarian historians to have been more than six million men strong in the spring of 1942—sufficient at any rate to open a second front in Europe.

It soon became obvious, however, that the governing circles of

Britain and America had no intention of opening such a second front, their long-term goal being to let Germany and the Soviet Union wear each other down. The Allies preferred to wait, and it was even said that they started secret negotiations with the Germans for a separate peace instead of giving the Soviet Union real and effective assistance.

So the Wehrmacht high command, knowing its rear to be safe, concentrated its combat strength on the Soviet-German front. It is now known that on 1 May 1942 the German armed forces comprised 232 divisions, 10 brigades, and 6 air fleets. Of these, 178 divisions and 8 brigades, i.e., nearly eighty per cent of Germany's ground forces, plus 4 air fleets were engaged against the Red Army in the East. Germany's allies had an additional 39 divisions and 12 brigades and air-force units on the eastern front.

Although no longer in a position to launch an attack against the Red Army along the whole length of the front as in 1941, the Wehrmacht was still strong enough and had sufficient reserves to deliver serious strategic blows in individual sectors.

Meanwhile the Soviet government, making its own preparations for the summer offensive in ignorance of its allies' true intentions, was counting on the fact that simultaneously with the Red Army's attack the Anglo-American forces would launch an offensive against Germany from the West. Accordingly the Soviet chiefs of staff were instructed to prepare the army and navy for a large-scale offensive operation.

Then Churchill went to Moscow in August 1942 and announced officially that the opening of the second front had been postponed. The memorandum that the Soviet government handed him in reply reads in part: '. . . The Soviet high command planned its military operations for the summer and autumn on the assumption that the second European front would be opened as agreed in 1942. . . . The refusal of the British government to open a second front in Europe in 1942 . . . aggravates the situation of the Red Army on the front and is prejudicial to the plans of the Soviet high command.'

But there were other mistakes as well. In the Hungarian history of the war that I have already quoted they are analysed as follows: 'The high command overestimated the successes of the winter offensive and failed to take into account the fact that the German army had got over its defeat, recovered its effectiveness, and amassed considerable offensive potential. The Soviet armed forces, although fortified by substantial munitions supplies and the experience gained in previous engagements, still lacked the necessary technical superiority and were less mobile than the enemy. In the circumstances the plans for the 1942 summer offensive ought to have involved keeping the Red Army temporarily on the defensive in order to rob the enemy of his advantages and create the proper conditions for successful resumption of offensive tactics. This would have made it possible for the Soviet troops to break the force of the Fascist attack on prepared terrain and from favourable defensive positions, and to do so with fewer losses. In addition this would have meant creating at a much earlier stage of the campaign the conditions that turned the war radically in our favour.'

As a result of these errors on the part of the Soviet high command the troops in the southern sector of the front were insufficiently prepared for a defensive operation against enormously superior enemy strength. In July the Germans shattered the front with a series of powerful blows and started advancing swiftly in the direction of the Volga and the northern Caucasus.

I noticed around this time that Central was beginning to pay particularly close attention to our reports concerning the German operations in this southern sector of the front. At the director's request, from July onwards I marked particularly important telegrams as 'urgent' so that they could be decoded first. I continued as before to write all the telegrams myself in German.

In July the Red Army, engaged in heavy defensive fighting against the Nazi forces thrusting towards Voronezh and Voroshilovgrad, tried to check the advance of Field Marshal von Bock's army. During this period we passed Central information about certain changes in the plans of the German high command.

Bock's armoured and mobile divisions succeeded in breaking through the front, and in accordance with the German plan of attack as put into practice by Rundstedt, commander-in-chief of the army group 'South', they pursued their thrust towards the Volga and Stalingrad.

According to information received by Louise, what the Germans had in mind was this:

First they intended to reach the Don-Volga line (without

advancing further in the direction of the Caucasus). Then General Küchler's army group was to start a thrust from Lake Ilmen, break through the sector between Leningrad and Moscow, and by-pass Moscow to the north. Having done this, he was to turn south; Bock, once he had reached the Volga, was to turn north; and the two army groups were to join up east of Moscow. With Moscow encircled, a concentric attack was to be launched on the capital.

Louise's well-informed source doubted whether the German high command had the strength at its disposal for so extensive an operation as the encirclement of Moscow, and in view of the increased fighting efficiency of the Red Army at this period his doubts appeared justified. Nevertheless the Wehrmacht was still strong and capable in favourable circumstances of dealing out some powerful blows. The only reason why the Germans failed in 1942 to carry their eastern campaign to a victorious conclusion was that the Red Army's stand before Stalingrad broke the force of the Wehrmacht and shattered the German general staff's rosy hopes.

Hitler was confident that he would have his revenge for 1941: he would launch a fresh attack on Moscow and demolish the capital of the hated Bolsheviks. Today, when so many documents have been published and books written about the Second World War, this is common knowledge. We, however, knew Hitler's intentions at the time, having received word of them from a number of sources.

In the summer of 1942 I received fresh proof, this time from Finnish diplomatic circles. The information came through Grey, who reported to me in June *via* Long and Pakbo about Hitler's meeting with the Finnish president, Mannerheim.

According to our informant, who was present during part of the interview, Hitler's surprise trip to Finland had been prompted by Mannerheim's having informed Berlin on 15 May that Finland intended to conclude a separate peace with the Soviet Union, whereupon Germany had immediately stopped provisioning the Finnish army.

Hitler told Mannerheim that his key strategic concept was the offensive against the line Astrakhan-Stalingrad with the purpose of cutting the Soviet Union off from the northern Caucasus; subsequently he proposed to overrun the Caucasus and take Baku, at the same time launching an attack on Moscow. . . .

He promised the Finnish president an immediate loan of four SS divisions to help him maintain order and agreed to extend Finland's eastern frontier to Lake Ladoga after the war.

In return Hitler demanded that the Finnish positions be defended more forcefully, that the Finns take part in the attack on Leningrad, and that the Finnish army mount a vigorous operation in the direction of Murmansk.

The Germans, as is well-known, registered some important successes in the southern Soviet-German sector during the first phase of the campaign, launching a powerful attack on a broad front. The enemy army groups pursued their thrust in two directions: towards Stalingrad, and towards the northern Caucasus.

Our reports to Central confirmed that Hitler meant to carry out the German plan of attack essentially unchanged. In August, for example, I sent off the following telegram:

4 August 1942. To the director.

Via Long.

According to information received from the highest military circles, Hitler has set them the target of taking Maykop and Groznyy in August. The Wehrmacht high command has stated that the oil-wells destroyed by the retreating Russians could be made operational again within six months.

They reckon that the Russian oil will cover the Wehrmacht's total requirement. All the top oil experts are currently in Berlin, awaiting orders to proceed to the northern Caucasus.

Dora.

Agnes confirmed this with a report from Berlin. In his view the Wehrmacht high command was planning as before to overrun the northern Caucasus as far as the line Stalingrad-Astrakhan-Groznyy-Maykop, although the tough resistance encountered towards Stalingrad and the relatively easy advances made in the northern and western Caucasus had given rise to some discussion in the high command and at Hitler's headquarters.

The Germans planned to take Stalingrad on 27/28 July. They were also weighing up the earlier (first) plan of the Wehrmacht high command regarding a thrust through Baku and Persia to the Persian Gulf, but everything pointed to the fact that they would go back to that plan only if Japan joined the war against the Soviet

Union. Agnes stressed that, in spite of Germany's military successes, Japan was sticking to its wait-and-see attitude.

For the Red Army general staff it was important to know not only the enemy's intentions and any modifications of his strategic plans but also the number and strength of the German units engaged in the southern sector of the front, the reserves and munitions at the enemy's disposal, and the amount of his losses. In a telegram of 25 August 1942, for example, the director asked:

1) Where is Hitler's headquarters? 2) Do the 73rd, 337th, and 709th divisions and the SS division 'Reich' exist and if so where are they deployed? We have information to the effect that the 337th and 709th divisions have been moved from west to east and the 73rd division and the SS division 'Reich' from east to west. Where are they at the moment?

It was Salter who answered these questions for us and in addition obtained detailed information about the deployment of German troops in France. On 30 September 1942 the director informed us that this information of Salter's had been extremely useful and expressed his particular appreciation.

CHAPTER 17

'Taylor'

As the battle of Stalingrad got under way, Christian Schneider, the man we called 'Taylor', turned out to be surprisingly well-informed about the Wehrmacht's operations. His reports, which reached me *via* Sissy, were so concrete and detailed that we began to wonder whether someone was not using Taylor to slip us false information. What made it even more curious was that Taylor, a mere translator at the International Labour Office, had no facilities for getting hold of information of a military nature; up to now we had neither expected nor received really valuable intelligence from him, and we were consequently amazed when he started coming up with material of the very first importance. A leak of these proportions, had the enemy come to hear of it, would have sown consternation in the ranks of the German general staff.

Moreover, as Sissy now informed me, it had been Taylor who, more than a year before, had told her that Germany was on the point of attacking the Soviet Union and had even given her the exact date, which I had then radioed immediately to Central. The whole thing needed thinking about. . .

I passed on Taylor's first reports to the director with a feeling that at last we had hit upon a really important source. I had no means of checking his reports myself, however, and until I got a reaction from Moscow I was plagued with doubts as to whether what we were transmitting was true or false.

To my surprise the director, usually wariness itself, showed quite exceptional interest in the material we were giving him and suggested we try and activate Taylor as fully as possible. He also recommended, however, that in order to give ourselves a clear picture of the man's true potential we should give Taylor the following assignment: let him list the German formations fighting in the southern sector of the front, and let him also find out and report how many German prisoners of war were currently interned in the Soviet Union—the latter of course on the basis of information at the disposal of the German general staff. It was no easy assignment.

Yet the answer came back within a few days. Taylor's report, which I encoded and had radioed to Central immediately, was as follows:

15 August 1942. To the director.

From Taylor.

1) Herewith the numbers of practically all the German formations engaged from 1 May in the southern sector of the eastern front, particularly between the Don and the Donets, in the Donets Basin, and on the Crimean peninsula:

Armoured divisions: the 7th, 11th, 14th, 16th, and 22nd.

Mobile divisions: the 18th, 60th, and 70th.

Fast mobile divisions: the 5th, 99th, 100th, and 101st.

The 49th army corps, comprising 2 mountain divisions.

Infantry divisions: the 15th, 22nd, 24th, 28th, 35th, 50th, 57th, 62nd, 68th, 75th, 79th, 95th, 111th, 113th, 132nd, 164th, 170th, 211th, 221st, 226th, 254th, 257th, 262nd, 298th, 312th.

The 61st tank regiment. One Bavarian SS brigade, 1 artillery brigade (including the 20th Küstrin heavy artillery regiment); 1 mixed SS detatchment of regimental strength consisting of Danish and Norwegian volunteers and German SS units.

2) The number of German prisoners of war currently interned in the Soviet Union is 151,000.

Dora.

It would have been difficult for me in Switzerland to check whether these figures in fact tallied with the formations engaged in the southern sector of the Soviet-German front. Theoretically a certain amount of checking would have been possible, for example by talking to the men returning from the eastern front for treatment in the Swiss hospitals and sanatoriums in German hands. These men were a useful source of information and one that we did on occasion activate. Further information could have been obtained from journalistic circles in Berne, Vienna, and Berlin. But all this would have taken time. It was much easier for Central to check the credibility of Taylor's information because all they had to do was compare it with their front-line reconnaissance reports. Checking the number of prisoners of war was even simpler.

Central expressed themselves satisfied with Taylor's answers and from then on regularly asked for information from him.

It became increasingly clear that Taylor had a pretty good idea of what the German military leadership was up to. Where was all this valuable information coming from, and how did a German emigrant with a relatively humble office job get hold of it? Taylor's secret remained impenetrable: he parried all our enquiries by saying that he had given his word and could reveal nothing. Central asked us several times to find out what sources Taylor was drawing on, but we had to content ourselves with not knowing for fear of losing a valuable man. We did so the more readily for the fact that Taylor occasionally hinted that he might soon be in a position to satisfy our 'importunate curiosity', as he ironically put it. We had no alternative but to wait.

During that difficult period, with the Germans marking up provisional victories on the Don, before Stalingrad, and in the northern Caucasus, the 'veterans' of our Swiss group—Pakbo, Sissy, Long, and Salter—also put in some fruitful and resourceful work, repeatedly furnishing me with important intelligence reports.

The Soviet high command was acting on the assumption that Germany had at its disposal fresh reserves that, if they were to be used to reinforce the German troops in the fierce fighting before Stalingrad, would constitute a considerable danger. Central instructed us to find out and report whether there was in fact a reserve army available in Germany or whether this was just a bluff.

Salter quickly obtained the relevant information from a source of his called 'Lili', and I radioed Central accordingly:

There is no so-called reserve army in Germany; there are a number of formations consisting of recruits and older men, amounting to not more than 20 divisions altogether.

This information was based on data obtained from various German military circles. It did not account for those called up in August 1942.

It was also about this time—mid-July 1942—that we received the first wind of the fact that German scientists were experimenting with nuclear fission—the first stage in the manufacture of the atomic bomb. Central communicated a special word of thanks to all those who had been involved in getting hold of such a strategically vital piece of scientific intelligence.

The information pouring in to me all the time had to be passed on as quickly as possible, and I can tell you I had my hands full. I spent the day working on my Geopress maps, keeping up with my correspondence, reading the newspapers and the scientific literature, and listening to the radio news bulletins that reached neutral Switzerland from every country involved in the war. My evenings and nights I spent locked in my study, writing and encoding the telegrams.

I tried to keep my Geopress business trips to a minimum, but I still had to do plenty of travelling in order to maintain contact with the various members of the group. I usually took the encoded telegrams to Rosa and Maude myself, though sometimes I sent my wife Helene. Keeping contact with Sissy in Geneva also took up a lot of time, but not as much as going to see Pakbo and Jim, neither of whom knew or could be allowed to know my address. To take Jim his encoded telegrams I had to go to Lausanne, and Pakbo I met in a variety of places.

After a while I got my wife to help me with the encoding, and later on, at the express request of the director, I involved Jim as well. From July 1942 (and not from the beginning of our collaboration, as for reasons of his own Foote claimed in his book) I took Jim his telegrams in German.

This speeded things up considerably, of course, although both Helene and Jim really had enough on their plates already. Helene looked after the business side of Geopress, did all the typing, and also had her courier work, on top of being the mother of two children. Jim had his radio-operating, and in addition Central set him special assignments that were not directly connected with the work of the group.

The telegrams marked 'urgent' were transmitted mainly by our Geneva operators, Jim getting only those that could stand a delay of a day or two. But whenever I or one of my couriers (Rosa sometimes went in Helene's stead) had time for a trip to Lausanne we took Jim the 'urgent' telegrams and he transmitted them from there.

We all took a certain degree of exhaustion for granted, but on top of the fatigue and tension that are the intelligence agent's constant and inevitable companions there was that extra nervousness that was shared by the entire country. Right through the spring and into the early part of summer, Switzerland expected the Germans to invade. The general mobilization decreed by the government made a hole in our organization too: Pakbo was called up, which meant that I lost contact with some of our best sources, including Long, Salter, Louise, and Agnes.

Fortunately this situation did not last. Pakbo managed to get himself demobilized and was back in Berne before very long. In fact large numbers of reservists were sent home again as a threat of occupation receded. We received reliable information that the heat was off, and we stopped our preparations for going underground.

Around the middle of July we heard that the head of the Geneva office of the organization responsible for processing Germany's munitions orders had received a coded telegram from the German high command instructing him to call off preparations for a Fascist *putsch* in Switzerland since the Swiss had got wind of those preparations and obtained proof that they were being financed from Germany. It being of the utmost importance to Germany that the Swiss munitions industry should continue supplying it with war material, the man was advised to break off contact with the Geneva Fascists for the time being.

This report reached us *via* Sissy from a new acquaintance of hers who was later to supply us with further important information.

Switzerland and the Swiss were to some extent reassured, but they went on trembling in fear of their treacherous northern neighbour and his insatiable ambitions right up until the end of the war.

CHAPTER 18

The transmitter and the oscillator

On 27 October 1942 something happened that spelled danger for our organization: the Swiss police raided the Hamels' place in the rue de Carouge, searched both flat and shop, and arrested Edouard.

Olga Hamel informed me immediately and I hurried to a rendezvous with her outside the city. There she told me the whole story.

The police arrived about nine o'clock one evening. It was just coming up to Edouard's transmitting time, and he was connecting up the set and the aerial and getting everything ready. Suddenly the couple heard a noise from the shop below: someone was hammering on the locked and bolted door. Guessing that it was the police, Maude snatched up the encoded telegrams lying on the table, dashed into the kitchen, and threw them in the stove. Then she picked up the set, ran with it out through the back door and down into their small storage cellar, laid it in the hole that had already been dug for it, and shovelled the earth in on top. The lock and bolts held for a few minutes more while Maude cleared up the last suspicious traces. As she returned to the flat, footsteps could already be heard pounding up the stairs.

Wasting no words, the police pushed Edouard aside as soon as he had opened the door, burst into the flat, and started searching. They worked their way systematically through the entire house. They failed to find the transmitter buried in the cellar, but they did discover, hidden under the parquet flooring, the reserve set that Edouard was knocking up out of spare parts in his few free moments. The police took it out, put it on the table, and had a good look at it. Fortunately it was not yet finished and had no Morse key attached. Furthermore, as a camouflage, Edouard had built the transmitter into an oscillator of the kind used for medicinal purposes. Oscillator and radio operate on the same principle, both of them emitting short waves. If the Morse key and one or two other parts are missing, even an expert may find it hard to distinguish the one from the other.

Edouard accordingly told the police that this was a medical appliance that he was building himself because one could not buy them. He suffered from neuralgia, he said (producing a doctor's certificate to this effect), and was treating himself with the appliance, not being able to afford a doctor.

The police replied that they must still arrest him for concealing a short-wave set even if its purpose was therapeutic, and they took Edouard and the set away with them.

A day went by, two days went by, and still Edouard did not return, though neither was Maude summoned for questioning. At last, on the third day, they let her husband go home.

Edouard had stuck to his story and played his part convincingly. The police could bring no evidence, and the examining magistrate was obliged to release him. The doctor's certificate worked strongly in his favour, as did the fact that, built as it was into an oscillator housing, and in its half-finished state, the transmitter constituted an exact copy of its medical relation. The police experts admitted that Edouard's home-made appliance did in fact bear more resemblance to an oscillator than to a short-wave transmitter, and it was their evidence that tipped the scales in his favour.

The police interrogation did something towards dispersing our fears. It emerged that the Hamels' place had been raided not with a view to finding a secret transmitter but for the purpose of seizing illegal publications. The Geneva police had arrested Hamel's brother the day before as he was delivering left-wing socialist literature to an illegal address. His brother had nothing to do with our group, nor did Edouard have anything to do with illegal party work, but the arrest of the brother led inevitably to the raid on the Hamels. The Swiss monitors had not yet discovered our Geneva transmitters at that time. In any case the Swiss had very few monitoring devices, and most of them were used to keep a close watch on any German aircraft penetrating Swiss air space.

So we were somewhat reassured, although the incident had of course drawn the police's attention to Edouard.

When subsequent police enquiries likewise failed to come up with any evidence that Edouard had been operating an illegal transmitter, his case was handed over to a court martial for further investigation. Luckily the police records and the confiscated transmitter for some reason stayed on the shelf there for six months; Edouard was not troubled further and was able to continue his work.

Then, at the end of May 1943, he received an unexpected summons to appear before the court.

Three days before the hearing I instructed him to stop transmitting and receiving and to find a good hiding-place for the new reserve set that he was working on in his spare time. These precautions, however, turned out to be superfluous.

The court martial heard Edouard's case on 2 June and failed to establish that any particular felony had been committed. The sentence was surprisingly lenient: ten days' suspended for illegal possession of a short-wave appliance for medicinal purposes. The whole affair, which could have had serious consequences for us, ended by letting us off with a mild shock.

CHAPTER 19

Rosa's boyfriend

Rosa, twenty-three in December 1942, was the youngest member of our group. She was a quiet, reserved, sensible girl, and she was devoted to the cause we all served. But beside all these positive qualities she had one major negative quality: she lacked that sixth sense of circumspection that people who work 'underground' usually only acquire after years of experience.

When we recruited this daughter of an old Internationalist it was in the confident expectation that time would turn her into a valuable combatant on the underground front.

After several months spent in trying her out, drilling her in the rules of conspiracy, and teaching her how to operate a radio set, by the autumn of 1942, as I have said, we had Rosa maintaining contact with Central on her own.

Helene and I visited Rosa regularly during the day or in the evening. There was nothing to arouse suspicion about this; the neighbours doubtless took us for French tutors or for relatives of hers. On the contrary, it would have aroused suspicion if, as a student, she had lived too much on her own.

Rosa worked pretty well. She began her transmissions on the dot, she transmitted the encoded texts without any mistakes, and her courier work was disciplined and punctual. As far as we could see she observed all the rules of conspiratorial work. And yet the worst thing happened that could have happened.

Rosa fell in love.

It must have been around September 1942. Rosa met at the hairdresser's a good-looking young man called Hans Peters, who worked there. Peters was a German but had been living in Switzerland for some time already. He undoubtedly did everything to make the girl fall in love with him. He gave her to understand that he was a member of an underground resistance group, that he was an anti-Fascist, even that he was a Communist. Rosa told us this with utter conviction later, when the arrests started among the members of our group and our suspicions extended to, among other people, Rosa's lover.

Lack of experience of the ways of the world and in particular of the enemy's insidious methods in this case played a fateful and decisive role. Rosa believed her admirer's every word and forgot that it was her duty to be permanently on her guard; head over heels in love, she lost all control over herself. But what was even worse, she told neither myself nor my wife anything about it.

It did not emerge until after the war that the hairdresser Hans Peters, resident in Geneva, had been a member of the semi-legal National Socialist organization founded in Switzerland in the thirties and had been recruited by the Gestapo as a secret agent. He was in close touch with a man called Hermann Henseler, who was on the staff of the German consulate in Geneva. Henseler was himself a German secret agent and was the man who paid Peters his money.

Peters played his cards skilfully, and eventually Rosa became his lover. They slept either at Peters' place or at Rosa's, to which after a while she invited him. In this way a German agent gained access to the flat from which one of our group's transmitters was being operated. It is not difficult to imagine the rejoicing at Gestapo headquarters when Peters' report came in!

I must say something at this point about the so-called '*Rote Kapelle*' Special Detachment at Himmler's counter-intelligence headquarters whose task it was to track down Soviet intelligence agents operating in Europe.

The history of how the *Rote Kapelle* Special Detachment was set up and how it operated can be pieced together from the archives and from statements made by members of the German secret service interrogated after the war. The work of the organization has also been described in detail by W.F. Flicke, to whom I have already referred.*

Kapelle means 'band' or 'orchestra', and the *Rote Kapelle* or Red Orchestra was what the Nazis called all the Soviet intelligence groups operating in Europe whose transmitters they had been monitoring since the beginning of the war against the Soviet Union. In 1941 the Abwehr, the SD (*Sicherheitsdienst* or security service), and the Gestapo succeeded in tracking down our

*W.F. Flicke, *Die Rote Kapelle*, Kreuzlingen, 1949.

colleagues in Brussels, in Holland, and subsequently in the German capital as well. Yet even with Holland, Brussels, and Berlin out of action, the German monitors reported that the transmitters in France and Switzerland were still carrying on a lively dialogue with Moscow.

On hearing this, Himmler personally gave urgent instructions that a small number of reliable, qualified members of his secret political police should get together to form a special group. Dubbed the 'Red Orchestra' Special Detachment, this group of Gestapo officers worked in close collaboration with the SD and with radio reconnaissance.

In the summer of 1942 the detachment arrived in Paris, first setting up its staff headquarters in the SD building (previously the home of the French Sureté) in the rue des Saussaies and subsequently moving to its own building in the boulevard de Courcelles.

The 'Red Orchestra' detachment later came to be known as the Pannwitz detachment because from the summer of 1943 onwards it was headed by SS-Hauptsturmführer Heinz Pannwitz, an experienced criminal-investigation officer from the Gestapo's Prague office.

In Paris the detachment's agents started looking for the Soviet intelligence organization whose radio link with Moscow the Abwehr's radio direction finders had already been observing for more than a year. Some of those agents were sent into the unoccupied zone because it was thought that the leader and several members of the Belgian-Dutch group had gone into hiding there after successfully escaping arrest in 1941.

At the same time the detachment launched its operation against the Swiss group. The Germans knew that two of our transmitters were operating in or near Geneva and the third in Lausanne. They now had to find them, which in cities of the size of Geneva and Lausanne is no easy task. Their biggest problem, however, was having to conduct the search in neutral territory; while behaving quite correctly towards the official representatives of the German Reich, the Swiss government took energetic steps to block any operations by Himmler's secret service on Swiss soil.

In the summer of 1942 the Germans were still not able to decipher our telegrams, piles of which were gathering dust on the decoding experts' desks. They realized, however, that even if they managed to pin-point the transmitters, catch the radio operators, and seize the equipment, their success would be incomplete. The Germans knew from experience that our organization could replace all that as long as its leader remained at liberty.

So the German secret service adopted a new, more cunning approach. As W.F. Flicke describes it, the essence of this method was first to ascertain the illegal organization's technical line and then, by tracing that line, to get hold of the relevant documentation, the code-key, the list of agents, and so on. They could thus, Flicke says, kill two birds with one stone: they wiped out the particular intelligence group concerned and they also—which was no less useful—got into radio contact with Moscow and could begin to feed Soviet Intelligence false information.

In pursuance of this policy the Germans, having monitored and located a transmitter, kept not only the radio operator under observation but also the people who brought him the information to be transmitted. Sustained observation of this kind put them on the track of other people and other addresses. They also put *agents provocateurs* onto the suspects to try and get into their confidence and insinuate themselves into the organization. Once the circle of addresses, agents, and contacts was observed to be complete, the arrests began.

In searching for our group, German Counter-intelligence used more or less this method, the only difference being that their agents had a much more difficult time of it in Switzerland than they had had in Germany and the occupied countries.

It emerged from the correspondence files of the Gestapo after the war that in August 1942 two of its agents, Hermann Henseler and Hans Peters, had been given the assignment of trying to infiltrate the Soviet intelligence organization in Switzerland. One of these agents had succeeded in establishing close relations with a certain Margarete Bolli, who turned out to be a radio operator.

What did not emerge, and what still remains unclear, is how the Gestapo agent Peters knew that Rosa was the person he was looking for or that she was a radio operator and a member of our group.

Quite patently the Germans did not know the whereabouts of Rosa's transmitter before their agent made her acquaintance. To find it by monitoring they would have had to use direction finders in the city itself, systematically checking district by district and house by house. (A year later the Swiss police did just that—possibly on the basis of data supplied by the Germans—and were successful.)

The only thing that could have made the German agents suspicious of Rosa was her regularly meeting people who were being watched by the Gestapo or the SD. Rosa was in contact with Pakbo, Jim, Helene, and myself; apart from us four, the only person who knew her address was Edouard, who had installed the set in her flat.

Which one of us could they have been watching at that time, i.e., in August 1942?

The Gestapo and the Swiss police may well have had their eye on Pakbo since long before the war as a progressive journalist, an anti-Fascist, and the head of a socialist press agency. Then there was Edouard's arrest by the federal police, though that was not until October. And there were a number of people—the *agent provocateur* Zweig ('Aspirant') was one of them—who could have given the Gestapo information about my wife's and my own Communist past.

However it came about, the fact of the matter is that in August/September 1942 the 'Red Orchestra' Special Detachment picked up the trail of our group.

I have no idea how much Rosa told her 'Communist' boyfriend, whether for example the gullible young thing volunteered the information that she was in radio contact with Moscow, but this much is certain: Peters was permanently on her heels, searched her flat for the transmitter whenever opportunity offered, and was able of course to observe Rosa when she met me or my wife or when she left Geneva on an assignment. So he was undoubtedly able to establish that Rosa was in touch with Pakbo and Jim, which represented a very great threat to the existence of our organization.

If we had known what a serious mistake Rosa had made we could still have found a way of protecting the group—by swiftly reorganizing our contacts, for example, by breaking off relations with Rosa and taking away her transmitter, and by moving Jim to a different flat. Some of us would have gone underground to carry on directing the work of the group from there.

But we had no inkling of where the enemy was coming at us from.

CHAPTER 20

Enter Schellenberg

Himmler was clearly dissatisfied with the time it was taking to hunt up the rest of the underground intelligence groups in Europe—and particularly in Switzerland—that his organization had already monitored. The SS chief decided to make an approach to the Swiss secret service and try in this way to obtain the necessary information and freedom to operate on neutral territory. He entrusted his top-secret mission to his pupil and favourite, SS-Brigadegeneral Walter Schellenberg.

Schellenberg, a leading SD officer and a member of the Nazi élite, timed his cleverly devised Swiss operation very well. Germany was enjoying its greatest military successes on the eastern front. The Wehrmacht's assault divisions were threatening Stalingrad, and there was fierce fighting in the foot-hills of the Caucasus Mountains. It looked as if it would take very little to break the resistance of the Soviet army in the southern sector of the front. In western Europe, on the other hand, there was no sign of preparations for an Allied landing and the opening of a second front, and Germany's rear was relatively undisturbed.

Schellenberg reckoned—and he was right—that with the situation on both the military and the political fronts in Germany's favour the Swiss would be more approachable and readier to make concessions as regarded the activities of the German secret service. He set himself the ambitious goal of establishing personal relations with Oberstbrigadier Roger Masson, the head of Swiss Intelligence and Counter-intelligence as well as of Switzerland's frontier defence. It was a tempting prospect to make contact with this influential officer of whom it has been said that 'he trusted, albeit almost against his will, in the victory of the German Reich'.* The author of that statement, the former German general staff officer Wilhelm von Schramm, can hardly be accused of prejudice in this respect.

*W. von Schramm, *Verrat im Zweiten Weltkrieg* ('Treason in the Second World War'), Düsseldorf, 1967, p. 266.

Masson, in common with Swiss government circles in general and with the majority of the leaders of political and economic life, wished at all costs to avoid any kind of tension between Switzerland and its powerful northern neighbour. Back in 1940 he had shared the opinion of most members of the Swiss government in putting the chief blame for such tension on the Swiss press with its continual criticism of the Nazi regime. Another man who shared that opinion was of course Goebbels at the German ministry of propaganda.

Schellenberg and Masson met four times altogether—twice in 1942 and twice in 1943. Their first meeting, on 8 September 1942, took place on German soil, in the little town of Waldshut on the Swiss-German frontier. Five weeks later Schellenberg crossed the frontier himself, and Masson received his guest at Schloss Wolfsberg, a chateau near Ermatingen on Lake Constance, where the two men held talks from 16 to 18 October. The chateau was the property of Paul Meyer-Schwartenbach, a friend and confidant of Masson's. Meyer, who before the war had made his living by writing detective stories, was responsible during the war—despite his occupying the rank of major in Masson's intelligence organization—for handling Switzerland's war supplies to the German army together with Schellenberg's aide, SS-Sturmbannführer Hans W. Eggen. This was evidently so lucrative a business that by 1942 he already owned a chateau at which he was able to arrange meetings between German and Swiss intelligence officers.

The third and fourth meetings also took place on neutral Swiss territory. It goes without saying that these occasions were kept top-secret, only one or two confidential agents and the two protagonists' body-guards knowing about them.

It is not known exactly what the two intelligence chiefs talked about at their meetings in 1942. Possibly Schellenberg merely put out feelers and did not at first try to put any pressure on his colleague. At any rate he appears to have made a great impression on Masson, who told Bernard Barbey, General Guisan's aide-de-camp, after the September meeting: 'We [meaning himself and Schellenberg] operate on the same wave-length.'* A fine admission on the part of the head of Intelligence of neutral Switzerland.

*Jon Kimche, *Spying for Peace,* Foreword to second edition.

Schellenberg, a past master of provocation and deception, undoubtedly did not show his whole hand immediately to an opponent as familiar as Masson was with the rules of behind-the-scenes intrigue. It is unlikely that at those early meetings he gave Masson any concrete information about the 'Red Troika' or asked for his help in tracking down our organization. But it is not impossible that Himmler's envoy gave his opposite number to understand the disturbing nature of the circumstances that had made it necessary for him to leave Berlin on this secret mission to Switzerland.

One thing stands out a mile: Masson can hardly have failed to realize that so exalted a personage as SS-Brigadegeneral Walter Schellenberg must have had a very important reason indeed for seeking to establish a confidential relationship with him. What could it be? What was Schellenberg after in Switzerland?

Pretty obviously he was after an intelligence organization that was operating against Germany.

CHAPTER 21

'Lucy'

I have already mentioned how in the summer of 1942 we started getting some extraordinarily high-quality information *via* Sissy from Taylor—and how Taylor resolutely blocked all our attempts to contact his source directly.

Around the middle of November, however, as Soviet troops were beginning to encircle Paulus's army outside Stalingrad, Taylor dropped Sissy a hint to the effect that his German friend, the man who provided the information, was prepared to supply Soviet Intelligence regularly with material of interest to it. After first securing permission from Central, Sissy asked Taylor to talk things over frankly with his friend and persuade him to come in with us.

According to Taylor, his friend had been furious to learn that the exceptionally valuable information from the eastern front that he had been passing (*via* Swiss Intelligence) to the British was not being used by them but was simply being thrown into the wastepaper basket. The successes of the Red Army before Stalingrad were undoubtedly also influential in prompting him to offer us his services. Taylor informed Sissy that he and his friend were prepared to help the Soviet Union without payment, only wanting their expenses covered, because they were aware that the Soviet Union was Hitler's bitterest enemy and that the outcome of the war depended upon the resistance it put up.

But Taylor also made a condition: his friend would only work with us as long as we made no attempt to discover his real name, his address, and his profession. All Taylor would tell us was that the man lived in Luzern.

I asked Central whether we should accept this unusual condition. My view was that we should, in order to avoid losing contact with this extremely well-informed man who possibly had a whole group behind him. After carefully weighing up the pros and cons the director agreed, pointing out, however, that Sissy too must take precautions and that Taylor must under no circumstances give away to his friend her name and address—a counter-condition that Taylor accepted.

In this way our group came to include, in November 1942, a man who was to play a very great part in our future work. I gave him the codename 'Lucy'—an allusion to the place where he lived. As with all the other codenames, I used it only in my telegrams to the director.

Wanting to put Lucy's usefulness to the test, I set him, even before I received the director's answer, a special assignment: I asked him to find out what the German general staff knew about the Red Army, about the deployment of its troops on the front, about its commanding officers, and so on. Lucy informed me *via* Taylor that he was prepared to do this.

Either three or four days later Sissy handed me a typewritten report of several pages. The information Lucy provided absolutely staggered us. All our questions were answered exhaustively. He gave the deployment and strength of various Soviet divisions, named their commanding officers, and quoted the German general staff's evaluation of those officers. Marshal Shaposhnikov, chief of the Red Army general staff, was spoken of with the highest respect; in fact the Germans referred to him as a genius. They also had very flattering things to say about the middle levels of command in the Red Army. Individual front and divisional commanders, however, came off rather less well. The Germans of course obtained this information from their front-line reconnaissance units and from interrogating prisoners, since as Paul Carell writes: 'The German side had no insight into the major strategic plans of the Soviet high command . . . There was no German reconnaissance service in the higher ranks of the Soviet officer corps.'*

From then on Central set Lucy some of the most complicated assignments, all of which he fulfilled superbly.

Lucy's real name did not emerge until after 1944, when our group had been sprung and the trials began. That was the first time we heard the name Rudolf Roessler. After the war dozens of books and articles were written about him, and the debate about the 'Roessler problem' still goes on in the columns of the Western press.

*Paul Carell, *Verbrannte Erde* ('Scorched Earth'), Frankfurt-am-Main, 1966, p. 441.

Today the figure of Rudolf Roessler is fairly well defined, but different European circles and organs of the press hold widely divergent views as to his activities. Some consider Roessler 'the best intelligence agent of the Second World War'; others see him as 'a true German patriot and a fighter against Fascism'; others again feel that he betrayed his fatherland and the German people. A similar spectrum is covered by the world's judgement of the still unknown but allegedly highly-placed officers who supplied Lucy with military information.

Rudolf Roessler was born of a middle-class family in the ancient town of Kaufbeuren in southern Bavaria. His father, an important forestry official, gave his children a strict Protestant upbringing.

With the outbreak of the First World War the barely seventeen-year-old Rudolf, carried away by chauvinistic zeal, volunteered for the front. Life in the trenches probably had a sobering effect on him, because on his return he did not even think of pursuing a military career but instead took up art and journalism. A liberal democrat in politics, Roessler wrote theatre criticism, edited a newspaper in Augsburg in the twenties, published a literary magazine in Munich, and in the thirties headed with romantic enthusiasm and considerable competence the 'national-christian' People's Theatre League, founded to counterbalance the left-wing *Volksbühne,* the People's Theatre in Berlin.

He married a simple working-class girl, formerly a sales assistant in an Augsburg department store. When the Nazis seized power in Germany the couple emigrated to Switzerland and became bitter enemies of National Socialism. In 1934 Roessler founded in Luzern the Vita Nova publishing company, of which he was both proprietor and managing director.

The emigrant Roessler decided to fight the hated Hitler regime with the same weapon as his anti-Fascist friends in Berlin had chosen—the razor-sharp weapon of intelligence work.

Probably before the war began Roessler established contact with the so-called 'Buro Ha', the secret branch of Swiss Intelligence that had been set up with the blessing of General Guisan, commander-in-chief of the Swiss armed forces. The Buro Ha took its name from the man who headed it: Major Hans Hausamann.

Recruiting Roessler was a tremendous coup for Swiss Intelligence. At the time when he offered his services to the Buro Ha he was in all probability already in touch with important sources who were prepared to wage secret war on the Third Reich. Roessler's intelligence material came from members of the resistance movement, some of whom held high public office in Germany and others of whom had emigrated to Switzerland. Who these people were, how this anti-Nazi organisation came into being, and how the information got from Berlin over the frontier to Roessler are questions that have to this day received no clear-cut answer.

This much, however, is certain: Rudolf Roessler cooperated closely with Swiss Intelligence and supplied it with military information that came out of Germany. This is proved by various archives as well as by Roessler's own admission when, after the war, the Swiss authorities made him stand trial.

Roessler's case was heard by the federal court, beginning on 2 November 1953. As part of his defence he represented his standpoint in a way that typified his whole attitude. I quote:

'They call me a spy. A spy, as everyone knows, is a person who breaks the recognized rules of warfare to mislead the enemy—he may for example gain access to the enemy's territory by wearing the enemy's uniform—or who gets hold of important secrets by means of deception, fraud, and possibly the use of violence as well. Not even the charge against me maintains that I have ever acted in this or any similar way.'

Basel University history professor Edgar Bonjour, in a report commissioned by the Swiss government on Swiss foreign policy during the Second World War, adds that Roessler and myself 'cannot be called spies in the true sense of the word. They did no spying themselves but collected, arranged, evaluated, and passed on, partly with their own transmitters and partly by courier and post, the reports submitted to them by their agents.' According to Bonjour, not only Roessler's declaration as quoted above could apply to us both but also his statement: 'I can say with a clear conscience that I did not see any infringement of Switzerland's foreign relations as being a possible consequence of my actions.' The same author adds that Roessler could 'rightly hold this view, especially since Switzerland and the Soviet Union were not at war and his host country came to no harm by what he passed on to the Russians.'

There is no doubt that at first Roessler worked exclusively for the Swiss. Then, as war broke out, the other intelligence services of the anti-German alliance started receiving his information as well.

And very valuable information it was too, coming as it did from military and government circles inside Germany. According to Accoce and Quet, Roessler gave the Swiss advance warning of the German attack on Poland and of the Wehrmacht's intention to overrun Belgium and Holland and carry out a flanking movement to encircle the British and French armies—the operation that of course ended with the capitulation of France; he also gave them the Germans' plans for the campaign against the Soviet Union and the plans of other major military operations.*

On the other hand Roessler gained access to the important body of material that Swiss Intelligence was collecting about Germany—some of it flowing in to Masson's military intelligence headquarters, NS 1, some of it into the Buro Ha, both of them in Luzern—and was able to analyse and evaluate it. This material included statements by deserters, smugglers, and refugees from Germany and the occupied countries, information collected in talks with the German soldiers and officers being treated in Swiss hospitals, and finally—this was a sore point with pro-German members of the Swiss government such as Marcel Pilet-Golaz—the reports of Switzerland's military attachés and consular officers abroad. According to Jon Kimche, the Buro Ha had its own link with the Wehrmacht high command, with Hitler's headquarters, with sources close to Himmler, and even with leading circles in Finland. Although the Buro Ha was nominally subordinate to Masson, there was considerable rivalry between these two pillars of Swiss Intelligence. In fact Masson disapproved of Hausamann's department so heartily that he denounced it to Pilet-Golaz for anti-German activities.†

Roessler, at any rate, was sitting pretty. He was able to compare this vast mass of material with his own sources and draw the necessary conclusions.

General Guisan, who hoped for a League of Nations victory as Switzerland's only chance of escaping German occupation, did not forbid his subordinates to contact the Allied intelligence services.

US Intelligence was of course represented in Switzerland by Allen W. Dulles, later director of the CIA. Dulles arrived in

*Pierre Accoce and Pierre Quet, *La Guerre a été gagné en Suisse.*

†See Jon Kimche, *Spying for Peace,* chapters 4 and 5.

Switzerland in November 1942 as a member of the American diplomatic mission. Edgar Bonjour has this to say about Dulles's activities:

'The American intelligence chief was concerned as he explained it to keep Washington and London as well as Allied headquarters in Italy supplied with the information that was streaming in from Switzerland's neighbours, passing them that information either by radio or by courier. In Dulles's view the talks he held with Swiss politicians and intelligence officers constituted a counterpoise to Masson's contacts with military representatives of the Axis powers. In this way the balance required by Swiss neutrality with regard to the belligerent nations was restored.'

Thanks in part to Roessler, General Guisan found himself in possession of important intelligence material about Germany—material of potentially enormous value to Germany's opponents. What was he to do with it? Was he simply to file it away? As far as Guisan was concerned, the situation was clear: '. . . the only thing that could stop the conquest of all Europe by the Nazi regime was a military defeat in the field, . . . and there would be no prospect at all if the Russians collapsed. Could the Swiss do anything to help them in holding out?'*

Bonjour writes that those responsible for Switzerland's neutral foreign policy nevertheless had to bear in mind the fact that 'the Russian armies were making an effective contribution towards destroying National Socialism, which was also in the immediate interests of Switzerland', and he too recalls that, if Russia had collapsed or been thrown back to the Urals, Hitler would no longer have tolerated the existence of democratic, neutral countries in the stronghold of Europe.

*Jon Kimche, *Spying for Peace,* p. 88.

CHAPTER 22

'Werther', 'Olga', 'Anna', and the rest

One of my purposes in writing this book is to do what I can to set the record straight, and on the subject of Lucy and his sources the record is a pretty tangled and distorted one.

From the end of 1942 onwards, then, Rudolf Roessler's anti-Nazi intelligence sources in Berlin also fulfilled assignments set them by our Moscow headquarters. I have mentioned already that, apart from Taylor, no one in my group knew Roessler's name. We did not even know for certain that he was working for Swiss Intelligence as well as for ourselves; that was just a guess. Taylor handed the reports to Sissy, and Sissy passed them on to me. I condensed them into telegrams, which I then encoded and radioed through to Moscow marked 'from Lucy'.

I never met Roessler myself—then or later. Again apart from Taylor, the only members of my group to do so were Sissy and Jim, who saw him once in the autumn of 1944. What, therefore, are we to make of the passage in Pakbo's 'memoirs' where he claims that I told him 'one fine May morning in 1941' that I had found a first-class informant named Rudolf Roessler and asked him, Pakbo, whether he could 'make enquiries about him'? Pakbo goes on for a whole page about how he managed to discover all.* Curious memoirs indeed—as Pünter appears to have conceded himself in an interview he gave the *Tribune de Genève* soon after publication: 'I have no proof that Radó knew Roessler; I am simply relying on memory. I seem to recall Radó asking me to find out something about Roessler before the German attack on the Soviet Union. But I wouldn't swear to it. This was more than twenty-five years ago, you realize . . .'†

Drago Arsenijevič, the Yugoslav I have already mentioned, who published a book in 1969 rehashing most of the misinformation

*Otto Pünter, *Der Anschluss fand nicht statt,* p. 124.

† *Tribune de Genève,* 18 December 1967.

already on the market at that time, spins Pakbo's web of fantasy further. According to Arsenijevič, I discovered Roessler's identity through 'shadowing and private research' on the part of Paul Böttcher and Christian Schneider.*

The information Lucy passed on to us reached him from a variety of government departments in Germany. To help Central keep track of where the information came from I gave these sources suitably allusive codenames.

'Werther', for example, was the Oberkommando der Wehrmacht or German army high command—to spike all speculations to the effect that the name referred to a particular officer of the German general staff whose doctoral thesis had been on Goethe's great work, *The Sufferings of Young Werther.* Wilhelm von Schramm's statement that 'Werther was an invention of Roessler's' is likewise without foundation.†

'Olga' was the Oberkommando der Luftwaffe, the air force high command. Accoce and Quet, seizing with their customary resourcefulness on the fact that this happened to be the name of Roessler's wife, declare that the codename was chosen by Roessler's Luftwaffe informants as a tribute to that lady.‡ It was not.

'Anna' stood for Auswärtiges Amt—the German foreign office.

The other codenames too—'Teddy', 'Ferdinand', 'Stefan', and 'Fanny'—referred not to persons but to sources of information. Lucy handed his reports to Taylor or Sissy with an indication of their origin: whether 'from the army high command', or 'from the air force', or 'from the foreign office', or whatever it might be. When I encoded the telegrams I indicated the source with one of the above codenames, which were known only to the director and myself.

Furthermore, to correct another of Accoce and Quet's mistakes, Rudolf Roessler only became 'Lucy' in November 1942, when we established contact with him on a regular basis. Before that, all we had received from him were bits and pieces that Taylor had passed on to us without telling Roessler he was doing so.

It goes without saying that at this highly critical stage of the war

*Drago Arsenijevič, *Genève appelle Moscou.*

†Wilhelm von Schramm, *Verrat im Zweiten Weltkrieg,* p. 103.

‡Pierre Accoce and Pierre Quet, *La Guerre a été gagnée en Suisse,* p. 98.

Central were very interested in knowing who these people were that Lucy got his information from and where and in what capacity they were employed.

There was more to this than mere curiosity. If we wanted to be sure that his information was reliable, if we were to avoid falling into a possible German counter-intelligence trap, we had to know his sources. Given the seriousness of the situation before Stalingrad and in the northern Caucasus, one can appreciate why Central attached such importance to whether or not Lucy's reports could be depended on.

Besides, what Lucy told us about the intentions of the German military leadership was often so detailed and thorough as to be scarcely credible. Moreover his information came direct from Berlin, and it came very fast—although it is highly unlikely that, as Foote claimed in his book, we sometimes heard about decisions of Hitler's headquarters 'within twenty-four hours' of their being made.* It is equally improbable that, as other sensation-seekers have claimed, we in Geneva occasionally received word of changes in the Germans' operational plans, regrouping of divisions, and so on before the commanding officers concerned on the eastern front.

It was of course extremely important for Central to know exactly how fresh Lucy's intelligence was, and on 10 March 1943 the director instructed me to ask Lucy always to give the date of origin of his reports, in other words the date of dispatch from Berlin. He started doing so, and I was able to check how long the information was taking to come through—namely between three and six days, assuming Lucy's dates were correct. For example, the Berlin dispatch date of the telegram I sent Central on 6 May 1943 had been 2 May, my telegrams of 13 May were based on reports dated 6 and 7 May, my telegram of 30 May gave the date of origin as 25 May, mine of 10 July gave 6 July, and so on.

To begin with, as I have said, Central treated the information they received from Lucy with great caution. After a thoroughgoing analysis, however, they dropped their suspicions and urged us to work as closely as possible with Lucy. Lucy was prepared to do so, and after a while he even showed signs of dropping the veil of secrecy, telling Taylor this and that about the positions and intelligence potential of his Berlin friends. But he still flatly

*Alexander Foote, *Handbook for Spies,* p. 94.

refused to give away their real names and ranks because, as he said, it could turn out to be disastrous for them. Appreciating this, we stopped pestering him with questions.

There is every indication that Lucy's secret remains intact to this day. An interesting admission in this respect is that of Allen W. Dulles, ex-director of the CIA, in his book *The Craft of Intelligence*: '. . . the Soviets developed a fantastic source located in Switzerland, a certain Rudolf Roessler (codename, 'Lucy'). By means which have not been ascertained to this day, Roessler in Switzerland was able to get intelligence from the German High Command in Berlin on a continuous basis, often less than twenty-four hours after its daily decisions concerning the Eastern front were made.'*

So even the director of the CIA, who spent part of the war in Switzerland heading American intelligence activities against Germany, has no idea who Roessler's informants were. Incidentally we find even Dulles accepting without question Foote's groundless claim and even boosting it to 'often less than twentyfour hours'.

Generaloberst Franz Halder, up until 1942 chief of the general staff of the German land forces, worked the same vein of fantasy when summoned as a witness at a trial in 1955.† He repeated his testimony twelve years later in the German magazine *Der Spiegel*: 'The instigation of practically every German offensive in the German high command was betrayed to the enemy by a member of the high-command staff immediately it was planned and even before it reached my desk. Throughout the entire war we never managed to plug this leak.' ‡ Halder does not actually say so but his tone suggests that this was the only reason the Germans did not win the war.

But the record, as usual, is held by Accoce and Quet: 'At this period of history [they are talking about the summer of 1942], for the space of more than a month, not more than *ten hours* elapsed between a decision being made at the Wehrmacht high command

*Allen W. Dulles, *The Craft of Intelligence,* Weidenfeld & Nicolson, 1963 p. 111.

† See Paul Carell, *Verbrannte Erde,* p. 84.

‡ *Der Spiegel,* 16 January 1967.

and Moscow hearing about it. In fact in one instance it took less than six hours [!].'*

Finally, the usually circumspect Jon Kimche in this case also finds the temptation too great for him: 'As with the "Viking Line" [The NS 1's line to the Wehrmacht high command], this [information] often dealt with troop movements and operational orders which Radó sent to Moscow often before they had been received at the German operational headquarters, or had been carried out.†

Another riddle is how Rudolf Roessler maintained so regular and reliable a liaison with his Berlin informants.

The Western press has put up a wide variety of hypotheses. Some authors are of the opinion that Roessler and his Berlin friends used the courier service of the German embassy in Switzerland; others are convinced they were in radio contact. The courier hypothesis strikes me as possible in the case of one or two reports a week. It would also explain why the Germans' well-organized radio-reconnaissance service failed to monitor Roessler's hypothetical transmitter. On the other hand, no courier could possibly have taken Roessler's assignments to Berlin and brought back the answers as quickly as in fact occurred. The pace of exchange maintained would have required the services of several couriers commuting permanently between Berlin and Berne, which was of course out of the question.

The radio hypothesis is even less convincing. Accoce and Quet claim that Roessler's Berlin friends had equipped him with a transmitter and a code before the outbreak of the war and that, co-operating as he was with Swiss Intelligence, Roessler need fear neither informers nor the police but could calmly switch on his set at any hour of the day. His friends—so Accoce and Quet go on—used official channels, transmitting their encoded reports straight from the Wehrmacht high command's radio headquarters at Camp Maybach in Zossen, near Berlin. In view of the countless coded telegrams being transmitted by this station all the time, no radio monitor's suspicions would have been aroused; the radio link between Roessler and Berlin was thus invulnerable.

In my opinion this idea does not hold water. For a start Accoce

*Accoce and Quet, *La Guerre a été gagnée en Suisse*, p. 232.

†Jon Kimche, *Spying for Peace*, p. 91.

and Quet make the silly mistake of claiming that it was Taylor, alias Christian Schneider, who taught Roessler how to operate a transmitter. I happen to know for a certainty that Schneider never worked as a radio operator and had not the vaguest notion of radio technology. As for Roessler working independently with a transmitter of his own, people who knew him during that period say that he would not have known what to do with it. But I have an even sounder reason for doubting this hypothesis: if Lucy had had his own set, the Germans would have monitored it as surely as they monitored so many clandestine transmitters.

In all probability, then, Roessler neither received nor passed on his telegrams himself.

What of the possibility that he made use of an official transmitter? It is conceivable that his information passed through official channels—through the German embassy in Switzerland or through the German consulate. Hans Bernd Gisevius, the German vice-consul in Zurich and subsequently an active participant in the so-called 'conspiracy of the generals' and an organizer of the attempt on Hitler's life on 20 July 1944, was in touch with Allen Dulles from late 1942 onwards.* Gisevius may have approved of what Roessler was doing and placed a radio operator at his disposal.

Or there was another possibility—the 'Buro Ha', with which Roessler had been co-operating since before the war. In both cases the German monitors would have picked up official transmitters. It is hardly likely that they would have suspected their own embassy or consulate of espionage, and against the intelligence service of a neutral country they were powerless without irrefutable proof that the Buro Ha's transmitter was in touch with sources in Germany.

The Germans never found Roessler's Berlin sources—at least there is no trace in the archives of the Gestapo and the SD or in the work of the Abwehr radio-reconnaissance officer W.F. Flicke of their having done so.

I do not know the answer myself, but I can contribute a couple of pointers.

The first dates from the early days of our association with Lucy.

*See Jon Kimche, *Spying for Peace*, pp. 108 f.

Central and I both encouraged Sissy to sound Taylor out about where Lucy got his information from and how. Sissy managed to get out of Taylor the fact that Lucy possessed a vast 'data bank' in the form of press cuttings, records of conversations with highly-placed Germans, and the results of talks with German soldiers convalescing in the German-owned sanatoriums in Davos. Furthermore, Wilhelm von Schramm notes how 'porous' the frontier between Switzerland and Germany was, 'spanned as it was permanently and effortlessly by the German language, even by the Allemannic dialect of that language, as well as by an extraordinary number of close family, cultural, and business ties and by interlocking capital arrangements, which were never broken off. Added to all this were the fact that more than 150,000 German citizens were permanently resident in Switzerland, and during the war some 8,000 German emigrants as well, and the fact that the inhabitants of the towns and villages along the frontier were allowed by the conventions of "local frontier traffic" to work on the other side.'* Of those German citizens, incidentally, even as late as 1943, 30,000 were members of the Nazi party; three years earlier, according to Baron Sigismund von Bibra, counsellor at the German embassy in Berne, who headed the Swiss party, the membership figure had stood as high as 100,000.†

Finally, as the Bonjour Report has now made official, as it were, the Swiss general staff's intelligence service under Roger Masson built up a widely ramified intelligence network in the early months of the war to collect military and political information from the Axis powers. 'Intelligence headquarters had its people in the frontier patrols that questioned immigrants and those who made use of the local frontier traffic facilities. The Swiss intelligence service, with a staff of only ten at the outbreak of the war, grew during the war to a hundred and twenty.' Bonjour further writes: 'Intelligence exploited a wide variety of possibilities. It received reports from the Swiss customs and frontier defence, censored post, telegraph and telephone communications, monitored the radio, analysed the domestic and foreign press, and interrogated deserters, refugees, internees, and Swiss returning from abroad. Its most valuable source were the reports of its agents,

*Wilhelm von Schramm, *Verrat im Zweiten Weltkrieg*, pp. 197f.

† Alphonse Matt, *Zwischen allen Fronten*, Frauenfeld, 1969, p. 196.

whose connections in some cases extended into the potential enemy's highest councils, to the German war ministry, and to the Führer's headquarters.'

These sources provided a dense and many-layered mosaic of intelligence material, analysis of and deduction from which could often come up immediately with the right answer concerning troop movements within the German army. Roessler said as much himself in November 1953, when the Swiss put him on trial for espionage. Referring to the file of 20,000 cards and newspaper cuttings that had been found in his possession, he explained that by arranging and analysing already published political, economic, and military information as well as information obtained in other ways he had built up a first-class store of material that served as the basis for his intelligence reports.† The Buro Ha too devoted a great deal of attention to the German press.‡

In the mosaic method of intelligence collecting some of the pieces may of course be missing and others have been placed there by a deliberately misleading hand. But our Moscow headquarters was able to check part of our reports against those of their front-line reconnaissance, and when they were in doubt about something they did not use it. Or the director would set us a control question when something failed to tally with information he had already. This sometimes happened in connection with Lucy's reports, though mostly in the first few weeks of our working together; later there was less occasion for doubting his information, probably because he started checking his sources more thoroughly himself.

But of course the card-index method by no means goes all the way towards explaining how during the Second World War Lucy managed—if not within twenty-four hours, at least within three to six days—to get intelligence material of the first importance to me from Berlin. It seems to me that the unequivocal answer to this question emerged from the discussion broadcast by Swiss television on 15 and 22 May 1966 on the occasion of the publication of Accoce and Quet's book. (Incidentally I was once asked to take part in such a discussion myself, but in view of the attitude that the

† See Wilhelm von Schramm, *Verrat im Zweiten Weltkrieg,* p. 318, and Jon Kimche, *Spying for Peace,* p. 92.

‡ See Alphonse Matt, *Zwischen allen Fronten,* p. 183.

Swiss authorities persist in maintaining towards me I turned the invitation down.) During the course of that television discussion, extracts from which were published as an appendix to the French edition of Pakbo's book,* Dr Xaver Schnieper, Roessler's closest friend, said that the reports went through on the Wehrmacht's service telephone line from Berlin to Milan and that a courier brought them from there to Roessler in Luzern. These were probably the two couriers that Roessler mentioned on his arrest in 1944.

Even during the war, Luzern and Milan were not more than five or six hours apart by express train; conceivably, though, the couriers did not need to go as far as Milan but only to the frontier station, Chiasso (three or four hours)—and here the opportunities were plentiful, with German goods trains plying across the frontier in both directions every ten minutes or quarter of an hour, as I had observed myself. Central's questions and requests for information probably reached Berlin by the same route; in an article published in December 1966 Wilhelm von Schramm said that Schnieper had once told him so in conversation.† Schramm, a logical, pragmatic, and by and large circumspect historian—except when his anti-Communism occasionally makes him swallow even Foote's and Flicke's wildest assertions—refers to the television discussion in the book I have already quoted: 'Berlin stopped trusting its Italian Fascist ally during the war and after the Allied landing in Africa established more and more official agencies in Italy, ostensibly to supply the Wehrmacht's "Afrika-Corps". A special munitions Kommandantur was set up in Milan, and it is not impossible that the German authorities there were in direct touch with Berlin and also organized the shuttle-service between Milan and Luzern. It is even possible that the authority in question was SS, because from as early as the end of 1942—i.e., the battle of Stalingrad—onwards leading SS officers started consolidating their lines of retreat.'‡

Swiss Intelligence—both the Buro Ha and Masson's NS 1—benefited from this phenomenon as well, both organizations

*Otto Pünter, *Guerre secrète en pays neutre*, Lausanne, 1967, pp. 256 f.

†See 'Die rot-weiss Kapelle', in *Frankfurter Allgemeine Zeitung*, 13 December 1966.

‡Wilhelm von Schramm, *Verrat im Zweiten Weltkrieg*, p. 118.

having contacts in the highest military and political circles in Germany. Bonjour writes: 'It seems at first astonishing that the Swiss intelligence service should have received information from the highest levels of command in the German army. The explanation is this: individual Germans who on ideological grounds privately condemned the Nazi regime seized every means that offered itself of overthrowing the hated dictatorship. One such means was to leak important military and political secrets abroad. They passed this information to Switzerland in the tacit hope that it would find its way to the enemies of the oppressor, damage the totalitarian system, and ultimately lead to military defeat.' In this way Swiss Intelligence was able to keep the government and the general staff well in the picture with regard to Germany's most secret military and economic affairs—and Roessler was in two-way touch not only with the Buro Ha, as we have seen, but also with Major Mayr von Baldeck of the NS 1. According to Bonjour, 'this Swiss officer was probably aware that Roessler was passing the information he gave him on to the Russians but saw nothing reprehensible in this mutual-assistance arrangement since it was all done with a view to toppling Hitler, protecting the country from war, and hastening the approach of peace.'

This does not, however, mean that Roessler's only direct sources of intelligence were the Buro Ha and the NS 1, as a number of authors have tended to claim in recent years. On the contrary, Paul Carell compares the vague and in some details incorrect reports of the Buro Ha before the battle of Kursk with the highly precise information provided by 'Werther' and draws the conclusion that this source was exclusive to Soviet Intelligence. Hausamann for his part said in a television interview in May 1966 that it was not Roessler who had received information from him but the other way round, and that he had been able to establish that Roessler's information was 'extraordinarily accurate'. And Alphonse Matt, in his 1969 book about the work of the Hausamann agency, writes that Roessler 'regularly supplied the Buro Ha, *via* a contact man, with information that was generally of exceptional quality'.†

The most fantastic hypothesis of all I have saved up for the end. Malcolm Muggeridge, ex British Intelligence, citing his close

†Alphonse Matt, *Zwischen allen Fronten,* p. 191.

acquaintanceship with Alexander Foote, who he claimed was in touch with Roessler during the war (not true), revealed in *The Observer* of 8 January 1967 that Roessler's information had come from the British intelligence service. According to Muggeridge the British managed during the war to break the German army's secret code. Wanting to keep the fact dark, but at the same time wanting to bring the information they thus collected to the attention of the Russians, they employed Roessler as go-between (how, Muggeridge does not say). Anyone in his senses will of course be satisfied with Hausamann's declaration in the *Neue Zürcher Zeitung* the following week: 'It seems to me utterly fantastic that the British should first have passed this material to Roessler and that it should then have been passed by him back to the British.'*

But the ultimate solution of the riddle we must leave to time. All we can say now is that the contact between Lucy and his informants was ingeniously and expertly organized and worked perfectly.

*Neue Zürcher Zeitung, 11 January 1967.

CHAPTER 23

The 'Red Orchestra' Detachment in action

In the latter part of 1942 German counter-intelligence agents succeeded in tracking down and arresting a number of Soviet intelligence agents who had at various times been in touch with individual members of our Swiss group. In September they got 'Niggi', a Swiss national living in Brussels who knew Sissy, and on 12 November 1942 they picked up Kent, whose Brussels group had been blown in 1941.

The reader will remember that Kent was the man who came to see me in March 1940 on the director's instructions to bring me my code and my transmission timetable and teach me how to use the former. Kent went into hiding after the Brussels mishap, and he hid so effectively that it took the Germans almost a year to find him. It was not until the 'Red Orchestra' Detachment sent its agents into unoccupied France and seized so many members of the French group that Kent too was caught in the net.

The collapse of the Belgian and French groups indirectly dealt our group in Switzerland a severe blow. The sad but undeniable truth is that some of our colleagues found the threats, blackmailing manoeuvres, and tortures of the Gestapo more than they could bear. They not only admitted that they had been working for Soviet Intelligence but, as can be verified today, gave details of that work and told all they knew about the Swiss group. In this way the Gestapo got hold of pretty full details about myself—my name and codename, my profession, my Geneva address, and other particulars including the size of my family and the number of languages I spoke. But the most precious thing of all that was thus handed to them on a plate was the key to the code I had been given on that day back in 1940.

From then on—i.e., from about December 1942 onwards—the German radio-reconnaissance experts were able from time to time to decipher and read certain of my telegrams to Central and certain of the instructions the director sent back.

It should, however, be noted at this point that from the autumn of 1942 onwards I had been in the habit of giving some of my telegrams to Jim in German for him to encode for transmission. Jim's code they did not know, which meant that they were unable to decipher his telegrams—and the telegrams I took Jim or sent him by courier twice or three times a week were precisely the most important and most urgent ones, because I knew that his Morse was exceptionally quick. Incidentally, even after December 1942 the Germans managed to decipher only a fraction of my telegrams (according to Schramm, in 1943 they were reading one in ten) because they did not have enough cipher experts available.

As soon as they had the code-key, of course, the Germans also tried to decipher the telegrams that had been piling up since they had started monitoring the exchange between Switzerland and Moscow in 1941. But in 1941 a lot of my telegrams had gone out on Sonya's transmitter; Sonya's transmitter had not been monitored, and in any case the Germans did not know her code either. Referring to the approximately 250 monitored and deciphered texts in the German and Swiss archives, Schramm writes that in the first year of the war the Germans picked up only a fraction of our telegrams and of those were able subsequently to decipher only about thirty.*

According to Flicke—and here I think we can believe him—his German counter-intelligence chiefs were dismayed and appalled to learn what high-quality information the 'Red Troika' was collecting and passing on to Moscow.† Now that they could decipher some of it the Germans were able to draw up a list of the codenames of our sources and the members of our group: Dora, Pakbo, Sissy, Louise, Long, Salter, Rosa, Taylor, and so on. Then in December 1942 a new crop of names started turning up in the telegrams: Lucy, Werther, Olga. . . The Germans of course had no idea who was behind these codenames, but they could see that our informants sat in very high places in the Wehrmacht and elsewhere. They also learned (although very much later) from the telegrams that passed between Central and myself that Lucy's information did not come to me direct but *via* Sissy. At the time, however, they did not know for certain who Sissy was. Even 'Niggi', whom they had arrested, did not know her real name.

The only name the Gestapo had was my own.

*Wilhelm von Schramm, *Verrat im Zweiten Weltkrieg,* pp. 105, 111, 146.

†W.F. Flicke, *Agenten funken nach Moskau,* p. 21.

PART 3

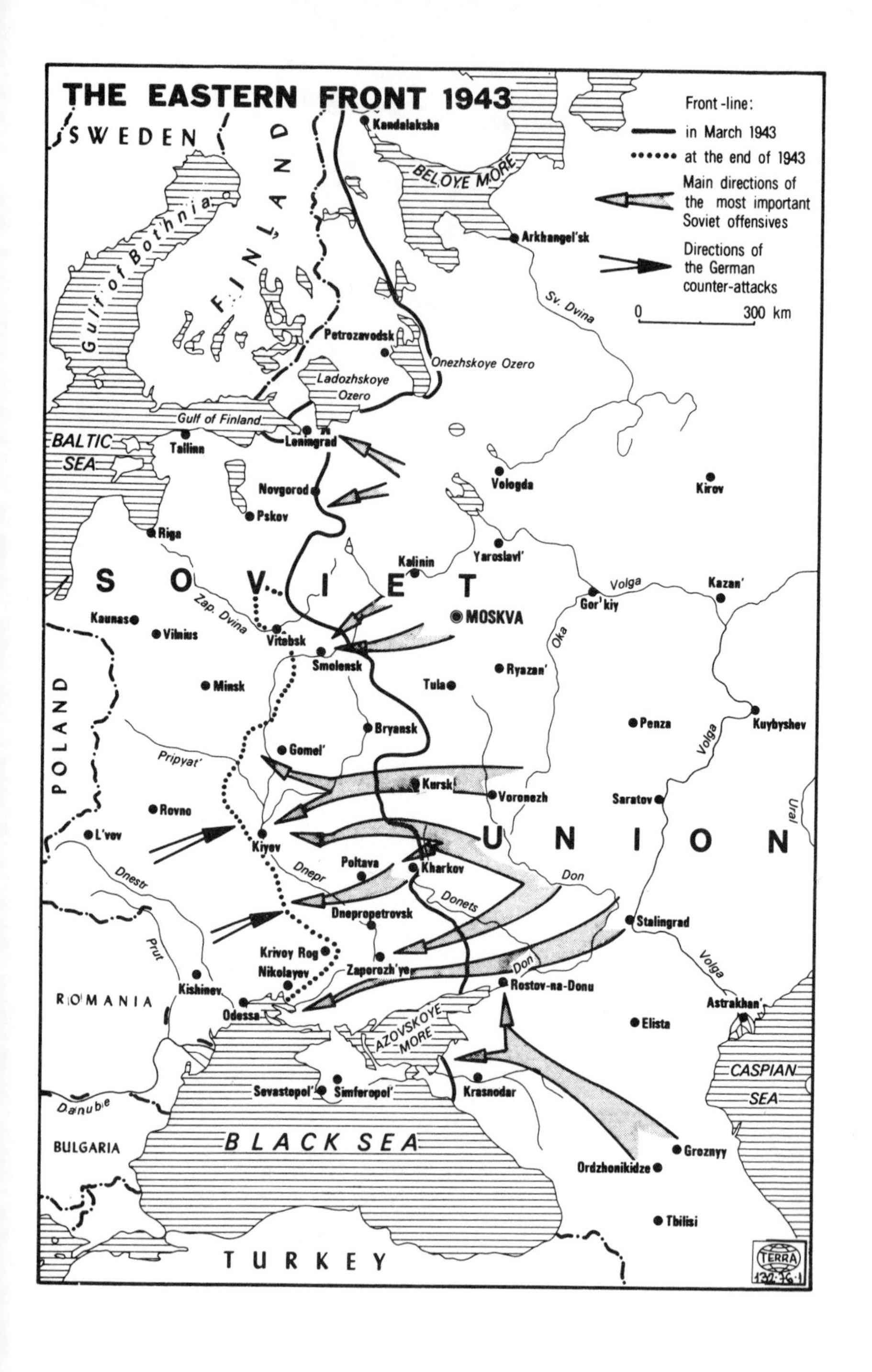
THE EASTERN FRONT 1943
Front-line:
in March 1943
at the end of 1943
Main directions of the most important Soviet offensives
Directions of the German counter-attacks
0
300 km
SWEDEN
FINLAND
Gulf of Bothnia
Kandalaksha
BELOYE MORE
Arkhangel'sk
Sv. Dvina
Petrozavodsk
Onezhskoye Ozero
Ladozhskoye Ozero
Gulf of Finland
BALTIC SEA
Tallinn
Leningrad
Novgorod
Vologda
Kirov
Pskov
Riga
Kalinin
Yaroslavl'
SOVIET
Volga
Kazan'
Gor'kiy
Zap. Dvina
MOSKVA
Kaunas
Vilnius
Vitebsk
Smolensk
Oka
Ryazan'
Tula
Minsk
POLAND
Bryansk
Penza
Kuybyshev
Gomel'
Pripyat'
Volga
Kursk
Voronezh
Saratov
Ural
Rovno
L'vov
Kiyev
UNION
Dnestr
Dnepr
Poltava
Kharkov
Don
Donets
Dnepropetrovsk
Stalingrad
Prut
Krivoy Rog
Zaporozh'ye
Don
Nikolayev
Rostov-na-Donu
Volga
Kishinev
ROMANIA
Odessa
Astrakhan'
Elista
AZOVSKOYE MORE
CASPIAN SEA
Sevastopol'
Simferopol'
Krasnodar
Danube
BULGARIA
BLACK SEA
Groznyy
Ordzhonikidze
Tbilisi
TURKEY
TERRA

CHAPTER 24

The Battle of Stalingrad

Early in 1943 the German troops in the southern sector of the Soviet-German front suffered a crushing defeat.

The mighty battle raged over nearly forty thousand square miles of the Volga and Don steppes and lasted almost six and a half months, from 17 July 1942 to 2 February 1943.

The Red Army high command, under no illusion as to the importance of the engagement, determined to launch a concentrated counter-attack and smash the enemy forces massed in the Stalingrad region. The operation, which was on an unprecedented scale, was executed in brilliant style. Marshal A.M. Vassilevsky, then chief of the Red Army general staff and as such involved in working out the plan of battle, looked back on that time in an article published in *Pravda* on the twenty-fifth anniversary of Stalingrad: 'Our troops needed a total of only five days to complete the encirclement of the more than 300,000 man strong German army group. Twenty-two enemy divisions and a number of units sent as reinforcements were caught in one gigantic trap.'*

On 2 February 1943 the encircled army group was completely wiped out.

Lucy, as I have said, brought his group in with us in the autumn of 1942. One of his first reports contained the information:

The German army high command sees no possibility of the Soviets' assembling troops in the uninhabited semi-desert known as the 'Black Fields' south-east of Stalingrad. The flank of the German army is consequently unprotected here.

As Marshal Zhukov mentions in the memoirs I have already quoted, it was this very region (Sarpa-Zaza-Barmanzak) that was chosen on Vassilevsky's recommendation as the starting-base for

*A.M. Vassilevsky, in *Pravda,* 2 February 1968.

the November counter-offensive on the left wing of the Stalingrad front. Zhukov cites General Jodl, the former chief of German operational staff, as having said after the war: 'We had no idea of the strength of the Russian troops in this region. Previously there had been no troops here at all, and then suddenly they attacked in such strength that they made a decisive difference.'*

Lucy's report prompted a series of detailed questions from Central:

9 November 1942. To Dora.

Where do the Germans' rear defensive positions run south-west of Stalingrad and along the Don? Where have defensive positions already been built on the lines Stalingrad-Kletskaya and Stalingrad-Kalach? What are they like? What type of fortifications have been built on the line Budennovsk-Divnoye-Vershne-Chirskaya-Kalach-Kachalinskaya-Kletskaya and on the line Dnepr-Beresina?

Director.

Here are some of the other questions we were asked to answer during the battle of Stalingrad:

10 November 1942. To Dora.

Check through Taylor and other sources:

1) What is the current position of the 11th and 18th armoured divisions and the 25th mobile division that were previously engaged in the Bryansk-Bolkhov sector?

2) Is Weich's army group already in existence? Composition and staffs?

3) Is there yet a Guderian army group? Which armies belong to it? Where are their staffs?

Director.

26 November 1942. To Dora.

Send particulars of concrete measures by the German high command in connection with the Red Army's Stalingrad offensive.

Director

*G.K. Zhukov, '*Memories and Reflections*', pp. 422, 431.

2 December 1942. To Dora.

The most important job to be done now is to find out exactly what reserves the Germans have behind the eastern front.

Director.

(It must have been a day or two after this that we heard from Taylor that certain German generals—foremost among them Paulus, the commander-in-chief of the army nearest Stalingrad—wanted to give up the Stalingrad and northern-Caucasus sectors, because on 4 December Central asked us as a matter of urgency to give more details regarding Taylor's report. Hitler, of course, did not allow these plans to go through, and the fierce German counter-attacks continued.*)

7 December 1942. To Dora.

What military units are on the way to the eastern front from the West and from Norway, and what units are on the way from the eastern front to the West and to the Balkans? Please give numbers.

What plans does the German high command have in connection with the Red Army offensive? Will the Wehrmacht only fight defensive engagements or is the German high command planning counter-attacks in any sector of the eastern front? If so, where, when, and with what forces?

Director.

We did what we could to keep Central supplied with the information requested, and particularly their question of 2 December (repeated on 22 and 25 December) about the German reserves behind the front Werther managed to answer with great precision, giving the numbers and positions of the reserve divisions.

Central's reaction was swift and positive:

16 January 1943.

. . . The information received from Werther was extremely important.

18 January 1943.

. . . Our thanks to Werther for the information about the Caucasus front.

*Paul Carell, *Unternehmen Barbarossa*, pp. 517-20.

22 February 1943.

. . . Convey to Lucy our thanks for her excellent work. The last report from her group concerning the middle sector of the front is extremely important.

Director.

Three months earlier, on 5 November (my birthday), as the battle of Stalingrad was building up, I had been told that I had been decorated, and subsequently it was confirmed: I had been invested with the Order of Lenin.

Stalingrad was the signal for a series of crushing blows delivered by the Red Army. The attack went on for two and a half months, and the Germans lost everything that they had paid such a price for.

In January 1943 the Red Army secured a further important victory: it broke through the German positions and relieved Leningrad. The heroic city, besieged from the mainland and from the sea for nearly eighteen months, was free at last.

It was the beginning of a decisive year. The Red Army followed up with a concentrated offensive along the entire front, and in view of the changed strategic situation Central entrusted our group with new intelligence assignments.

CHAPTER 25

Ups and downs

In Switzerland the news of the German defeat spread like wildfire, although the German newspapers and radio stations behaved as if nothing had happened; they had in any case brought no word of the encircled army for months.

In the Swiss papers—which did not get the Soviet war communiqués and, basing their reports as they did on the BBC, had trouble finding their way among the multitude of tiny villages on the Don steppes—my maps were published. These showed how the ring was being drawn tighter. I learned subsequently that German diplomatic circles had lodged a protest with the Swiss authorities concerning my 'lying sketch maps of the war theatre' as they had appeared in the press. The spokesman of the German foreign ministry, Paul Schmidt (who after the war became Paul Carell, the war historian I have several times quoted), really flew off the handle on one occasion at a press conference. According to the Bonjour Report he threatened the Swiss press in the following terms: 'There'll be no room in the new Europe for those Swiss journalists that write against it. They may wake up one morning to find themselves somewhere in the steppes of Asia, though an even better solution might be to promote them to the hereafter.'

After Stalingrad, however, it was not long before the German press and radio were forced to publish the grudging admissions released by Goebbels's ministry.

In sharp contrast to the popular mood was the reaction of the Swiss government to the Soviet victory. As Edgar Bonjour points out: 'At the end of 1942 the federal government was concerned to avoid any expression of sympathy towards the Russians.'

I need hardly say with what enthusiasm I and my people received the news.

It had been a critical period for the Soviet Union, and certain of my associates had recently been taking a gloomy view of the future, wavering in their belief in a successful issue to the fight against Nazism and beginning to doubt the usefulness of our work. They included members of the resistance movement, and it became necessary for me to meet and talk to some of these comrades. In such cases I assumed the role of agitator or political counsellor.

We were in touch with the *Maquis* or French partisan army fighting in Haute-Savoie, the French *département* lying to the south of the Lake of Geneva. It so happened that at the same time as the German divisions broke through to the Caucasus the partisans in Savoy found themselves in a particularly difficult situation. The Germans had forced them back into the mountains and onto the ice-fields of the Alpine glaciers; they were short of food and munitions, and on top of all this came the bad news from the eastern front. The men lost heart and began to wonder whether it was worth fighting any more, now that it seemed they could expect no help; perhaps it would be better if they laid down their arms and split up.

Word of their poor morale reached me through the member of our group who maintained contact with them. Somehow we must cheer these brave fellows up, he told me; we must do something to restore their fighting spirit. I knew I was not supposed to intervene, but as a Communist I could not sit back and see even a single partisan unit break up, abandoning the fight against the occupier.

At my request the man organized a meeting at the frontier with representatives of the partisans. They turned up promptly at the appointed place. Being accustomed to secrecy and caution, they of course made no attempt to find out who or what I was and asked no unnecessary questions. I told them that under no circumstances must they surrender their arms to the enemy. I tried to convince them that sooner or later Germany must inevitably be defeated, and that they must believe in this as firmly as they believed in their own lives and in their country's destiny—otherwise France would never be freed.

I learned later to my great satisfaction that the Savoy *Maquis* did not give up but withstood the siege of the Nazi troops in the mountains and even began to take retaliatory action.

This was not to be my last meeting with the partisans. In 1944, when the Swiss police were looking for me, it was the *maquisards* that helped my wife and myself to slip across the frontier.

It was really impossible for Helene, Jim, and myself to process, encode, and pass on to Central the information streaming in every day—some twenty typewritten sheets, even when edited by myself into our highly economical style. I was getting between four and five hours' sleep, if that. The physical and nervous strain was enormous. So, with the director's consent, Sissy and Pakbo began to take some of the load off my shoulders.

We were taking a big risk, of course, in revealing the secret of the code key, however reliable my associates might be. But passing on the information came first, and we could not allow there to be any delay. In particular, the reports from Lucy, Werther, Olga, Teddy, and our other Berlin sources had to be sent off to headquarters immediately they came in.

Writing the text in clear, however, remained my responsibility alone. Sifting the incoming material and condensing it into telegram style was something I could leave to no one else. None of them would have been prepared to do it in any case, whereas I as the former head of a telegraph and press bureau had a lot of experience in this field.

Lucy's important material of course had priority; we encoded it at once and either I or my wife took it to the radio operators.

Our radio link with Central remained stable except on those days when the overworked operators (Central's or ours) made mistakes. In such cases the transmission would be repeated. As soon as Central had confirmed receipt we burned the encoded material. That was a strict rule. Our four operators, then, continued to maintain a normal connection, although the strain was enormous and growing greater all the time. They seemed to me to be all right, though.

Only Edouard's situation caused me some concern (I knew nothing, of course, of Rosa's meetings with Hans Peters); the sentence had been quashed, but the search of the Hamels' shop and flat and Edouard's arrest had undoubtedly left traces. I was convinced that the police were keeping an eye on him and that Edouard now figured on the suspicious persons list. If, however, the police or Counter-intelligence were to put Edouard and his wife under observation, it would be a simple matter to find out whom they were meeting.

According to the elementary rules of conspiracy we should have broken off all contact with the couple immediately. In a case like that the set must be hidden away, and work in the flat or house concerned can only be resumed when one is a hundred per cent sure that it is no longer under observation. The director expressed himself on this question in a telegram of 30 October 1942:

Prepare substitute rendezvous for Rosa, Pakbo, Jim, and Sissy in order that this group can maintain contact with us in the event of your being temporarily unable to look after operations. Tell Jim what has happened, and take extra precautions over rendezvous and delivering the telegrams to Jim. Bear in mind, dear Dora, that the work of your organization is now more important than ever before; you must do everything to see that it continues.

Director.

The trouble was, we simply could not afford the luxury of getting rid of two expert and experienced radio operators. Jim and Rosa would never have got through the work. Moreover the situation at the front at the end of 1942 was very bad, with the enemy on the Volga and in the Caucasus. It was not a time in which we could stick rigidly to the 'classical' rules of conspiratorial work.

For this reason we waited only a short time, until the police appeared to have lost interest, and then Edouard and Maude began sending again. After a certain amount of hesitation Central gave their assent, because the situation at the front was becoming steadily more tense, but in his telegram of 6 November the director said expressly:

Let Edouard's case be a lesson. Screen immediately all contacts of all your people. Turn your attention particularly to your radio operators' contacts with political circles, especially Communists and left-wing socialists. Such contacts can endanger the whole organization. It is important that the radio operators' environments should be completely secure. Remember how vital it is that your organization be kept going.

Director.

In another telegram of 19 December Central again stressed the importance of this question;

On top of your measures to make the whole organization more secure, please do everything in your power to ensure that the work can continue. Just now this is especially important. Please take whatever action is necessary calmly, judiciously, and with circumspection.

Director.

In view of the risk that the police might descend on them again, I tried to make things safer for the Hamels. I began by looking for another place they could work from. I found one in a residential district not far out of the city. The house stood in the middle of a large, old-fashioned park. From the windows one had an unimpeded view in all directions, and anyone watching the house would have immediately been obvious. In future Edouard and Maude mainly worked there; only occasionally, when time was really short, did they use the reserve set in their own flat. Edouard organized an excellent hiding-place in the villa and fitted it with an electric lock. Even the most thorough search would hardly have discovered it.

These precautions taken, the Hamels once more threw themselves into the work with everything they had.

In the winter and early spring of 1943 we were busy supplying the Soviet troops with information concerning the offensive operations launched in the different sectors of the front.

On 20 January 1943 Central set me an assignment for which we had to push everything else to one side:

Find out what plans and concrete intentions the Wehrmacht high command has to counter the Red Army's offensive and above all how they mean to ward off or neutralize the Red Army's assaults. What differences of opinion are there in the Wehrmacht high command as regards the measures to be taken and the plans that have been adopted? Pass this order on to all members of Lucy's group....

On 22 February I was sent an even more detailed assignment for Lucy:

We have to know the Wehrmacht high command's plans as regards the Kluge army group in the middle sector. Everything you can tell us about the middle sector of the front is of the first importance.

Director.

These were weighty and difficult assignments. Only Lucy's Berlin sources could provide this kind of information, and yet again they came up with it: as at the time of the Stalingrad and Caucasus counter-offensive, Werther, Olga, and the rest sent in detailed reports of plans forged at the very highest level of command in Germany. Here is a sample of the information we sent Moscow at that time:

28 February 1943. To the director. Urgent.

From Werther.

The Wehrmacht high command is expecting the Soviet offensive to reach a climax in a major Red Army assault near Kursk in the direction Glukhov-Konotop. It is also expecting at least two army corps to try and break through between Bogodukhov and Konotop.

They fear this breakthrough because the reserves, including the 3rd armoured division, sent between 15 and 20 February to secure the Bogodukhov-Konotop road have been thrown across into the Donets Basin.

The Red Army breakthrough between Kharkov and Konotop is of decisive importance not only with regard to the German positions in the Poltava region but also as far as the Kremenchug-Romny-Konotop road is concerned, which the Germans may have to give up in March.

Dora.

In the Leningrad region too the Germans were losing ground as the Soviet high command assumed the initiative:

29 March 1943. To the director. Urgent.

From Werther. Berlin, 25 March.

The Russians have succeeded in breaking through the front in the sector covered by the 61st infantry division (which belongs to General Lindemann's 18th army).

The Germans have established that the concentration of Soviet forces on the lower Volkhov and in the Leningrad region is continuing. The German high command suspects that large quantities of war material have reached Leningrad over the last few weeks via Murmansk and Vologda as well as troops via Petrokrepost and by air.

Shipping in the Murmansk region is increasing as a result of the fact that the German air force is now weaker over the Arctic Ocean. Consequcntly the German high command is expecting increased Russian activity in the Neva, Volkhov, and Svir regions. The German high command has decided in the first place to accelerate construction of the 'eastern rampart', above all in Estonia and Latvia.

Because of the to some extent critical situation that has emerged on the Neva front, on 23 March part of the reserves stationed near Oredezh had to be thrown across. These reserves are also securing communications between Solzy and Detskoye Selo.

Dora.

As is clear from this report of Werther's, the Germans' offensive potential in the northern sector of the front was exhausted. Their plans to starve out Leningrad, take Murmansk, and join up with the Finnish army in the Karelian isthmus had all failed. The enemy now had to concentrate entirely on defence and try to hold out in the positions the Soviet troops had driven him back to in January. This was why the German high command, dismayed at the weakness of its positions in the south, started to build up what it called the *Ostwall* or 'eastern rampart', a line of strongly fortified defensive positions in the Baltic States. On 12 March 1943 Central set our group the assignment of collecting information about the fortifications the Germans were constructing, an assignment we later fulfilled.

Meanwhile so much important material was coming in that I was obliged to involve further members of the group in the work of encoding. Central gave me permission to teach Rosa and Maude certain details of the process. Rosa's job was to type whatever pages we needed from the code book. Maude performed only the simple initial operations involved; she never saw the text in clear. Sissy I had already involved in this work and she was now operating independently, having been told by Moscow the title of her code book and sent instructions as to how to use it.

CHAPTER 26

Schellenberg returns

Although German Counter-intelligence proceeded with the greatest discretion in its attempts to uncover our organization, there were various indications that something was up. We were pretty sure, in other words, that the Germans were on our trail. At the end of April we became absolutely sure—but more about that in the next chapter.

Meanwhile in March Walter Schellenberg turned up again in Switzerland. His 1942 talks with Roger Masson, head of the Swiss secret service, had evidently not been as successful as expected, and he had decided to take matters further.

In the spring of 1943 Schellenberg met Masson on two occasions that we know of. The first was on 3 March, at the Hotel zum Bären in Biglen, not far from Berne. Also present on this occasion were General Guisan, commander-in-chief of the Swiss armed forces, and his aide-de-camp, Colonel Barbey. The second meeting, which is the one that interests us, took place according to Schellenberg at the Baur-au-Lac Hotel in Zurich on 12 March. It was then that Schellenberg 'came to the point'. Both meetings were of course top secret, and at the second no one else was present to take notes of what was said, but if we can believe certain sources and the piecemeal admissions of the two participants it is not difficult to guess what their talk turned on.

Remember that at that time German Counter-intelligence was already in possession of the key to the code I was using and had deciphered some of the telegrams that their radio reconnaissance service had been recording. It will have been clear to Schellenberg from certain of these that the Soviet intelligence group operating in Geneva was in touch with Swiss secret service people and was receiving information about Germany from them. To the chief of the Reichssicherheitsdienst this must have come as a very nasty shock.

When on top of this the decoding experts brought him some of the reports from Lucy's sources in Berlin, Schellenberg was faced with the staggering but undeniable fact that top-secret information had been leaking from no less an authority than the Wehrmacht high command. It must have occurred to him straightaway that those responsible must be high-ranking officers, possibly even generals, who had access to confidential general-staff documents. But who could the traitors be? And how did they communicate with one another?

The interests of Germany demanded that something be done about this without delay, and the SD chief went rushing off to see his Swiss opposite number again in the hope of worming out of him what he knew about this conspiracy at the heart of the Reich. As Wilhelm von Schramm puts it: 'It was self-evident that these talks were to set things up for the liquidation of the "Red Troika".'*

In 1949, when his case came up before the Nuremberg War Crimes Tribunal, Schellenberg gave an evasive answer to the question that touched on his reasons for getting together with Masson: 'It had been my intention to organize a regular exchange of intelligence material with Masson. I had to give up the idea, however, because Masson would not play . . . .' He appears to have given the British a much fuller account of his meetings with Masson when he fell into their hands in 1945. He spent the three years up until Nuremberg in London, where he undoubtedly initiated the gentlemen of the Intelligence Service into all the secrets of Hitler's Reich.

The French journalists Accoce and Quet suggest that at the 12 March meeting in Zurich Schellenberg came right out with the fact that 'he was aware that certain generals in the Wehrmacht high command were hatching a plot against Hitler'. (According to von Schramm, Schellenberg had already broached this subject with Masson on 9 September 1942.†)

So much has been written about the 'conspiracy of the generals' that there is no need for me to repeat the details here. I first heard about it through Pakbo, whose informant had got his information *via* the ex-mayor of Leipzig, Karl Friederich Gördeler, from the Wehrmacht high command headquarters in Berlin's Bendler-

*Wilhelm von Schramm, *Verrat im Zweiten Weltkrieg*, p. 268.

†Wilhelm von Schramm, *Verrat im Zweiten Weltkrieg*, p. 267.

strasse. A telegram of mine sent to Moscow on 20 April 1943 contains a reference to it:

. . . The so-called second string of generals who wanted to get rid of Hitler in January has now decided to liquidate with him the circles that support him.

One thing is clear: this plot against Hitler, which caused such a stir and so ignominiously miscarried, can be looked at in the light of a 'family squabble' among leading circles in Germany. The sole aim of the 'opposition party' was to conclude a separate peace with Britain and the United States in order that they could then direct their entire might against the Soviet Union. The conspirators sought to replace the dictatorship of the Führer by a military dictatorship, in other words by a regime that would be acceptable to the Western powers and with which the latter could conclude an agreement to the detriment of the Soviet Union. An exception was the group around Count Stauffenberg, which regarded co-operation with the Soviet Union as a possibility for the future.

Schellenberg started out with the assumption that the sources who were passing military information to Switzerland were anti-Hitler men of whose existence Himmler's secret police were already aware. If Masson knew about the plot against Hitler, Schellenberg argued, his Berlin informants must belong to that circle, and consequently it was on the cards that they were betraying vital state secrets to the Swiss. Schellenberg already had proof that Masson was receiving top-secret information from high up in the Wehrmacht chain of command. Why else should Masson have asked so anxiously at the 3 March meeting whether it was true that troops under the command of General Dietl were fitting out for the invasion of Switzerland? (We heard about this too from our own informants.) Masson's information was correct—except that the troop movements on the Swiss frontier had no other purpose than blackmail. Schellenberg, playing along, hastily assured Masson that he would use all his influence as well as that of his friends to persuade Hitler to drop his plan for occupying Switzerland.

On 23 March 1943, eleven days after Schellenberg and Masson's Zurich meeting, General Guisan's aide, Colonel Barbey, wrote in his diary: 'Met an ecstatic Masson. He has heard from Eggen

[Schellenberg's aide]: Schellenberg says we can be "pleased with him". The danger of occupation is past; Switzerland is no longer in the dock as far as the Wehrmacht high command is concerned. The plan regarding Switzerland has been definitively shelved.'*

If this is true, the head of the Swiss secret service committed a grave mistake in telling Schellenberg something he had learned through Rudolf Roessler's sources or through his own department's link with Berlin, the picturesquely named 'Viking Line'. Nevertheless, all Schellenberg's attempts to blackmail Masson with hints to the effect that the Führer was planning to occupy Switzerland got him nowhere: Masson was not prepared to part with any information about his intelligence network, nor did Schellenberg discover whether the Berlin informants of the NS 1 belonged to the group involved in the plot against Hitler or whether they constituted a separate group confining itself strictly to intelligence work.

Aside from all this, however, there are many indications today that Schellenberg exerted constant pressure on Masson to make him hunt down the Soviet intelligence group operating in Switzerland. Exactly when they reached agreement on this point is difficult to say; very probably it was at their Zurich meeting in March 1943, though it may have been somewhat later. At any rate, this much is certain: the head of Swiss Intelligence agreed to do so—and eventually did so, as we shall see.

He agreed because he felt indebted to Schellenberg for lifting the threat of invasion and because he did not want to lose his favour. But for the moment he did nothing about it, having no intention of compromising his own sources in the German capital. He was able to stall by saying that he had no information as yet about a Soviet intelligence organization in Switzerland. And by stalling, by seeking to gain time, he in effect furthered our work, because by 1943 time was already telling against the 'Thousand Year Reich'. The Red Army was on the offensive, pushing back the German positions along a broad sector of the front. And every day our organization survived was of the greatest value to Moscow.

Schellenberg undoubtedly suspected that his Swiss counterpart was playing fast and loose with him. The regular reports coming in from his monitoring service convinced the SD chief that the 'Red

*Bernard Barbey, *P.C. du Général,* Neuchâtel, 1947.

Troika' was still very much at work, and as time was getting short he determined to mobilize his entire network of agents in Switzerland in order to run us to earth. He hoped to compel Masson to take action by handing him on a plate evidence that would lead him straight to our people in Geneva and Lausanne.

In the spring of 1943, on Schellenberg's instructions, the German network in Switzerland mounted the first direct operations against our group. And they had plenty of agents available.

The spies were trained at the SD base in Stuttgart, which went under the inoffensive name of 'Alemannischer Arbeitskreis' or Alemannic Work Circle. The head of this organization, which came directly under Schellenberg, was SS-Sturmbannführer Klaus Hügel. The Swiss Fascists got together with him a number of times in 1940 and 1941 with the knowledge of the Swiss head of state, as foreign minister Pilet-Golaz was later obliged to admit before the Swiss parliament. And in February 1942 Hügel was received with full honours by the Zurich city council as official representative of the city of Stuttgart.* Hügel's school trained three hundred men at a time. Many of these were sent to Switzerland where they mainly picked up information among the German citizens resident in the country.

Then there was also the F Bureau in Berne, a branch of German military Counter-intelligence. The subversive activities of this hotbed of Nazism in Switzerland were shrouded with the veil of diplomatic status: the head of the F Bureau, Hans Meisner, was the German consul-general. He was in direct radio contact with Berlin. At one point in their book Accoce and Quet furnish further proof of their ignorance by confusing the SD or Sicherheitsdienst with the military counter-intelligence organization, the Abwehr. Lieutenant-commander Meisner was an Abwehr man.†

Schellenberg's agents could have operated in neutral Switzerland exactly as they operated inside Germany had it not been for the energetic protests of the Swiss federal government. The strict controls enforced by the latter, which knew no mercy as far as Nazi spies were concerned, meant that Schellenberg's men had to proceed slowly and very carefully. Nevertheless, in the spring and summer of 1943 the German agents in Switzerland were extremely

*Alphonse Matt, *Zwischen allen Fronten,* p. 168.

†Gert Buchheit, *Der deutsche Geheimdienst,* p. 285.

active. We knew nothing about this part of the SD's and the Gestapo's operation against us; we could only see what went on 'above ground', as it were.

An interesting footnote to this part of the story is that the SD, probably for reasons of rivalry, failed to provide the Abwehr with adequate information about the 'Red Troika'. Only from April 1944 onwards did all German counter-intelligence operations in Switzerland come to be placed under the F Bureau in Berne.*

*Gert Buchheit, *Der deutsche Geheimdienst,* p. 285.

CHAPTER 27

The monitors move in

At the end of April 1943 the Swiss papers reported that German radio direction finders mounted on lorries had appeared on the French shore of the Lake of Geneva, allegedly to locate an illegal French transmitter. In actual fact the monitoring was being done from three sides—from the French, Italian, and German frontiers—and they were not looking for a French transmitter but trying to get a more precise fix on our transmitters in Geneva and Lausanne—'they' being in all probability the Abwehr's radio reconnaissance experts working hand in hand with the Gestapo people from the 'Red Orchestra' Detachment in Paris and with Schellenberg's agents.

I found the report most disturbing. Maude's transmitter had undoubtedly been picked up, because the villa she was working from now was in the rue Florissant, less than a mile from the Swiss-French frontier. Rosa's transmitter in Geneva and Jim's in Lausanne were also well within reach of short-range direction finders.

In fact as far as German Counter-intelligence was concerned this operation was only of secondary importance. I have mentioned already how W.F. Flicke stresses in his book the futility of arresting a network's radio operators when you strongly suspect—as the Germans did in our case—that the network will immediately resume contact with its headquarters from other points, which it will then take you further months to locate. The people the Germans really wanted to get at were Werther, Teddy, Olga, and all the others on Lucy's Berlin line.* There are other indications that this was so, and it is one of the reasons why the Germans were not in such a hurry over measures of reprisal against our Swiss group as they might have been.

The search went on, however, and with the help of archive

*W.F. Flicke, *Agenten funken nach Moskau,* pp. 311 f.

material now available we can follow its carefully prepared course. Two members of the staff of the F Bureau in Berne, Captain Hans von Pescatore and Corporal Willy Piert, subsequently fell into Allied hands and confessed to the subversive activities undertaken by the F Bureau in Switzerland, admitting that their job had been to track down the 'Red Troika' people.

Let me briefly recapitulate what the Germans knew about us at this period, i.e., in early 1943.

Pescatore and Piert stated under interrogation that they had made a thorough study of the organizational structure and principles of operation of the Soviet intelligence service but that they had encountered enormous difficulties in working on foreign soil. Nevertheless the captain and his staff did manage to get hold of a certain amount of information. They discovered, for example, Sissy's real name—Rachel Dübendorfer—as well as her address and domestic circumstances. Not that this was necessarily their doing entirely; some of the information the Gestapo may have got out of Niggi, the courier I mentioned as having been arrested in Brussels the previous September.

The Germans also knew a lot of codenames, as they featured in the telegrams they were monitoring. These, however, told them nothing. The F Bureau, for example, possessed a copy—decoded—of the telegram the director sent me on 23 April 1943 asking for certain specific details regarding Sissy's and Lucy's Berlin sources. One can imagine the impatience with which the Abwehr people awaited the reply! Luckily Roessler was an extremely circumspect man and gave no personal or professional particulars of himself, Werther, Olga, or any of the others. This did not stop the Germans monitoring our transmissions, though; probably they assumed that sooner or later the secret of these names was bound to come out.

According to the statements of Pescatore and Piert the Abwehr had been able to decode my telegrams to Central since the arrests in France at the end of 1942. According to Flicke's account the big breakthrough came in March 1943, though even then they could sometimes only read part of the text. A Swiss police inspector put it even later; Paul Böttcher, who was arrested in Geneva in 1944, said that the inspector had told him during the course of his interrogation: 'The Germans have been monitoring and deciphering all the telegrams the Russians have sent from Geneva since the summer of 1943.'

We know, however, that when the Abwehr did get hold of the code-key they were also able to decipher some of the telegrams they had monitored during 1941 and 1942. And in that period our telegrams had given the real names and professions of virtually all the members and informants of our organization in order that Central could evaluate the information accordingly. If the Germans had managed to read those telegrams they would have had no trouble tracking down our people.

How did it happen that those telegrams did not fall into the Abwehr's hands? I can suggest two reasons. One is that the Hamels were still by way of being beginners in those early days and that consequently the majority of the information had gone out through Jim, who had been given his own code by Central for his exclusive use. This code, as I have said, the Germans did not know. The second reason is that only a fraction of those 1941 and 1942 telegrams was ever monitored. Flicke puts the figure at fifty per cent, and of those fifty per cent they managed to decipher only ten per cent—i.e., five per cent of all telegrams sent. I should point out that I changed the code every day, and if for some reason the Germans missed the first group of figures giving the place of the code book, even with the code book in their hands they could not or could only with the very greatest difficulty decipher the telegram.

So the codenames remained all they knew, and the greater part of our informants remained safely incognito.

As soon as I read that there were enemy direction finders in the vicinity of Geneva I decided I had to do something. I immediately informed Central:

29 April 1943. To the director.

According to the newspapers here the Germans are looking for an illegal transmitter in the Geneva region. This is probably Maude's transmitter, which is only one kilometre from the frontier. To make it more difficult to locate I suggest that Maude work on the 48 metre wavelength on even days and on 45 metres on odd days, beginning on Sundays, Wednesdays, and Fridays at 23.00 GMT, on Mondays and Thursdays at 23.30 GMT, and on Tuesdays and Saturdays at 24.00 GMT. I also suggest she work alternately from the old and the new places. For this purpose we will set up a reserve set in the old flat. More than six months have gone by since the search at the old flat and we can assume that the investigation is closed.

Dora.

(According to Flicke this telegram was deciphered, though not until later, and from that point on of course the Germans had a pretty clear picture of Maude's transmitting activities.*)

A day or two later came the reply to my proposal:

. . . Maude can adopt the new schedule from today 5 May. The old schedule remains valid until 10 May, however, and can be used if need be.

Central categorically forbade us to use the reserve set in Edouard's flat and even to keep it there on the grounds that the search business could not be regarded as closed. A new flat was to be found for Maude, and I was to organize this as swiftly and circumspectly as possible. I was also informed that we must train a new radio operator as soon as possible and set up a third transmitting station in Geneva, meaning that with Jim's in Lausanne we would have four altogether.

At the beginning of May I heard that the Germans had mopped up the illegal French transmitter they had been looking for just over the frontier and I began to hope that perhaps the radio direction finders had not been after us at all. There was no guarantee any more, however, that our radio link with Moscow would remain secret; Edouard, Maude, Rosa, and Jim were daily working for several hours at a stretch with no change of locale because we could not find a flat that was suitable, and this was of course dangerous.

In answer to the director's telegram of 5 May agreeing the new schedule for Maude I reported that it was impossible for the time being to accommodate the reserve set in a new place. Nor was it going to be an easy job to find and train a new operator to man it. We were well aware that a mere change of schedule was not enough

*W.F. Flicke, *Agenten funken nach Moskau,* pp. 330 f.

in the present situation. We needed new places to work from and we needed new, trained operators. But all this would take time. We were banking on our assumption that, even if the Germans should have discovered our radio link with Moscow, our radio operators were in no immediate danger as long as the search was being conducted on the other side of the frontier. The situation would of course deteriorate if the Germans were to let their bloodhounds loose in Geneva or Lausanne. But for that the enemy needed time—which also meant time for us to do something.

Early in the summer we had to face a major setback: 'Bill', a secretary at the German military purchasing commission in Geneva, was blown. She was a member of Sissy's group and she had given us some useful information. Deeply concerned, Sissy told me at our next meeting that the girl had been given the sack because it had been discovered that confidential information was leaking out of the office. The accusation had apparently been made openly by an officer who Bill was convinced was a Gestapo man. The girl of course denied everything but was dismissed all the same. We did not know at the time what had tripped her up. Now one can see more clearly: German Counter-intelligence evidently established on the basis of monitored telegrams that the girl belonged to our organization because they mentioned the place where she worked. For example:

2 May 1943. To the director.

From Bill.

Mannerheim has been holding talks in Geneva with General Müller, who represents the Wehrmacht high command on the commission responsible for purchasing Swiss munitions for the German army.

Dora.

It is possible the Germans also deciphered the following two telegrams to Moscow:

18 May 1943. To the director.

From Bill.

According to information received from sources close to General Müller, in the second half of April Germany was making preparations to occupy Switzerland on account of the attitude adopted by the Swiss at the talks. The Germans were counting seriously on the help of the fifth column that has been built up in the Swiss officer corps. Head of the fifth column in Switzerland is Baron Mitternich, the official delegate to the Red Cross. They planned to occupy only the industrial region, leaving open to the Swiss army the option of withdrawing into the mountains. The occupation idea was shelved because the Swiss made concessions at the trade talks.

Dora.

28 June 1943. To the director.

From Bill.

According to information from the German munitions office the Germans are currently working on a new type of tank, the Panther, which is supposed to be a modified Tiger with heavier armour-plating and increased mobility.

Dora.

With material of this kind to hand it was of course a simple matter to spot where the information was coming from and find out who must be responsible.

Bill got off with a dismissal, but for the rest of us the affair might have had graver consequences. I instructed Sissy to break off all contact with the girl because the Germans would undoubtedly be keeping her under observation. Fortunately Bill knew neither who Sissy was nor where she lived.

We did not know that Sissy herself was already blown by this time.

But there was a lot we did not know. It emerged later that in 1943 we had in fact had more than sufficient reason to be alarmed. Not content with monitoring our transmitters, deciphering our telegrams, and sicking *agents provocateurs* onto us, the Germans went to the lengths of exerting pressure on the Swiss government through diplomatic channels to make them take steps to paralyse our work. In 1943 the Reich's representatives in Switzerland five times requested my arrest, naming me in their memoranda as a Soviet agent who was collecting intelligence against Germany in the territory of the Swiss Confederation. They clearly hoped that the Swiss authorities would either intern me or expel me from the country, in which case the Gestapo would be waiting for me as soon as I stepped across the frontier.

Luckily for me the Swiss did nothing of the sort. The federal government took no notice of the Germans' memoranda. A number of years later the Swiss papers reported that, at the time, the Swiss government had not understood what the Germans were talking about (what—arrest a well-known member of the scientific profession?); they simply did not believe I was a Soviet intelligence agent. Well, maybe they did not. As the *Gazette de Lausanne* wrote on 2 February 1949: 'Various public figures protested at this affront to a geographer who was widely known and whose presence in Switzerland did the country credit.' I think it more likely, though, that political reasons prompted the Swiss not only not to hand me over to the Germans but not to intern me either.

The Swiss military leadership, as I have said, looked to an Allied victory as offering the only guarantee that Switzerland would escape invasion by the Germans. For this reason the federal authorities took an indulgent attitude towards the Allies' intelligence agents, thereby making the latter's work easier. Only occasionally, when the Germans lodged a diplomatic protest against the anti-German nature of some foreigner's activities, did they reluctantly step in and do something. This happened, for example, with Long and Salter. The Germans probably knew the two men's backgrounds, suspected them of anti-German activities, and sent sharp notes of protest to the Swiss government. Thus pressurized, the authorities placed the two temporarily under police observation, but not for any length of time. The federal police of course had a pretty good idea that Long and Salter were working for Gaullist Intelligence, but they had no intention of placing any serious obstacles in their way because their work not only did not compromise the security of Switzerland but indirectly served Swiss interests.

In this complex and in many respects perilous situation, then, our group pursued its work in the spring of 1943 on the threshold of the operations that were to decide the war.

CHAPTER 28

Preparations for the decisive battle

The Red Army continued its offensive. In March 1943 there was fierce fighting in the middle sector of the front, defended by the troops of Field Marshal Kluge, and in the Ukraine around Kharkov and in the Donets Basin, where the defence was in the hands of Manstein's army group 'South'. The Soviet operation to free the northern Caucasus was nearing its conclusion. The main fighting here was on the roads leading to Novorossiysk and the Taman Peninsula, these being the key points as far as taking the Crimean bridgehead was concerned.

Central asked us to find out above all what the Germans were planning for these sectors of the front, which were of crucial importance to the Soviet high command. As usual we passed on this assignment *via* Sissy and Taylor to Lucy, and as usual the answer came back before long:

8 April 1943. To the director. Urgent.

From Werther. Berlin, 3 April.

The difference of opinion between the Wehrmacht high command and the army high command [Oberkommando des Heeres, as distinct from navy and air force] *has been overcome by deciding provisionally to postpone continuation of the offensive against Kursk until the beginning of May. This decision was helped along by the fact that Bock, Kluge, and Küchler were able to show that more and more Soviet forces are being concentrated all along the northern sector and in particular in the Velikiye Luki and Leningrad regions. They pointed out how dangerous engaging the available reserves prematurely could be.*

Manstein for his part stated that he could not hold the southern sector of the front and Kharkov if the Red Army continued to command such a magnificent deployment zone as that in front of Kursk.

In any case neither the Wehrmacht high command nor the army high command is thinking in terms of an all-out offensive operation, either generally or in southern Russia and the Caucasus.

The army high command believes that well-organized Russian offensive operations are possible only in the following regions: Leningrad, Orel, the Kuban estuary, Novorossiysk, and the Kerch peninsular.

In the opinion of the army high command new, powerful Russian offensives in the Lake Ilmen region and to retake Kharkov are out of the question before 10 May. It is also presumed that the Russians will not take up positions or launch a major offensive in the Velikiye Luki region before then.

On the basis of this assessment of the situation on the eastern front, only the air fleets of Keller and Richthofen and the air-force units stationed on the Kerch peninsula have been to some extent replenished. Otherwise the Germans consider that the Soviet air forces on the Leningrad front and in the Novorossiysk and Temryuk areas are stronger than the German.

Dora

It is now known that Hitler put his signature to Operational Order No. 6, in which he appointed 3 May as the earliest date for the beginning of 'Operation Citadel', on 15 April 1943.* On 20 April, however, Lucy passed us a report from Werther to the effect that the deadline for the beginning of the German attack on Kursk, originally set for the first week in May, had been postponed. A few days later Werther came up with something more precise:

... The new deadline for the German attack is 12 June.

Early in May we received and passed on the following information:

2 May 1943. To the director. Urgent.

From Werther. Berlin, 27 April.

The German high command and Manstein are increasingly examining the possibility that the Soviets may be going to launch a

*See *Kriegstagebuch des Oberkommandos der Wehrmacht* ('War diary of the Wehrmacht high command'), Frankfurt-am-Main, 1965, vol. 3, pp. 1425 ff.

co-ordinated attack on the Crimean peninsula on land, sea, and in the air. Consequently exceptional measures have been taken to engage air-force and naval units in order to hold up the Red Army's preparations in Batumi, Poti, and Sukhumi. By defending the Kuban bridgehead the German military leadership hopes to be able to avoid a battle for the Crimea.

They plan to back up this defence by starting their offensive operations in time. The 1st tank army under Kleist has been designated to launch attacks and create at least a threatening situation in the neighbourhood of Rostov and Voroshilovgrad in order to relieve the German defences on the lower Kuban and in the Novorossiysk region, take the pressure off the Crimea, and so cut down the danger threatening the whole German position in the Balkans.

The 1st tank army, however, is for the time being unable to carry out the task it has been set because it is in need of both manpower replacements and fresh supplies of artillery and aircraft. The plan is to have this army ready for the above-mentioned offensive operations by 15 May. General Konrad, commanding the troops in the southern Kuban area, has received orders to hold his positions until that date at whatever cost.

Dora.

Apart from this kind of intelligence concerning the intentions of the German military leadership, in the spring of 1943 we also collected other important information of a military and political nature, not only from Lucy's Berlin friends but also from some of our older sources.

For example, Moscow was interested in knowing where the Wehrmacht staff had its different headquarters. Long came up with something here, which he got through his own connections:

. . . One headquarters of the Wehrmacht high command is in East Prussia, in Rastenburg, and Hitler has three other headquarters: Obersalzberg, near Berchtesgaden; Neuruppin, near Berlin; and Lapfen, near Königsberg, in East Prussia.

Lucy was able to fill in another piece:

. . . A permanent special staff operates at the field staff headquarters of the German high command on the eastern front

near Baranovichi, no matter where the high command itself is at the time.

In April we received the following detailed report from Werther:

1. Composition of the 4th tank army, under the command of General Hoth: the 3rd, 25th, and 27th armoured divisions, the SS division 'Viking', the 12th, 26th, and 103rd mobile and light divisions. Temporarily attached as reinforcement are the 9th and 11th armoured divisions; the 6th and 7th armoured divisions have been detached for reorganization. The 4th tank army's preparations for the summer operations cannot be complete before some time in May.

2. On 2 and 3 April there was a conference at the German high command to discuss the plans for spring, summer, and autumn 1943 and the distribution of reserves.

The conference opened under Göring's chairmanship without Hitler, then Hitler arrived and also took part.

The conference revealed the existence of fundamental differences of opinion between Göring on the one hand and Bock and Halder on the other (Halder had been invited to attend in an advisory capacity).

Halder and Bock declared that they were not in agreement with the measures planned concerning the deployment of the newly organized army and air force reserves. Bock stated that he could take no responsibility for a decision that did not allow for reinforcement of the army and air force in the West.

Göring was supported by Dönitz, Keitel, Manstein, List, Zeitzler, Fromm, Milch, and Jeschonnek, all of whom were present at the conference. Kluge, Küchler, and Rundstedt, i.e., the commanders who would have supported Bock, were not invited to take part.

The differences of opinion were allegedly smoothed out during the course of the conference.

According to information from general-staff officers, Bock holds the post of supreme commander of the army.

The 4th tank army mentioned by Werther suffered heavy losses when the Germans embarked on a counter-offensive in the Kharkov region and had to be replenished with fresh forces to get it on its feet again.

Around this time we also received information from Werther about the deployment of German long-range bomber groups:

... There are German long-range bomber groups with the 1st, 2nd, 3rd, and 6th air fleets and in the far north. Of these the 3rd group belonged until February to the 3rd air fleet under Sperrle; from March onwards it forms part of the 2nd air fleet stationed in western Sicily under Kesselring. Also with the 2nd air fleet are three long-range bomber groups under Wing Commander Giese. The 18th group is attached to the 3rd air fleet stationed in Holland and attacking English coastal areas. The 19th group belongs to the 6th air fleet and is in action in the Crimea.

Olga reported from Berlin about how successful the Soviet air force's bombing raids against German military targets had been, and how worried the Wehrmacht commanders were:

... The latest bombing raids flown by the Soviet air force against eastern Germany have led the German high command to the conclusion that the Soviet military leadership is for strategic reasons paving the way for the Red Army's offensive by carrying out a systematic bombardment of the principal eastern-front supply bases.

The destructive effect of the Soviet air-force raids on industrial plant in Tilsit and Insterburg was far greater than that of the raid on Königsberg.

The German high command is assuming that the Soviet bomber command has organized a group consisting of a minimum of 400 long-range bombers for the counter-offensives against Germany.

In April I received some important information concerning the location of military training camps and the reserves stationed in the German hinterland:

17 April 1943. To the director.

From Olga.

Newly-organized German units:

1. One tank regiment of the 14th armoured division is being re-formed at Camp Zeithain, another tank regiment of the same division at Bautzen.

2. The 11th infantry division recently arrived at Camp Wieber in Hesse for re-formation.

3. The 94th infantry division is in process of re-formation at Camp Königsbrück.

4. The 294th infantry division has been waiting in Lower Austria for transport to the front since 31 March.

5. The 29th mobile division will be ready to proceed to the front on 20 April.

6. The newly-organized 305th infantry division will also be ready for transport to the front on 20 April.

7. By 10 May the following divisions will be ready for transport to the front: the Waffen-SS division 'Deutschland', the 41st, 295th, and 371st infantry divisions, and the 60th mobile division.

8. Ready to move by the end of May will be two newly-organized armoured divisions, at least one mobile and eight more infantry divisions, and possibly a mountain-infantry division as well.

Dora.

Central were of course extremely interested in information about the German munitions industry:

28 March 1943. To Dora.

1. Request you fill out Teddy's information about armoured-vehicle types with tactical and technical particulars: thickness of armour-plating, armament, speed. We very much want details of the monthly output of armoured vehicles.

2. It would also be useful if Teddy could give us the monthy figures for aircraft production in Germany and Italy and details of German military-aircraft types.

Director.

We answered these questions to some extent in our telegram of 14 April with some important data from Teddy concerning the trials of the new B-1 Tiger, a heavy tank of which the Germans had great hopes and which they used in the summer of 1943 against the Soviet fortifications in the Kursk-Orel-Belgorod region:

...In the opinion of the commander of the 10th tank army, General Fischer, and of the tank officers sent to Tunis by Guderian this tank is of only limited suitability for attacking fortified

positions. In mobile fighting in which air forces play a significant part it fails to show to advantage because of its limited speed (26 kph). In addition the tracks are insufficiently protected, though the rest of the armour-plating is fully adequate. Of the 17 tanks of this type so far lost in Tunis, 13 were put out of action by British aircraft. The vehicle's poor speed makes it easy to bomb.

Teddy gave more details in another report:

... On the open road or on flat, hard ground the maximum speed is 36 kph. The armour-plating is 88-100 mm thick; reports from the front are positive as to its stopping capacity.

Knowing the Tiger's tactical and technical details and its combat potential was extremely important to Moscow. On the basis of such information the Soviet military leadership was able to take steps before the battle of Kursk to provide the kind of anti-tank weapons needed to destroy this new and powerful assault vehicle.

Regarding tank and aircraft production in Germany, I quote a sample of the information Teddy provided in April and May:

... Under pressure of the transition to defensive warfare, since December 1942 the German high command has been stepping up production of fighter planes and close-combat aircraft, concentrating particularly on the following types: Messerschmidt 109, Focke-Wulf 190, Ju-87, and Ju-88.

In March the German armoured-vehicle industry produced 320 units of type T-3, between 400 and 410 units of type T-4, and 90 units of type B-1 [the Tiger].

Around the same time we heard this from Long:

... German industry, including that in Austria and Czechoslovakia, manufactured 700 armoured vehicles in February and aims to boost monthy production to 900 units.

Another aspect our sources in Germany and the occupied countrie's observed and reported on was the location and extent of the damage inflicted by Allied air raids on enemy munitions plant.

Here, for example, is a report from southern Germany received in early April:

. . . The last RAF raid destroyed half the Bosch works in Stuttgart. Production has been brought to a standstill for the time being. The Mercedes factory in Untertürkheim has orders to boost tank production by 30 per cent.

Shortly afterwards we received a report from an engineer employed at the Siemens works in Nuremberg. He told us that British bombers had inflicted such heavy damage on the plant that munitions production was down to 15 per cent. Another target that was badly hit was the MAN (Maschinenfabrik Augsburg-Nürnberg) works, which it took the Germans all of three months to repair.

Olga reported:

. . . The RAF raid of 13 March on the Krupp works in Essen put the following departments out of action: the gun-barrel foundry, the armoured-vehicle production line, the steam-locomotive production line, the machine factory, the boiler factory, and the tube rolling mill.

The 4 April raid also knocked out the heavy army lorry production line and virtually all the departments producing infantry equipment. In all these departments production is temporarily at a standstill.

In its July raids the RAF destroyed Gelsenkirchen goods station. The Mannersmann gun-barrel foundry and the same company's big rolling mill in Schalke, near Gelsenkirchen, were completely destroyed and the railway-truck factory in Cologne was badly damaged.

A spinning mill in Reutlingen, one of the main suppliers of parachute silk, has been working at one-quarter capacity since the end of May as a result of bomb damage by British aircraft. Raw silk stocks are running low because there is nothing coming in from the Far East.

The US air force raid of 10 August destroyed several major depots of the United Ballbearing Works in Schweinfurt, which has meant a big drop-back in supplies for tanks and lorries. Half the town was flattened.

Another of Olga's reports concerned German losses—3,175,000 dead, seriously wounded, missing, or captured in the period from the beginning of the war up until 3 April 1943. How nearly exact this information was is confirmed by figures that have become available since the war: from June 1941 to the end of June 1942 the Germans lost 1,980,000 men on the eastern front, and between October 1942 and March 1943, according to army high command figures, a further 1,324,000, which makes a total of just over 3,300,000 for the eighteen-month period.

In 1943 Germany was subjected to a new 'total mobilization', and I close this chapter with a telegram I sent the director in the spring of 1943, collating information received from Olga and Teddy in Berlin:

. . . Result of the 'total mobilization' for the army since 1 January 1943:

286,000 men called up as fit for front-line duty. Between April and 1 June a further 290,000 already mustered troops will report to the army.

The army has been replenished with units fit for garrison duty, construction work, etc.—95,000 men altogether. A total of 57,000 young volunteers have been deferred.

In February and March the army is being replenished by means of the unscheduled mobilization of 108,000 men fit for front-line duty and 62,000 men fit for garrison duty and construction work.

Only 190,000 convalesced sick and wounded will be returned to the army in January, February, and March.

In the same period SS troops will receive between 80,000 and 120,000 replacements.

Dora.

CHAPTER 29

Behind-the-scenes diplomacy

Another essential aspect of our work in the spring of 1943 was scouting information about the political and diplomatic manoeuvres of Germany and the satellite countries. For example:

25 April 1943. To the director. Urgent.
From Olga and Anna.
The Germans suspect that the Polish government in London is coming to the conclusion that in the present situation German occupation of Poland constitutes a very much smaller danger than Soviet occupation.
Hitler, Göring, and Ribbentrop are confident that with the tactics they are using they can not only get the frontiers drawn to the disadvantage of the Soviet Union but also poison Anglo-Russian relationships, which could affect the future course of the war.

Dora.

Around the same time Salter got wind of something:

....Mannerheim arrived in Switzerland on 17 April and is staying in Lugano, ostensibly to convalesce after a serious illness. The Swiss government had forbidden the press to report his visit.

A few days later we heard:

...Mannerheim is in Interlaken, negotiating with the United States. The Finns have decided not to try to open negotiations with the Soviet Union directly and are insisting on American mediation. They are demanding the 1939 frontiers and want a US guarantee against the possibility of Soviet occupation.
Mannerheim is also negotiating with the Americans on Germany's behalf about concluding a peace treaty with Germany.

At the end of April Mannerheim was in Geneva, where he met League of Nations secretary Lester and asked whether the League of Nations could not lend a hand in Finland's attempts to conclude a separate peace with the Soviet Union on condition of being granted multiple guarantees. Lester was extremely guarded and said he must first take advice in London and New York.

And at the end of May Olga reported from Berlin:

. . . The purpose of Mannerheim's visit to Switzerland was to make it officially known to the Allies and to Russia that Finland wishes to undertake no further commitments to Germany in 1943.

The Finns wanted to stress with Mannerheim's trip that they are not interested in the conference recently held by Germany's allies under German chairmanship.

Earlier my own countrymen had flown one of these diplomatic kites in the direction of the Soviet Union:

2 March 1943. To the director. Urgent.

The commercial attaché at the Hungarian embassy in Berne, Mérei, has approached Long to ask whether the Gaullists could not act as intermediary between Hungary and the Soviet Union. According to Mérei a change of government is imminent in Hungary. There are two candidates for prime minister of the new government: Count Bethlen and Rassay, the leader of the Democratic Party. Both wish to conclude peace with the Soviet Union.

Mérei asked Long whether he could pass on to the Soviet Union via the Gaullists a list of Hungarian questions designed to prepare the ground for peace talks. Long said he would let him have an answer after consulting the Gaullist Committee. Mérei has returned to Hungary but will be back for a short visit in a few days' time. Request immediate instructions.

Dora.

This attempt to sound out the Soviet Union with a view to a compromise peace was doomed to failure. Hitler would undoubtedly have blocked any step leading to a weakening of his Reich's defences.

The Hungarian government later resumed its kite-flying—not towards the Soviet Union this time but in the direction of Britain and the United States. A report from Pakbo, which I received on 23 May and passed on straightaway, said that Horthy was preparing to visit Switzerland in order to contact the British with a view to concluding a separate peace. On 28 May Lucy too reported that Horthy and Antonescu (of Rumania) would be coming to Switzerland to hold talks with the British. Again of course the Germans nipped these approaches in the bud.

Other reports from various sources indicated that the differences of opinion in the Axis camp on matters of war and peace were on the increase:

21 April 1943. To the director.
From Werther.

1. On his last visit to see Hitler Tsar Boris of Bulgaria was forced to promise that Bulgaria would enter the war on the side of Germany and Rumania if there was any question of the Dardanelles and the Bosphorus being occupied by Russian or British troops, because it was to be expected that Turkey would submit to Anglo-American and Soviet political pressure and finally go over to their side.

2. The Germans promised Tsar Boris that as a preparatory measure they would post a German army in the Balkans that could in an emergency forestall the Anglo-Russian invasion by taking the Dardanelles in the summer of 1943. As in February/March 1941, possible marshalling areas for the German army are the Tundkha-Maritsa region and the approaches to Adrianople [Edirne].

3. The Germans forced this promise out of Tsar Boris in order to be in a position to play a political trump card on the occasion of Mussolini's then imminent visit by showing him that the combined German-Bulgarian assault on the British Middle-East zone would make things easier for Italy.

Dora.

Mussolini, however, was not as impressed as Hitler had hoped he would be:

29 April 1943. To the director.
From Long.

At their last meeting Mussolini categorically refused to comply with Hitler's request that Italy send fresh troops to the eastern front. He also stated that Italy was not interested in the projected German attack on Turkey because Italy's strength was exhausted.

After the meeting with Mussolini Hitler quickly contacted the rest of his satellites to prevent them from following Italy's example. The heads of state of Bulgaria, Hungary, and Rumania promised on a visit to Germany that they would remain loyal to the Axis but said that they were not prepared to go on taking an active part in the war.

Dora.

This refusal to continue playing an active role did not mean that these countries definitively withdrew from the war but only that they did not wish to send any more divisions to the Soviet-German theatre of operations, where Hitler's allies, particularly Italy and Rumania, had already made great sacrifices. Indeed they no longer had the strength to take part in the hostilities in the east.

In 1943 Hitler put the main burden of the fighting on the Soviet-German front on the shoulders of the German people, although he continued to demand that his allies lend him effective assistance in the other theatres. Above all the Führer placed his hopes in his Axis partners, Italy and Japan:

19 April 1943. To the director.

From Olga.

Japan has promised the German high command that it will use its fleet air arm and its submarines to step up Japanese activity against the American's Australian shipping lines and the Indian shipping lines of the British, these operations to reach a climax should the Anglo-American allies try and attack Sicily in an attempt to secure free passage to the Mediterranean through the Sicilian Channel. The Germans were at great pains to make the Japanese see that their operations must come to a climax now, while Bizerta and Tunis are still in Axis hands and not after they have fallen.

The Germans again requested that the Japanese bomb northern Australia in order to distract Anglo-American attention from the landing in Europe. So far Japan has refused to comply with this request on the grounds that it does not have enough long-range bombers.

Dora.

But Japan's operations in the Pacific came too late to rescue the situation in the Mediterranean. The North African front was in acute danger. Harried by the Allies, the Italian and German troops under the command of Rommel surrendered one town after another, retreating all along the coast. The total loss of this strategic bridgehead would of course expose Italy to direct attack by Anglo-American forces from the south. In this connection Werther reported:

...Following the meeting between Hitler and Mussolini, Rommel has been instructed to hold out as long as possible. This at the insistence of Italy, which has demanded that Tunis and Bizerta be defended stubbornly.

In May the situation in the Mediterranean theatre became even more critical. The Germans were extremely worried because the destruction of Italy would rob them of an effective army. As Olga informed us:

... The German high command has decided in the event of an Allied landing in southern Italy to leave the decisive fighting to the Italians, with the German army defending only the eastern Adriatic coastal region, the Piave Line, and South Tyrol.

This is considered necessary in case Italy should switch to the Allied camp or quit the Axis.

At the end of May we sent Moscow another telegram dealing with a related question:

30 May 1943. To the director.

From Werther, 25 May.

The Wehrmacht high command is making preparations to force Bulgaria to join the German defensive front in the near future. To put more pressure on the Bulgarians the German troop presence in Serbia is being rapidly reinforced. The intention is to declare the

Bulgarian Balkan zone a threatened area without regard to the Turkish and eastern Mediterranean situation.

This decision is consistent with the Wehrmacht high command's basic view that as far as the defence of Germany is concerned the Balkans are more important than Italy.

Dora.

As things started to get hot for Mussolini the behind-the-scenes diplomacy intensified, with Il Duce's former supporters making hopeful approaches to the Anglo-American camp. Rome in early 1943 saw a spate of secret meetings between official and unofficial representatives of the warring powers.

Once again the Vatican served as a kind of central clearing-house. In February Cardinal Spellman, who was in touch with Wall Street and with Allen Dulles in Switzerland, arrived from New York. We know now that the American cardinal contacted Baron Weizsäcker, the German ambassador to the Vatican, and on 3 March met Ribbentrop in Rome. At the request of Allen Dulles, who masterminded all America's European intrigues, Spellman also held talks with the Pope.

Word of the general content of their talks reached me in Geneva and was duly forwarded to Moscow:

2 April 1943. To the director.

From the Vatican.

1. The Pope and Cardinal Spellman talked mainly about post-war policy, the Pope paying particular attention to the question of church participation in the solution of social problems after the war. In the Pope's view there can be no serious talk of peace and what can be done in peacetime before Hitler's fall, which will bring with it the fall of Mussolini.

2. The Pope has instructed the French bishops not to obstruct the activities of France's Catholic youth and not to support General Giraud.

Dora.

It is interesting that the Pope recognized the inevitability of the collapse of the Fascist regimes of Germany and Italy. His instructing the bishops not to support the man whom Pétain had

Q

appointed to replace the German puppet Admiral Darlan (murdered in December 1942) as governor-general of the French North African colonies was no mere whim.

CHAPTER 30

More *agents provocateurs*

Around this time Jim received one of his special assignments from Central: he was to meet the courier of our French group, who was expected to arrive in Switzerland towards the end of March. The director's instructions were that Jim should merely hand the man from France some money, on no account letting himself be drawn into conversation about our work. Time and place for a series of alternative rendezvous were duly fixed: 28, 29 and 31 March in Lausanne and 4, 5, and 7 April in Geneva.

Jim arrived punctually at the first rendezvous in Lausanne. The courier, however, did not. The natural assumption was that something must have happened to delay him, and indeed, a number of days later, as Jim appeared at the appointed place in Geneva, a man came up to him and in broken French gave the correct password.

Jim was supposed to hand the courier a substantial sum in Swiss currency. Geopress was not bringing in very much at that time, however, and we simply did not have the requisite sum available; Jim only had a little money with him. He therefore agreed a new rendezvous with the courier and promised to bring the money then.

Otherwise the meeting went off as planned, though Jim had wondered about a couple of things: firstly the man from the French organization lived, according to his own admission, permanently in Switzerland, and secondly he was for some unknown reason unprepared for the conversation about the money. Reporting back to the director afterwards, Jim mentioned his doubts just in case.

The second meeting took place near the station in Berne on 6 May. We had still not been able to raise the whole sum and Jim only had part of the money with him. He handed the courier the envelope with the notes and said he would be bringing the rest to a further rendezvous. The courier replied that someone else might be coming to the next rendezvous in his stead. Apparently they had covered everything and Jim was about to take his leave when the courier abruptly pulled a large, bright-orange envelope from his briefcase and handed it to Jim without a word. Jim was somewhat taken aback because there had been nothing in Central's instructions about a delivery arriving from France. Nevertheless he took the envelope and hurried away.

He hailed a taxi in the square in front of the station, climbed in, and told the driver to step on it. Whose hare-brained idea had this been, putting the message in a bright-orange envelope? Anyone carrying it could be seen for miles! How was he supposed to disappear with a beacon like that in his hand? He had to get rid of it somehow—right away, and without anyone seeing. He felt it; it contained a hard object, possibly a book.

Spotting a public convenience, he asked the driver to stop. Once inside he ripped the envelope into little pieces and flushed them down the pan, but not before careful inspection had revealed that the offending item was of Swiss manufacture. Decent paper had long since disappeared from the rest of Europe and the only place where you could get an envelope of that type and quality was in a high-class Swiss stationer's. So the courier had brought the thing here and put his book in it. But why? Plagued by fresh doubts, Jim wrapped the book in the newspaper he had had sticking out of his jacket pocket to identify him at the rendezvous.

He made a wide detour through the outskirts of Berne to cover his tracks and then returned to the station. There he did his best to disappear in the crowd before boarding his train. Even then he did not use the normal route back to Lausanne but changed trains halfway and reached his flat only after a suitably roundabout journey, confident that he had shaken off anyone who might have been following him.

They had agreed a further meeting for 11 June. Three days before that date, however, Jim's suspicions were strengthened by an urgent telegram from Moscow. The director strictly forbade him to meet the courier again; Central were afraid the Germans had the man under observation. The telegram also said that the money would be transferred by other means and instructed Jim to remove the two telegrams from the cover of the book the courier had handed him, encode them in full, using his own code, and transmit them to Central; he was then to burn the book immediately.

It was a brand-new French publication and the pages were still uncut. Carefully tearing the binding open as the director had instructed him, Jim discovered two telegrams that he assumed came from our comrades working underground in France. He encoded them and sent them off.

Central rightly remained very much on the alert, stressed to Jim the potential danger of the situation, and told him to take security precautions:

2 July 1943.

We must conclude from the affair with the courier that Gestapo agents managed to tail you to your flat and find out your name.

Take the following steps immediately:

1. Remove all suspicious material from your flat.

2. Stop sending and hide your set somewhere else for the time being.

3. Prepare yourself for the possibility that the Gestapo may try provocation. If you are interrogated by the Swiss police, deny everything categorically.

4. You may have one meeting with Albert [i.e. me]. *Then we shall provisionally break off this contact. Discuss with Albert whether it would not be better if you went away to the Ticino until the autumn. Also discuss whether you should change your flat or even move to another town.*

If you can instal the set in a safe flat from which you can send twice or three times a month, call us when you have anything out of the ordinary. Remain calm and steadfast. If there is no proof, you are in no danger.

Director.

Meanwhile on 26 June Sissy had received the first of a series of phone calls from a man who asked for 'Mr Dübendorfer' (there was no Mr Dübendorfer, remember—Sissy's was a fictitious marriage) and refused obstinately to give his name, saying only that he had been asked to ring by 'a gentleman from Lausanne, Mr Foote' on behalf of certain people from France. The name said nothing to Sissy because she had no contact with Jim, but the episode, occurring at this time, made her understandably nervous.

At the end of April the Gestapo had arrested in Paris a member of the French group together with his wife and son. The man, whom Sissy knew as 'Maurice', had been a contact between Paris and Switzerland. He had contacted Sissy on three or four occasions, calling at her flat. So he knew her name and address. Sissy had also introduced him to Paul Böttcher, to her daughter Tamara, and to Tamara's fiancé. Maurice, in other words, knew a good deal more than a contact man needs to know.

Sissy learned of Maurice's arrest ten days after it had occurred. She told me immediately, and on 10 May I informed Central in one of my 'urgent' telegrams. This was the first word we had received about the new wave of arrests in France. It was extremely disturbing because there was no way of telling whether Maurice would hold up under interrogation, especially in view of the fact that they had his wife and son as well. We knew all about the Gestapo's methods...

The question Sissy had to face was this: were these 'certain people from France' really members of the French group who had escaped the clutches of the Gestapo and were trying to get in touch with Central through her? But in that case why had they made the mistake of asking for 'Mr Dübendorfer'? Since receiving the news of Maurice's arrest she was mistrustful of anything that had to do with the French group.

She found this 'Mr Foote' in the telephone book and asked a friend to ring the number for her. When Jim received the call and a complete stranger started talking about 'people from France' he said immediately that he knew nothing about the matter and there must be some mistake. Sissy's friend would reveal neither name nor address but gave Jim Sissy's private number and rang off with the request that he call it if he wanted to find out about his French friends. Jim traced the number to one Rachel Dübendorfer, a name he had never come across before, and decided that the whole thing was the work of an agent provocateur. He did not ring the number but instead informed Central and myself about the anonymous phone call to his flat. That was on 30 June—the very same day as I heard from Sissy about her anonymous calls.

Again Central were deeply disturbed and instructed Sissy too to drop everything for a while and let others maintain contact with her sources; they were convinced that here was evidence of a German Counter-intelligence operation against us. Sissy, however, saw no particular danger (as Jim had not, once he had satisfied himself that he was not being tailed) and refused to comply—especially since, as she claimed, Lucy had made it a condition of working with us that his contact with our organization should be through her and no one else, and if she went we would lose the source. All my efforts to persuade her to take a break were in vain, although I am convinced that Lucy, in spite of his cautiousness, would have been prepared to use another contact.

The result of all this was that in the summer of 1943 we were unable to devote our entire attention to intelligence work. By now we shared Central's growing conviction that the enemy had discovered our presence and was closing in for the kill. From now on our time and energies were divided between the work of gathering information and the problem of camouflage and security. The net of observation and provocation was being drawn tighter and tighter, but for us there was no retreat.

The war was about to be decided.

CHAPTER 31

Approaching the showdown

Somewhat sobered by the summer of 1943, the Germans realized that adopting a defensive strategy against the Red Army was not going to do them much good; in fact it would frustrate all their major military plans and be tantamount to an admission of defeat. Consequently Hitler's general staff decided to prepare another big offensive on the eastern front, hoping by this means to solve a number of politico-military problems that were beginning to emerge with disturbing clarity around this time. As Field Marshal Keitel, head of the Wehrmacht high command, put it at a conference in Berlin in May 1943: 'Political considerations force us to attack.'*

At the beginning of the year Hitler had proclaimed a massive programme to boost munitions production and increase the fighting power of the Wehrmacht. It became the chief task of German industry to turn out large numbers of heavy tanks and the newest types of aircraft for the eastern front.

I quoted in Chapter 28 some telegrams we sent in April concerning the specifications and combat potential of the new B-1 Tiger tank, which was designed for breaking through solid fortifications. Around mid-June Lucy reported that the German armoured-vehicle industry had been producing nothing else since towards the end of April. A few days later we learned that the Germans were trying out an even further-improved tank called the Leopard. This had heavier armour-plating than the Tiger, a larger-calibre gun, and greater manoeuvrability. The enemy later sent it into action during the battle of Kursk.

Also in June we received some fresh figures concerning German aircraft production:

*Gert Buchheit, *Hitler der Feldherr: Die Zerstörung einer Legende*, Rastatt, 1958, p. 366.

7 June 1943. To the director.

From Teddy.

The Luftwaffe high command is expecting the German aircraft industry to deliver 2,050 new military aircraft in May and 2,100 in June. Of these the Wehrmacht high command wants to send between 2,000 and 2,050 new bombers and fighters to the eastern front in June.

Dora.

9 June 1943. To the director.

From Long.

The new Messerschmidt G-G fighter is an improved version of the ME 109. Wingspan is 16 m, maximum speed 670 kph, and the Daimler-Benz engine develops 1,700 hp. It has two 15 mm cannon and two 7.1 mm machine-guns.

Dora.

The German military leadership was improving the army's technical equipment in every way and at the same time hurriedly training reserves to replenish the divisions bled in the winter and spring fighting. As always it was vital for the Soviet high command to know what reserves the enemy had at his disposal:

5 April 1943. To Dora.

Special assignment for Anna, Olga, Teddy:

1. We need a well-grounded report on the results of the total mobilization and the number of newly-organized units.

2. We want information about how many troops Germany's allies are sending to the eastern front and when.

3. Convey our thanks to Lucy and Long for their work. Our thanks too for the work you, Maria, Sissy, Pakbo, Maude, Edouard, and Rosa have been putting in.

Director.

The assignment was duly fulfilled. Lucy's Berlin informants reported that, according to the official account of the reserve army staff, on 15 April 1943 the German army had a total of more than forty fresh divisions in reserve; we supplied a list of the numbers and locations of these units.

In Germany the replenishment of the damaged divisions went ahead more or less according to plan, but in the satellite and occupied countries it was proving extremely difficult to raise new military units to send to the front. Only at the cost of enormous efforts was the Third Reich able to squeeze fresh help out of its exhausted allies:

2 May 1943. To the Director.
From Teddy.
Fellowing Horthy's visit to see Hitler it was decided that Hungary should place two army corps of ten divisions at Germany's disposal for the eastern front. Rumania will probably send the same. The four army corps are to be organized, equipped, and at the front by 1 June.

Dora.

As the following telegram shows, however, things did not work out quite as Hitler and his general staff had planned:

17 June 1943. To the director. Urgent.
From Olga, Berlin, 13 June.
Germany's allies currently have a total of 20 field divisions stationed on the Soviet-German front: 11 Finnish (3 in reserve behind the front), 5 Rumanian, 2 Hungarian, 2 Slovak (on guard duty behind the front).

Dora.

Clearly neither Hungary nor Rumania had been able to keep the promise.

Indeed the condition of Hitler's satellites was becoming critical, as we informed Moscow around the middle of May:

...All the German satellites, Rumania included, are against sending fresh troops to the Soviet-German front. The unreliability of the Bulgarian army is causing the Wehrmacht high command serious concern.

The Wehrmacht high command does not expect Turkey to start taking an active part in the war.

Olga told us that Horthy and Antonescu, instead of sending four army corps, sent a mere five divisions to the Soviet-German front—and this was on the eve of the crucial battle of Kursk. As for receiving any help from Turkey, the Wehrmacht high command had had finally to abandon all hope.

From now on Germany was fighting virtually on its own on the eastern front. The other two points of the Berlin-Rome-Tokyo axis could offer no significant aid. Italy was already on the verge of military collapse. Japan had all it could do to maintain its strategic position in the Pacific in the face of growing Allied pressure; there could be no question of the Japanese launching a relieving offensive against the Soviet Union from the east.

By the summer of 1943 Germany had lost a colossal number of men. Lucy passed us some figures from Berlin—just three days before the battle of Kursk began:

2 July 1943. To the director. Urgent.

From Olga.

German losses from the beginning of the war to 30 May 1943: 1,947,000 fallen, 565,000 captured, 1,080,000 severely wounded. In addition some 180,000 dead and wounded lost by the auxiliary troops. According to the 30 May figures Germany has lost a total of 3,772,000 men including 2,044,000 dead.

Dora.

A vast, bleeding wound in the body of the misgoverned and misguided German people. Yet the leaders of the Reich, indifferent to the nation's sacrifice, continued to march fresh millions off to the hell of war.

By the beginning of the summer campaign the manpower of the German armed forces had been increased by one and a half to two million as a result of Hitler's total mobilization. This brought them up to 10,300,000 men—or almost the level of the previous year. In the summer of 1943 the enemy faced the Red Army with 42 more divisions than he had attacked the Soviet Union with. Although the quality of those troops no longer stood comparison with their 1941 level, the Wehrmacht was still an extremely powerful and excellently equipped army. At the same time the strength and experience of the Red Army ranged opposite had been steadily increasing. The coming encounter promised to be a dramatic one.

Lucy and his Berlin informants continued to play the major part in answering Central's questions regarding the enemy's strength:

30 April 1943. To the director.
From Werther and Teddy.
Composition of the German armed forces on the eastern front and in the far north according to details released between 4 and 10 April:
1. The 2nd army includes: the 5th and 8th mobile divisions and the 45th, 62nd, 75th, 168th, 299th, and 499th infantry divisions.
2. The new 6th army (Manstein's army group) includes among others the SS armoured divisions 'Das Reich', 'Adolf Hitler', and 'Totenkopf', the 82nd, 208th, 211th, 216th, 231st, 254th, and 370th infantry divisions, and the SS division 'Gross-Deutschland'.
3. Composition of the 9th army (in Kluge's army group): the 6th, 78th, 129th, 162nd, 183rd, 256th, 292nd, 328th, 342nd, 385th, and 539th infantry divisions.
4. Composition of the 16th army: the 30th, 65th, 96th, 117th, 123rd, 207th, 223rd, 267th, and 290th infantry divisions and the 3rd mountain-infantry division.
5. Composition of the 3rd tank army: the 1st, 2nd, 4th, and 5th armoured divisions and the 10th, 14th, 25th, and 36th mobile divisions...

And so on; it was a very detailed report. At the end Werther and Teddy listed the various armies and their commanders.

Later we supplemented this collated report with fresh details taking account of the changes made up until the beginning of the summer:

13 June 1943. To the director. Urgent.
From Werther.
Drawn up on the Soviet-German front including the far north at the beginning of May, after reorganization and reinforcement, were a total of 166 divisions of the German army [at the beginning of April the figure had been about 140 divisions]. *They include 18 armoured divisions, 18 mobile and light divisions, 7 mountain-infantry divisions, 108 infantry divisions, 4 Waffen-SS divisions, and 3 air-force field divisions.*
In addition there are 3 armoured divisions and 6 infantry

divisions at the disposal of the army high command and 1 SS division at the disposal of the Wehrmacht high command.

There are a further 122 policing and replacement divisions in the occupied hinterland.

Dora.

Around the middle of June we heard something interesting from Teddy:

... Following an order of Hitler's issued at the end of May the Waffen-SS troops have been removed from the control of the Wehrmacht high command and now constitute an autonomous army parallel to the Wehrmacht and directly subordinate to Himmler and Hitler.

Teddy had already given us a detailed break-down of the Luftwaffe, comparable to the one we had put together from his and Werther's information about the army, when in June Lucy informed us that this Berlin source was now able to photograph documents in the secret archives of the air ministry, to which he had not had access before. From then on Teddy's reports were even more detailed and precise. For example:

28 June 1943. To the director. Urgent.

From Fernand [this was the name I gave to this new sub-source]. *Numerous air-ministry documents from the period January-May 1943 provide the following picture of effective air-force units:*

a) Fighter groups: 1st, 2nd or 'Richthofen', 3rd or 'Udet', 5th, 26th or 'Schlageter', 27th, 51st or 'Mölders', 52nd, 53rd, and 77th.

b) Fighter wings: 'Ost' and 'Aibling'.

c) Night-fighter groups: 1st, 2nd, and 3rd.

d) Bomber groups: 1st or 'Hindenburg', 3rd, 4th or 'General Weber', 6th, 26th, 27th or 'Boelcke', 30th, 40th, 51st, 53rd or 'Condor', 55th, 100th, and bomber group ZB-1.

e) Bomber wings for special duties: 323rd and 900th.

f) 'Stuka' groups [dive bombers]: *1st and 2nd or 'Immelmann 5'.*

g) Heavy-bomber group: 26th or 'Horst Wessel'.

h) Interceptor groups: 1st and 2nd.

Dora.

Back in mid-May Werther had told us:

. . . On 6 May the Wehrmacht high command estimated that the Russians have at least 750 long-range bombers, not including reserves, which convinced them that the Russian long-range bomber force is quantitatively as well as qualitatively superior to the German.

There was great agitation at the Wehrmacht high command on 6 May on account of the disorganization and paralysation of traffic at the Minsk, Gomel, Orsha, and Bryansk bases. The Russian heavy-bomber raids have ushered in a psychologically new situation for the Wehrmacht, limiting the high command's freedom of decision.

The abrupt increase of Russian bomber activity in the middle sector of the front on 6 and 7 May exceeded the worst expectations of the German leadership.

Our other sources too continued to supply us with important intelligence concerning, among other things, the morale of the German troops. Reports of conversations with the wounded German officers and men undergoing treatment in Swiss Red Cross hospitals gave us an excellent picture of the current state of their *Kampfgeist,* which made a useful supplement to the information about the Wehrmacht provided by Werther, Olga, Teddy, and Lucy's other Berlin sources.

CHAPTER 32

On the threshold of the Battle of Kursk

I now come to the most important phase of our intelligence work—the period immediately preceding the battle of Kursk. As always our chief task was to find out what the enemy had in mind.

What in fact were the enemy's principal strategic intentions in the summer of 1943?

The plan worked out at Hitler's headquarters laid down that the German counter-offensive was to begin at the Kursk salient. This was the outcome of the Red Army's winter and spring offensive, which had pushed the German line of defence a long way west, forming a Soviet bridgehead that extended over an enormous area comprising several Russian and Ukrainian *oblasti* or administrative districts. The Kursk salient lay between two large enemy army groups: from the north the right wing of the Germans' middle army group threatened the middle sector of the Soviet front; from the south the left wing of their southern army group was wrapped round the Soviet Voronezh front. This gave the Germans the strategic possibility of catching the Soviet troops in a pincer movement and moving in to destroy them.

Around the middle of April this plan, which was dubbed 'Citadel', received its definitive form. In his Plan of Operations No. 6 of 15 April 1943 Hitler stressed the importance of 'Citadel': 'This attack is to be given top priority. It must be carried out swiftly and successfully. The attack must place the initiative for the spring and summer of this year in our hands. All preparations must be made with thoroughness and care. In the direction of the main thrust the best units must be engaged with the best weapons, under the finest commanders, and plentifully supplied with ammunition.'*

The Germans accordingly planned to attack the Soviet troops in the Kursk salient on two fronts simultaneously—southwards from Orel with their middle army group and northwards from Kharkov

*Quoted in H.A. Jacobsen, *Der Zweite Weltkrieg in Chronik und Dokumenten, 1939—45*, p. 544.

with the southern army group—hoping thereby to cut off and destroy several Soviet armies. Subsequently the enemy intended to launch a second offensive, this one named 'Leopard', behind the Soviet south-western front. If this was successful the German military leadership was considering a thrust towards the north-east in order to circle Moscow and attack the Soviet central front from behind.

What about the men at the front who had to work out and carry out the projected operation—what did they think of it?

Field Marshal Manstein, commander-in-chief of the southern army group, wrote in his memoirs: 'If we managed to smash the enemy's armoured reserves in this battle we might be able to make a fresh thrust, either against his Donets front or elsewhere. Ultimately this was as important a goal of "Operation Citadel" as the elimination of the Kursk salient.'*

Von Kluge, commander-in-chief of the middle army group, spoke up in favour of the attack in a telegram to Hitler and Zeitzler, chief of the army general staff: 'Because of its enormous scope it will inevitably affect the main body of the Russian troops, including those north of Orel. If successful, the operation will pay maximal dividends. And that is of decisive importance.'†

Interestingly, we also have the opinion of a professional soldier on the other side. In May 1943 General Walter Bedell Smith, later chief of staff of the Allies' European expeditionary forces, gave this assessment: 'The Germans are making preparations on the Russian front for an offensive of unprecedented proportions . . . . The object of this major German offensive is to knock Russia out of the war or so paralyse the Red Army that any further resistance on its part shall be feeble and unsuccessful.'‡

The American general was exaggerating, of course; as an experienced army commander he ought to have recognized that, for all their ambitions, the Germans were no longer capable in 1943 of either 'knocking Russia out of the war' or 'paralysing the Red Army'—and especially not in a single offensive, no matter on

*Erich von Manstein, *Verlorene Siege* ('Lost Victories'), Bonn, 1955, p. 484.

†Quoted in *Voyenno-istoricheski Shurnal*, Moscow, 1959, no. 6, p. 91.

‡Quoted in Harry L. Butcher, *My Three Years with Eisenhower*, New York, 1945, p. 314.

what scale. That one had been answered unequivocally in 1941, and the Germans had taken the point.

The German high command several times changed the date of the projected operation in order that their troops should be optimally prepared. Originally set for the spring, it was eventually postponed to the middle of summer. The West German historian Martin Göhring gives as the reason for this that Hitler 'wanted to make sure of destroying the enemy. He waited for the tanks to be produced and all possible reserves to arrive.'*

That, however, is only part of the truth; there were numerous reasons why the execution of 'Operation Citadel' was repeatedly put off:

6 May 1943. To the director.

From Werther, Berlin, 2 May.

The re-formation of the mobile and armoured divisions is subject to delays. The deadlines for re-formation and readiness to move for the 60th mobile and the 16th armoured divisions have been postponed by four weeks because these units are insufficiently equipped with vehicles and tanks as a result of delayed deliveries.

Dora.

13 May 1943. To the director.

From Werther, 7 May.

The Germans have discovered significant concentrations of Russian forces near Kursk, Vyazma, and Velikiye Luki. The Wehrmacht high command considers it possible that the Russian high command is preparing preventive attacks for several sectors of the front simultaneously, each of the kind that Timoshenko launched against Kharkov last year to harass the German deployment.

Dora.

On 10 May I had sent off a similar report from Pakbo's sources to the effect that German front-line reconnaissance had discovered powerful Soviet troop concentrations in the Kursk sector and around Vyazma.

*Martin Gohring, *Bismarks Erben* ('Bismark's Heirs'), *1890—1945*, Wiesbaden. 1959, p. 383.

P

Lucy's Berlin people kept a close eye on the development and elaboration of the plan at German high command headquarters:

27 May 1943. To the director. Urgent.

From Werther, Berlin, 23 May.

1. In Kluge's and Manstein's army groups all preparations had been made by 20 May to get all second-line mobile and armoured units ready for action and send them up to the front. These troops will be on the alert on their lines of departure by 1 June.

2. The German high command intends to launch a limited-objective assault in the southern sector of the Soviet-German front in the first week of June. The purpose of this is to show the Russians that Germany is not worried about the situation in the west and that for the time being Russia is still fighting alone. The German high command is also concerned to chalk up some fresh military successes to bolster the morale of the German army and people.

Dora.

As both sides made their secret preparations, marshalling their forces in and around the Kursk salient, their respective intelligence and counter-intelligence services were engaged in a fierce duel of their own.

As far as the German military leadership was concerned, it was particularly important that 'Operation Citadel' should come as a surprise. They did everything they could to keep their troop concentrations secret for as long as possible and divert the attention of Soviet reconnaissance from the zone in which the army groups were getting ready for the attack.

At the same time German Intelligence was making tremendous efforts to ascertain the plans of the Soviet high command. We heard about this from Werther when he answered Central's question about which sections of the front the Germans were planning to attack:

28th May 1943. To the director. Urgent.

From Werther.

1. The army high command's plan may miscarry if the Russians, who have already repaired their lines of communication, attack swiftly and with great force south-west of Tula and in the Kursk region.

The German high command does not know and is trying to find out whether the Soviet military leadership is planning an attack in the middle sector of the Soviet-German front.

2. Since 15 April the Wehrmacht high command has had a special reserve in the Ukraine that does not come under Manstein's army group but is immediately subordinate to itself. This reserve includes the SS divisions 'Totenkopf', 'Reich', and 'Leibstandarte' that up until 15 April belonged to the newly-organized 6th army.

Dora.

The intelligence duel gave rise to a paradoxical and indeed tragic situation for the Germans: they knew that there were leaks in their mantle of secrecy, and they were powerless to plug them. In answer to Moscow's questions:

. . .Instruct Lucy and Werther to find out:

1. At which precise point of the southern sector of the eastern front is the German offensive going to begin?

2. With what forces and in what direction do they intend to make the thrust?

3. Apart from the southern sector, where and when are the Germans planning to attack on the eastern front?

I was able at the beginning of June to send off the following information:

2 June 1943. To the director. Urgent.

From Werther, Berlin, 29 May.

The execution of the German high command's operational plans for the Soviet-German front is running into steadily increasing military and organizational difficulties. The German high command has the impression that the Russians—from the way they are reacting to German troop movements—are determined to fight to maintain the front line as it is at present, to allow no German offensive to develop, and to strike hard wherever the German lines of communication favour their doing so.

So far the order to Manstein's army group to be on the alert on its lines of departure against Kursk by 28 May has not been revoked.

This is partly in consequence of the disturbing news that the morale of all Germany's allies is rapidly deteriorating.

The decisions made by the German high command since 10 May have been characterized by numerous contradictions, by an absence of political and military principle, and by bungling on a scale that is shaking people's confidence in it both in Germany and abroad. One has the impression that the German high command trusts neither its own strength nor its ability to arrive at right decisions.

As a defensive measure against the Red Army forces massed in the Kuban region the Germans have pulled their short-range air formations out of the Donets Basin and the Kerch peninsula and already engaged the greater part of them in the fighting. If this situation continues for any length of time, Manstein will be getting insufficient air support in the Rostov and Voroshilovgrad regions, and without adequate air support the 1st army cannot move into action.

Dora.

The purpose of the Red Army's massing troops in the Kuban region was to defeat the German army group on the Taman peninsula and gain control of the marshalling zone needed to retake the Crimea. That was one part of the plan of attack Soviet high command headquarters had worked out for the summer and autumn of 1943. The attacks launched against the Germans on the Kuban and subsequently in other sectors of the Soviet-German front enhanced the effect of the decisive battle of Kursk; they were intended, by pinning down a part of the enemy's forces, to make him nervous, rush him into making hasty decisions, and ultimately put off the beginning of 'Operation Citadel' for long enough to enable the Soviet high command to marshal its reserves and complete its preparations for repulsing the German offensive.

In this they were successful;

3 June 1943. To the director. Urgent.

From Werther.

The Germans were able to stem the Red Army breakthrough on the Kuban front to some extent only by means of counter-attacks involving heavy losses, and this only by engaging their second-line divisions and regiments.

Nearly half of Manstein's army group is involved in the fighting on the Kuban, including the coastal-defence troops from the southern Crimea and the north coast of the Sea of Azov. The Germans are in constant fear that the Soviet fleet will move against Feodosia and Kerch.

Dora.

The following telegram, too, brings out the uncertainty that had seized the German leadership:

11 June 1943. To the director. Urgent.

From Werther and Teddy, Berlin, 5 June.

Up until the change in the situation that took place at the end of May the German high command was planning to attack and break through the Soviet-German front with the following units: the 1st and 2nd tank armies, the 5th army, and the newly-organized XIth army corps consisting of five divisions and forming the assault wing of the 2nd army. It was not planned that all these units should attack simultaneously.

The German high command wanted first to launch a thrust against Voronezh and the lower Don with the 1st tank army and part of the 6th army.

Then around mid-May they were considering first throwing the 4th tank army and the XIth army corps against Kursk.

In spite of this indecision the alerted units of Manstein's army group are still on their lines of departure.

For the time being there are no concrete plans for offensive operations in the northern sector, between Leningrad and Lake Ilmen, or in the middle sector of the north-western front.

Dora.

Hitler's headquarters was also very disturbed about the unfavourable situation in the northern and middle sectors of the front, particularly in the area occupied by the divisions of Kluge's middle army group that were supposed to attack Kursk from the north:

23 June 1943. To the director. Urgent.

From Werther, Berlin, 17 June.

a) The battle positions of the Kluge army group's 4th army and particularly of the 2nd army have if anything deteriorated since 11 June because interrupted lines of communication mean that normal provisioning of the front is no longer secured.

b) Serious differences of opinion in the Wehrmacht high command. The Wehrmacht high command does not under any circumstances want to provoke a major Russian offensive in the middle sector of the front. It therefore considers that there is no longer any point in the German preventive attack in the southern sector planned for May and early June because it would probably trigger off a Russian counter-stroke in the middle sector of the front, where Russian concentration has been building up significantly since 1 June.

The attack on Kursk that the German high command was planning up until the end of May now looks riskier because the Russians have concentrated such powerful forces in the Kursk area since 1 June that the Germans can no longer talk in terms of superiority. Hitler, however, still wants an attack.

The attack in the Bolshov-Mzensk region is so far of only local significance, but because of the poor state of all German supply and communication lines in the Bryansk area it seriously threatens the security of the lines of defence north and south of Orel.

c) The Germans have discovered that the Red Army is carrying out troop concentrations between Belev, Kaluga, and Yuzhnov that constitute a threat to Kluge's army group.

Dora.

In spite of the various dangers and in spite of its misgivings, the German high command finally determined to take the decisive step. There was no putting off the date of the projected offensive any longer. It was already summer, and if the Germans wanted to achieve any serious results at the front they must act now.

The giants were in position, and we in Switzerland, with the help of our sources in Berlin and elsewhere, had done our bit to see that the Soviet giant was ready.

CHAPTER 33

'Aspirant' tries again

One morning in early August there was a ring at my door. My wife was out taking telegrams to the radio operators and my sons were at school, so my mother-in-law showed the visitor into my study. I offered him a seat but for the moment he preferred to stand.

'My dear Monsieur Radó,' he said abruptly in a tone of ironic merriment, 'don't you recognize me, then?'

I studied his broadly smiling face. I have a very poor memory for faces, but there was indeed something vaguely familiar about this one.

'Yves Rameau, alias Ewald Zweig, journalist,' he prompted. 'Forgotten me already? Paris. . .Kurt Rosenfeld. . .your famous Inpress!'

So it was. Yves Rameau, alias Ewald Zweig, alias 'Aspirant'—the scum the Gestapo had commissioned to try and infiltrate our group; we had known that for a long time. What could I do but put a good face upon this unexpected appearance of a self-styled 'old friend'?

As we behaved in the way people do who have not seen each other for a long time, talking of matters of no consequence and of shared acquaintances, I took a closer look at Rameau. He had not changed since the Paris days—a stocky, chubby-faced man in an excellently tailored suit; a self-satisfied, arrogant piece of work with whom I would much rather not have been conversing.

He took the proffered armchair, sprawled in it with his fat legs crossed, and gave his tongue the freedom of the air. He claimed, for example, to have two real pals—Joe Stalin and Al Dulles. I have no doubt he thought his bragging witty and was trying to get a rise out of me. Inwardly seething, I took it all with a smile. Nothing the man did was capable of surprising me, knowing as I did what he had stooped to in the past.

Ewald Zweig was born in Germany. The Kurt Rosenfeld of his

introductory remarks, a relative of his, was the man with whom I had founded the anti-Fascist news agency Inpress in Paris, and it was from Rosenfeld that I learned how Zweig had earned his living back at home. He had had a little scandal sheet and had collected various compromising items of information and documents concerning well-known public figures with which to blackmail the latter whenever a suitable opportunity arose. The business flourished and Zweig grew rich; his victims, trembling for their reputations, paid up and said nothing.

In 1933, as the Nazis began persecuting the Jews, Zweig fled to France, where he soon embarked on fresh ventures. It was not long before this skilful, bribable, totally unprincipled reporter found backers. He took French citizenship and assumed the name Yves Rameau.

Kurt introduced me to him in 1934, by which time he was already a well-known figure in Paris. He married an extremely beautiful emigrant Hungarian opera singer. He always had money—some of it undoubtedly from the coffers of the French secret service—he lived in style, and he threw brilliant dinner parties in his luxurious Paris flat. For my part I steered clear of him (so did Rosenfeld); there was something unsavoury about the air he breathed.

With the occupation of France in June 1940 Rameau offered his services to the new overlord. The Germans forgave him everything—the anti-Fascist articles he had written, his work for the French secret service, even his Jewish birth—and accepted. It was all the same to Zweig-Rameau whom he worked for—as long as they paid well.

His first appearance in Switzerland in his new capacity of Gestapo agent was in the spring of 1942, as I have recounted already (see Chapter 15). Then he had given out loudly in diplomatic, journalistic, and emigrant circles that he was a member of the underground resistance movement and a supporter of de Gaulle, sometimes even going as far as to state baldly that he was a Communist. Peddling stories of his heroic deeds and boasting of his prowess in escaping the clutches of the Gestapo in Paris, he had tried to pick up the trail of our group.

I had not seen him then; in fact I had not seen him since my move from Paris to Geneva in 1936, seven years before. I might have thought he would look me up sooner or later. But the Gestapo and the SD always waited carefully before playing their trump cards.

Rameau had been living in Switzerland for more than a year before his masters decided on an open confrontation.

And now here he was, this *agent provocateur,* this German agent, posing gaily and volubly as the 'good old friend and comrade in the common international fight against Nazism'.

He noticed, of course, that I did not believe a word of what he was saying, and possibly he suspected that I knew a few things about him, but I have to admit that his mask never slipped for a moment. Oozing self-assurance, he continued to play his role with an ability that must have been inborn.

I waited for his next move.

'Well, and how are things with you, Mr Radó?' I heard him ask with a jovial smile. 'Here am I talking my head off and you have said nothing at all. Forgive me—it's been such an age since I last saw you and your charming lady wife!'

He got up out of his chair, still gabbing away, and then abruptly turned to me and said: 'My dear Radó, I've come to see you on a most important matter.' The ironical smile disappeared from his eyes as he added: 'As important to you, I feel sure, as it is to me.'

In a conspiratorial whisper he started telling me about the Soviet intelligence group that had been blown in Paris, about how he had helped the people concerned and been forced to go into hiding from the Gestapo. Eventually they had caught him and packed him off to Vernet, a concentration camp on the Spanish border where he had made the acquaintance of an interned Soviet diplomat. He had managed to escape, however, and had got hold of a transmitter with which to contact Moscow, but he did not have a secret code. He ended by saying that he was in touch with the American consul in Geneva, to whom he could introduce me if I needed any help.

I informed him coldly that I was not interested, that I furthermore had urgent work to do, and that I therefore did not wish to take up any more of his time.

When the scoundrel had gone I sat down and began to think. What could he know about my work before the war? Obviously there was plenty he might have learned about my past and that of my wife. He might know that I was a Communist, for example, and that I had been in touch with the German Communist party during my time in Paris, That would not have meant a great deal, however, because the Germans did not need Rameau to tell them that I had been involved in the international working-class movement for years.

I was more concerned about something else. If Rameau was so soon in possession of details of the arrest of our people in France, the Gestapo had given him the information for a purpose—but how much had they given him? What had they got out of their prisoners? Did the Germans now know about our group, about our radio link with Moscow? What had been the purpose of Rameau's visit? To worm his way into my confidence? To scare me? Or just to snoop around? Had he perhaps counted on my not knowing he was a German agent? Had he hoped I would let the cat out of the bag by accepting his offer of an introduction to the American consul?

I informed Central that same night and soon had the director's answer:

7 August 1943. To Dora.

Yves Rameau is quite definitely a Gestapo agent. We are certain that the Gestapo was behind his visit, which we had anticipated and of which we had given you prior warning. He is trying to find out whether you have contact with us. Report in detail what he wanted of you. What did he know about you in Paris? You have to be very careful now. Give great thought to everything you say and do.

Director.

According to W.F. Flicke the Germans subsequently deciphered this telegram, so that from that point on they knew that their agent was blown. That would of course explain why Rameau never showed his face again; his employers evidently felt that there was no point in continuing this particular attempt at frightening us into downing tools for a while.

I should say at this point that even Central began to wonder whether, in view of the increasing precariousness of my situation implicit in this kind of Nazi provocation, it would not be better if I did in fact drop everything and disappear for a spell. Particularly during this period, however, with the fighting on the eastern front entering its most crucial phase, I could not conscientiously have entrusted the leadership of the group to anyone else. So I told

Central that, in spite of the growing danger, I thought it best that I should try and hold out for as long as possible.

Later Central told us that Zweig-Rameau-Aspirant not only worked for the 'Red Orchestra' Special Detachment in Paris but was also associated with the Deuxième Bureau of the French general staff (the Vichy government intelligence service) and with the Swiss secret service.

The Swiss agent Kurt Emmenegger, alias 'Q.N.' or 'Müller', quotes in his 1965 memoirs a report he made to his superior in Luzern on 28 July 1944: 'I know from reliable sources that a certain Yves Rameau is in the pay of the Swiss federal police [Bundespolizei or 'Bupo']. Rameau holds a special passport issued by the French [i.e., Vichy Fascist] authorities. His real name is Zweig, he is a German citizen, and he is an agent of the Gestapo. We [i.e., Swiss Intelligence] are expressly warned to avoid the man. Rameau is resident in Geneva. So far any action has been blocked by the personal intervention of Bundesrat von Steiger [the Swiss home secretary].... ' In a further memo of 26 November 1944 in confirmation of an oral report of 23 November, 'Q.N.' stated: 'This German agent enjoys Bupo protection and works for them. It was this Zweig, alias Rameau, who directed the Bupo's attention to the illegal Russian transmitters and as official delegate of the German authorities took steps against them in Berne [i.e., took the matter up with the Swiss government].'*

Let me take a little jump forward in time to complete the exposure of this corrupt provocateur. The scene is Paris and the time November 1944. The occasion: a mass meeting organized by the French to celebrate their liberation from the occupier. My wife and I went along. Suddenly, whom should we see bustling about the hall with pencil and reporter's notebook in his hand but—Yves Rameau! I do not think he had seen us. The then chief of the Paris police was a Communist. I got a message to him through some French comrades, telling him who Rameau was. In the interval the Gestapo agent was duly summoned from the hall, arrested, and carted off in a police car to the Cherche-Midi prison.

Not that he stayed behind bars for long. The Americans kicked up a great fuss about him, and a few days later the swine was free. I do not doubt he had found his new masters.

*Kurt Emmenegger, *Q.N. wusste Bescheid* (Q.N. was in the know'), Zurich, 1965, p. 93.

CHAPTER 34

How much did the F Bureau know?

We knew we were surrounded by *agents provocateurs,* we knew it was possible that our transmitters were being monitored, but what we did not know and could not know was that, as the archives now reveal, the Gestapo and the SD were themselves actively on the trail of our group.

By the summer of 1943 their agents had collected a wealth of material about us. Hans Peters, continuing his affair with Rosa, reported regularly to his superiors. And the F Bureau in Berne compared and analysed the information sent in by its other informants, who were keeping an eye on everyone they thought might be connected with the Soviet intelligence network operating in Switzerland.

The people at the F Bureau—Hans von Pescatore and Willy Piert and all the others whom Schellenberg had sent in after us—drew up a list of suspects. We know this from their depositions after the war, and we also know that, although they found out quite a bit, they by no means managed to unravel it all.

Their reports to SD headquarters in Berlin contained the names of all those whom they believed to belong to our group. A number of these were clearly derived from erroneous information, but the list included Rachel Dübendorfer, Otto Pünter, Sándor and Helene Radó, Edmond Hamel, Alexander Foote, and 'Rosa' (they did not know her real name). They knew that the last three operated the two transmitters in Geneva and the one in Lausanne. The list also gave our addresses and particulars (in Rosa's case these reached Berlin *via* Hans Peters and the Gestapo, independently of the F Bureau).

The Germans reckoned that I was the head of the group, and they thought that Pünter was my second-in-command. They knew a great deal about him in fact, but for some obscure reason they considered him to be chiefly responsible for the administrative and business side of the group's affairs.

Another thing they got completely wrong was the nature of the Sissy-Taylor-Lucy-Berlin connection—in other words the very group of informants that it was most important for the Abwehr to find and that they had already been groping after for six months. The only thing the F Bureau and the other Abwehr agencies had to go on was the part of our radio dialogue with Moscow that their experts had managed to decipher. On the basis of this Pescatore and Piert came to the conclusion that it was Sissy who headed Lucy's group of Berlin informants, and also that Sissy worked largely on her own, being only nominally subordinate to me, although she used the 'Dora' radio link to pass on her vitally important information. In fact they even thought that Sissy was not only in immediate touch with the mysterious Lucy but also somehow had a direct line to Werther, Olga, Teddy, and the other sources, possibly by means of a contact man in the German capital

But the greatest confusion in the minds of the Abwehr's 'experts' concerned the question of Lucy's identity. For all their enormous experience, their intuition, and the (admittedly contradictory) reports of their agents in every corner of Switzerland, Lucy remained as great a riddle to them as the other codenames.

As to how the information got to Lucy from the German general staff and the Wehrmacht high command, the staff of the F Bureau could put forward only one hypothesis: in their reports to Schellenberg they sought to show that the information did not reach Switzerland by radio but in all probability by diplomatic courier. According to Pescatore, the F Bureau further believed that Lucy and Taylor were one and the same person, for which there was not a shred of evidence.

All in all, then, although the Abwehr made a certain amount of headway as far as locating the members and radio operators of our group was concerned, they learned nothing of any importance about our sources—beyond their codenames, of course. Yet this, according to W.F. Flicke, had been their chief aim: first track down the sources, and only then eliminate the network.

August came, we were working in top gear, and in the vicinity of Kursk it was already becoming apparent that 'Operation Citadel' was going to be a flop on a grand scale. Given this situation, it is hardly to be wondered at that SD chief Walter Schellenberg lost his nerve. Realizing with dismay that his carefully worked-out strategy for tracing the 'Red Troika's' sources was not paying off, he decided that tougher, swifter action was called for. According to the terms of his pact with Masson, this was the job of the Swiss.

Central had for some time had an eye on this possibility and had asked me for my opinion back in June. I had found out what I could from sources close to the Swiss secret service and on 8 July informed the director as follows:

> ... *The Gestapo and the Swiss police do not work together. This is beyond doubt. Nevertheless there is still a chance that the Gestapo may draw the attention of the Swiss to us in future.*

Which is what happened, as we shall see.

CHAPTER 35

The Battle of Kursk

As June gave way to July the two combatants faced each other with enormously powerful concentrations of forces.

The Germans planned to throw a total of fifty divisions into their 'Operation Citadel'; a further twenty or so divisions were posted on the wings of the attacking army groups, ready to be rushed in to support the main force. In this way the German high command managed to engage more than a third of its eastern-front forces in the battle of Kursk.

Altogether some 900,000 German troops, nearly 10,000 guns and mortars, and 2,700 armoured vehicles and assault tanks were involved in 'Citadel'. The middle army group, attacking near Orel, was supported by the 6th air fleet with some 900 aircraft; the southern army group, attacking near Kharkov, had the 960 aircraft strong 4th air fleet to back it up. These units included 1,000 bombers, and a further 200 bombers were ordered up from other units. It was a mighty air force representing two thirds of the Luftwaffe units stationed on the eastern front.

In the night before the attack Hitler's appeal to the German soldiers was solemnly read out to the assembled troops: 'From today on you will be taking part in a major offensive the result of which may decide the outcome of the war. Your victory will more than ever convince the world that all resistance to the German army is ultimately futile .... The mighty blow that we are going to strike at the Soviet armies must shake them to their foundations.... Remember that everything depends on the issue of this encounter.'

The enemy had indeed placed all his hopes on the outcome of the battle of Kursk. For the German generals it was a matter of wresting the strategic initiative away from the Red Army and turning the course of the war in their favour.

On 5 July 1943 the Wehrmacht launched what was to be its last offensive on the eastern front. As W.F. Flicke bitterly observes:

'The very first day's fighting revealed how far out the Germans were in their estimate of the strength of the Soviet defences.' For the last three weeks it had been 'repeatedly brought to the notice of the Abwehr's radio monitoring service that the Russians were excellently informed as to every phase of the German preparations. They knew all the units that were at the front and standing by. German reconnaissance, on the other hand, was completely in the dark regarding the powerful concentration of forces taking place behind the Russian front in the salient between Orel and Belgorod.'*

The full extent of the inadequacy of German Intelligence on this crucial occasion emerged only after the German army had suffered a crushing defeat. It was not the Abwehr's first fiasco, but for some reason or another Admiral Canaris managed even this time to hold on to his job.

Whether or not Hitler or Himmler knew of this further failure of their secret service, the Wehrmacht was in top gear and there was no stopping it now. Not that it would have been impossible to change the plan of attack and regroup the German troops, but Hitler had pressing political and military reasons for not wanting to call off his summer offensive.

I do not propose to describe the battle of Kursk in detail; the interested reader will find plenty of literature on the subject. Let us instead follow the broad lines of the engagement as I and my people saw it in Berlin and Switzerland.

Lucy's Berlin informants kept a close eye on changes in the German high command's plans:

9 July 1943. To the director. Urgent.

From Werther, Berlin, 4 July.

The Germans have found out that, in response to the regrouping of Manstein's army now in progress, the Russians have marshalled powerful mobile forces in the Kursk region and to the east of Kharkov.

The Germans cannot allow further Soviet troop concentrations to take place to the west and south-west of Kursk because if the Russians launch an offensive there it will threaten the entire middle sector of the front.

*W.F. Flicke, *Agenten funken nach Moskau,* pp. 351, 350.

If an offensive is in preparation the Germans will be obliged to launch a preventive attack in order to steal a march on the Red Army before it can get its own attack under way and fall on the German defences in the middle sector. This would force the 3rd and 4th tank armies onto the defensive.

Dora.

Werther submitted this report on the very day when Hitler signed his appeal to the troops, less than twenty-four hours before the battle began. The exact time of the attack—set for 3 a.m. on 5 July—the Soviet high command learned from the deserters who crossed to the Soviet lines after the order to attack had been posted. This enabled the Soviet artillery to open fire on the enemy's batteries and observation posts before the German guns had got off a single shot.

What is particularly interesting about the report is the way it shows that the Abwehr had not managed to find out what the Soviet high command actually had in mind. Berlin was expecting the Russians to attack. And when the Soviet artillery suddenly opened up in the middle sector of the front, the Germans assumed that this was the preliminary to a large-scale offensive. In fact the Soviet plan was quite different: first the attacking enemy units were to be worn down in a series of defensive engagements, and only then was the Red Army to counter-attack.

As the following telegram shows, even on the second day of the battle the German high command was still not properly aware of what was going on in this sector of the front:

10 July 1943. To the director. Urgent.

From Werther, Berlin, 6 July.

a) A preventive attack by the German army had been considered but no order to this effect issued by 5 July, when the Red Army answered the German partial offensive in the Tomarovka region with a concentrated counter-attack. The Germans had launched this action on 4 July in divisional strength. Its purpose was to carry out a thorough reconnaissance, because the Germans are afraid that things will develop along the same lines as between Velikiye Luki and Dorogobush.

b) The army high command, after discovering the extent of the

Red Army's offensive action between Kharkov and Kursk, ordered the 2nd army to attack in the Kursk region.

On 6 July the German military leadership still sees the fighting as defensive and is bringing up fresh reserves, mainly via Kharkov, Lebedin, and Konotop. These reserves are being engaged cautiously, in exact proportion to the Russian pressure ....

Dora.

Suddenly the German generals realized to their dismay that they had misjudged the plans of the Soviet high command that the Red Army was not intending to attack for the time being. They immediately ordered their troops to storm the Russian positions:

11 July 1943. To the director. Urgent.

From Werther, Berlin, 7 July.

The army high command today launched a crucial attack on the Red Army's Kursk army group with the aim of encircling Kursk. The attack was made by the 4th tank army and parts of the 3rd tank army, now fully assembled in the Bryansk region. The army high command's first concern is to maintain superiority of strength on the thrust towards Kursk.

How the battle develops will depend on whether the Red Army high command decides to attack in the Kaluga and Smolensk regions, in other words whether it will allow the Germans to marshal virtually half of all their armoured divisions in the area between Orel and Volchansk.

To make sure of success the German high command is throwing in the greater part of the reserves belonging to Manstein's army group; these reserves are being brought up continually via Kharkov. The high command sees no danger to the right flank and the middle sector of Manstein's army group.

The German military leadership feels that the situation on the Orel-Bryansk line is less precarious because:

a) the Russian high command is hardly likely to launch a major offensive before there is some action in western Europe, and

b) Germany in any case stands to win nothing on the Soviet-German front by passive defence and is therefore forced to do something.

Dora.

An interesting point here is that the Germans hoped the Red Army would not venture to launch a major offensive as long as its allies failed to start anything serious in Europe. Here again the German strategists were mistaken. The Soviet troops delivered their crushing blows very much earlier.

For two whole days the Germans stormed the Russian lines without interruption—but also without much success, gaining on the northern front of the Kursk salient a total of ten kilometres, which they paid for with heavy losses.

Manstein's army, attacking the southern sector of the salient, also drove some way into the Russian defences but lacked the strength to break through. Several of the Germans' best divisions were destroyed in the fighting here. The German war historian Walter Görlitz has this to say about the defeat of the southern army group: 'Between 10 and 15 July powerful assault units of Field Marshal Manstein's army group succeeded in reaching the watershed between Don, Psyol, Seim, and Vorskla. Here their strength was exhausted . . . . The assault came to a standstill. Field Marshal Konev later spoke of the "swan song" of the German armoured divisions. The last battleworthy units were reduced to slag, and German armour was done for.'*

We heard about these losses at the time, in a report from another of Lucy's Berlin informants:

14 July 1943. To the director. Urgent.

From Teddy, Berlin, 11 July.

This information comes from the Wehrmacht high command operations staff.

1. The Wehrmacht high command has ordered air reconnaissance to keep day and night watch on Soviet troop movements in the Moscow-Tula and Kursk-Voronezh regions. To date the German high command's hopes that extensive Soviet forces would be moved from the Moscow-Tula region to the Kursk region have not been fulfilled. If the Germans fail to provoke this, the reserves earmarked for the western front and the Balkans will be kept on the Soviet-German front.

2. The 2nd and 4th tank armies are suffering unexpectedly heavy losses. Since 7 July half the attacking mobile and armoured

*Walter Görlitz, *Der Zweite Weltkrieg, 1939—1945*, vol. 2, p. 207.

divisions have had to be replenished with men and machines.

Dora.

As the first part of Teddy's report indicates, the Wehrmacht high command was certain that the fierce fighting in the Orel-Kursk-Belgorod salient would force the Soviet military leadership to strengthen its defences with divisions taken from other sectors of the front, in which case the Germans could throw in part of the reserves they had been keeping for the defence of their already threatened European frontiers.

Once again the Germans were mistaken. The Soviet high command had no need to withdraw troops from other fronts in order to defend the Kursk salient; it had sufficient forces there already, both for defensive purposes and for the subsequent attack. Here is further proof that the Germans had no precise information about the strength of the Soviet reserves marshalled in this vital area. They realized this to their horror a few days later, when they ran into a series of powerful counter-blows. Weakened by his costly advances, and having thrown practically all his reserves into storming the Kursk salient, the enemy was unable to parry those blows and began to retreat. By 23 July the lines between Orel, Kursk, and Belgorod were back as they had been before the German attack on 5 July.

'Operation Citadel', on which the German high command had placed such hopes and on which it had lavished such preparations, had collapsed. 'The last major German offensive in Russia,' writes Paul Carell, 'was finished, was lost .... As Waterloo sealed Napoleon's fate, ended his supremacy, and changed the face of Europe, so did the Russian victory at Kurst turn the tide of the war, leading directly, two years later, to Hitler's fall and, with Germany's defeat, the transformation of the whole world. Seen in this light, "Operation Citadel" was the decisive battle of the Second World War .... Not Stalingrad but Kursk [was] the fateful, crucial battle of the war in the east.'*

Marshall Zhukov likewise recognized the historical importance of the battle of Kursk in a passage in his memoirs: 'The crushing defeat of the main body of the German troops in the Kursk region paved the way for the subsequent broad offensive by the Red Army

*Paul Carell, *Verbrannte Erde*, p. 80.

that had as its aim to drive the Germans out of our [i.e., Soviet] territory, then out of Poland, Czechoslovakia, Hungary, Yugoslavia, Rumania, and Bulgaria, and after that to destroy Fascist Germany once and for all.'*

Even Field Marshal Manstein, former commander-in-chief of army group 'South', although he attempted to play down the Kursk disaster, acknowledged in the book he published after the war the fiasco it had represented for German strategy: ' "Operation Citadel" was the last German attempt to hold the initiative in the east. With its discontinuance, which was tantamount to failure, the initiative finally passed to the Soviets. To this extent "Citadel" was a decisive turning-point in the war in the east.'†

Finally we have the verdict of Winston S. Churchill himself: 'Three immense battles, of Kursk, Orel, and Kharkov, all within a space of two months, marked the ruin of the German army on the Eastern Front.'‡

One could go on for a long time, quoting the words of the Soviet Union's one-time allies in praise of the Red Army as well as the grudging, disillusioned statements of the defeated. What a pity that both parties were later to suffer so badly from loss of memory. Politicians and soldiers in particular should remember the lessons of the Second World War.

I quote Marshal Zhukov again, this time from an article published in Moscow in 1970:

'In an attempt to obscure the importance of the victory of the Soviet army a number of West German historians have raked up the old Nazi chestnut about the defeat of the Wehrmacht having been due to "treachery behind the front". "Moscow owed its victory to its spies" is the sort of way in which they represent the history of the battle of Kursk.

'What is the truth of the matter? In the spring of 1943 we got hold of—thanks to the brilliant work of Soviet Intelligence—a quantity of important data about the grouping of German troops preparatory to the summer offensive. After analysing this information and discussing it with the Voronezh and central-front

*G.K. Zhukov, *Memoirs and Reflections,* p. 506.

†Erich von-Manstein, *Verlorene Siege,* p. 473.

‡Winston S. Churchill, *The Second World War and an Epilogue of the Years 1945 to 1957,* Cassell, London, 1959, p. 715.

commanders and with chief of general staff A.M. Vassilevsky, we were able to draw from the enemy's probable plans certain conclusions that subsequently turned out to be correct. On the basis of those conclusions we worked out our plan for the battle of Kursk, and that plan likewise proved to be successful. First the Soviet troops wore down the enemy in defensive engagements; then, switching to the offensive, they smashed the enemy army groups in pieces.

'We cannot, however, regard the work of our intelligence service, excellent though it was, as having been the sole decisive factor behind our victory in the Kursk salient. Anyone with the slightest knowledge of strategy will be acquainted with the ingredients of success in war: reliable assessment of the overall situation, choosing the right direction of one's main thrust, a well-thought-out battle order, precise coordination of all services, self-confident and well-trained troops, adequate material and technical supplies, determined yet flexible command, modern mobility, and a host of other things besides are necessary if victory is to be achieved. All these elements together constitute the art of modern warfare. Only the fact that officers and men at every level of command were in possession of that art made it possible for them to carry off the magnificent victory of Kursk. That victory was the product of the experience of all officer ranks, careful preparation, determined execution of the plan prepared, and the heroism of the soldier masses of the Soviet army. An efficient intelligence service was a further factor in the sum total of factors making for success in this colossal engagement.'*

That hits the nail on the head, of course. As every serious war historian knows, the fortunes of war are in the final analysis decided on the battlefield. Intelligence work, although an extremely important part of military organization and one that gives the high command material assistance in the execution of its plans, is not of itself able to determine the outcome of hostilities.

*G.K.Zhukov, 'The glorious victory of the Soviet Union and the impotence of historical forgery', in *Communist,* Moscow, 1970, no. 1, pp. 80-94.

CHAPTER 36

The Eastern Rampart overrun

Following the catastrophe of Stalingrad and the successful advance of the Soviet troops—in the early months of 1943 they broke through the front in numerous places—the Germans, desperately worried about the worsening situation, hurriedly began constructing a strategic line of defence running from the Baltic to the Black Sea, the so-called *Ostwall* or 'eastern rampart', with which Hitler hoped to bring the Red Army to a standstill.

I mentioned before (see Chapter 25) how Central, familiar by now with what Lucy's Berlin sources could do, asked us back in March 1943 to find out all we could about the 'eastern rampart', work on which had already begun at that time. This information, if we could get hold of it, would help the general staff enormously in working out its plans for the offensive. make it easier for our troops to demolish the enemy's defences, and so save the lives of tens of thousands of Soviet soldiers.

We duly passed the assignment on to Lucy, but even his Berlin people had trouble finding what we needed; the 'eastern rampart' files were kept separately in special safes and were very difficult to get hold of.

It was Teddy who agreed to do it. Around the middle of April, however, he sent word that he was not able for the moment to take the secret documents out for copying. Instead of the actual documents he promised to send us detailed information about the plans for the rampart. The risk involved was enormous and Teddy had to proceed slowly and cautiously.

Finally, after about a fortnight, he passed Lucy some valuable data concerning fortifications in the northern part of the line:

30 April 1943. To the director. Urgent.

Very important: plan of the "eastern rampart'.

From Teddy.

a) In the northern sector of the rampart 2 lines are being constructed:

1. an anti-tank line, and
2. a line of defence.

b) The anti-tank line lies in the approaches to the defence zone and is designed to take units of up to infantry-division strength.

The line of defence forms the front line of the defensive sector. Its fortifications are for the most part staggered to a depth of only 10 km. . . .

Points c) and d) of the telegram go on to describe how the line of defence and the anti-tank line lie, ending:

. . .Blockhouses, wooden bunkers, and tank traps are being erected all over the approaches to the 'eastern rampart' as well as on the line of defence.

e) The orders received by construction group 'North' reveal an intention to conduct strategically important defensive engagements between the anti-tank line and the line of defence in the hope that the majority of the Soviet tanks and assault guns will not get as far as the latter.

Dora.

6 May 1943. To the director. Urgent.

From Teddy, Berlin, 1 May.

1. A largish consignment of railway guns is on its way to Russia. It comprises 203 mm and 280 mm long-range cannon as well as some French fortress guns and 152 mm and 203 mm naval guns. All are destined for the fortifications in the rear combat zone to complete the 'eastern rampart' fortifications system.

Some for example are headed for the fortifications along the Dnepr south of Kiev where railway battalions are laying some quite long railway lines. These branch off the main line west of Kharkov and south of Kiev and run to the west bank of the Dnepr. New railway guns are also being dispatched to the Dvinsk region and the Crimea.

2. The Germans are continuing to assemble further tank platoons, most of them for the 'eastern rampart' fortifications system.

Dora.

The Red Army general staff mobilized its reconnaissance units along the entire front as well as the partisan intelligence groups operating in the enemy's rear to complete its picture of the German army's plans to dig itself in. These reported where fortifications and anti-tank obstacles were being constructed, made sketch maps of the line of defence, blew up targets here and there, and derailed trains that were bringing up weapons and equipment for the 'eastern rampart'. The Soviet air force, now that it knew where the line of defence ran, bombarded it from the air.

I reported one of the partisans' successes in the following telegram:

16 May 1943. To the director.

From Olga.

At the end of April Russian partisans blew up a train between Vilnyus and Minsk, killing several hundred soldiers of the reserve detachment of the 241st East Prussian artillery regiment. This regiment belongs to the 161st infantry division.

Dora.

So the Soviet high command had a pretty good idea of the German defensive system in the spring of 1943—before the battle of Kursk began. This enabled it to prepare its troops accordingly and plan the thrusts that broke through the German defences in many places.

That summer and autumn the German line of defence proved incapable of halting the Red Army, nor were the Germans able to mobilize the necessary reserves for a counter-offensive. In blow after powerful blow the Soviet troops smashed the 'eastern rampart' to pieces and drove the enemy back towards the west.

The reports coming in from our Berlin informants gave us a vivid picture of the disastrous situation of the German army, retreating precipitately in all sectors of the front. The German military leadership was clearly in a state of nervousness bordering on panic, no longer capable of organizing resistance. I quote a telegram from that period:

1 September 1943. To the director. Urgent.

From Werther, Berlin, 28 August.

The order to withdraw the base organizations in the southern sector can probably not be executed. A planned retreat is practically impossible because Red Army pressure is increasing, losses in the whole Donets salient are high, and the Soviet air force is stepping up its activities in the German rear. Disbandment of the front can be temporarily achieved only by deciding to sacrifice the troops on the Kramatorsk-Gorlovka line of defence and in the Voroshilovsk region.

As of today the southern wing of the Donets front is in process of disbandment. South of Stalino and Makeyevka there is no line of defence prepared. It was to have been the fortified line of the River Miuss, but the Russians crossed that on 23 August. The concentrated counter-attacks near Senkov and Valki were frustrated by the superiority of the Russian troops. Preparations have been put in hand to evacuate Bryansk by detailing rear-guards to hold off the enemy and setting up bases on the eastern arc of the Desna along the line Shukovka-Trubchevsk.

Dora.

There was no stopping the advance of the Red Army. Soviet troops crossed the Dnepr, the Soch, the Desna, the Pripet, and the Beresina; they established a bridgehead on the Kerch peninsula from which to retake the Crimea; they harried the retreating Germans in the southern and middle sectors with a series of powerful frontal and flanking assaults; and as they went they liberated large numbers of Soviet towns and villages from the nightmare of occupation.

CHAPTER 37

The satellites start to waver

The series of major defeats suffered by the Germans on the eastern front shook the morale of even the most militant members of the Axis alliance. Their leaders, once in awe of the might of the Reich and its superbly disciplined army, no longer believed in a German victory. The political situation in the satellite countries became increasingly unstable as their peoples groaned under the burdens and privations of war. In the Mediterranean theatre too Hitler and Mussolini were losing one battle after another.

We endeavoured to keep Central regularly informed about the situation in Europe. Our main task was as before to collect strategic intelligence bearing on the Soviet-German front, but an important part of our work consisted in gathering information about the plans and operations of the Fascist bloc in the west, since this served to fill out usefully the general picture of events.

On 13 May 1943 the rump of Rommel's shattered Italo-German divisions surrendered in North Africa. They had been Mussolini's and Hitler's last hope. The North African front was a thing of the past.

On 15 May I passed on a report from Werther concerning certain details of the fall of Tunis, the last Axis bridgehead in Africa:

. . . Between 5 and 11 May only 3,000 soldiers managed to get out of Africa and over to Italy. The Germans' last Africa reports speak of the superior firepower of the new British Churchill tank and of the British armoured artillery, most of which is now equipped with American 105 mm assault guns.

Italy was threatened with invasion—a prospect that caused immense consternation at all levels of Italian society.

'Grey', our man in the Vatican, learned that the Pope had advised the Italian king to approach the English king and

Roosevelt direct and ask for an armistice before the Allies landed in Italy, as they were expected to do any day.

Hitler's other satellites were similarly disturbed:

21 June 1943. To the director.

Via Long, from a Hungarian diplomat who works at the embassy in Berne and has recently returned from a trip to Budapest.

1. Bakach [full name: Georgy Bakach-Bessenyey], *the Hungarian ambassador in Vichy, has been back to Budapest to persuade Kállay of the necessity of concluding peace with Russia. Bakach hopes to become Hungarian foreign minister.*

2. Ninety per cent of the Hungarian population is fiercely anti-German. The majority of Hungarian politicians want Kállay to break with Germany openly, but Kállay thinks the time is not yet ripe.

3. At his last meeting with Horthy Hitler demanded that a special detachment of the German general staff be accommodated in Budapest under the protection of German troops and that the Hungarian arms industry answer for a larger share of the production of war material for Germany. Horthy is disinclined to meet these demands.

Dora.

Our present knowledge of the situation in Hungary at that time reveals the second point of the above telegram to have been an exaggeration, no doubt due to wishful thinking.

Dissatisfaction with and resistance to the Nazi system was also building up in the countries Germany had conquered and occupied, notably in France. For example 'Diemen', a contact of Sissy's in Vichy, reported that in his opinion no more than five per cent of the population of France supported the Vichy regime and approved of its collaborating with Germany. Sympathy with the Soviet Union was gaining ground among the people.

He further informed us that sizeable groups of French partisans were active in the towns of Haute Savoie, Cantal, and Drôme and that they were in radio contact with London.

The activities of the Maquis were directed by the Conseil National de la Résistance, a body to which a number of political parties including the Communist party belonged. At the instigation of the Communist party the Council began to make preparations for a national insurrection, coordinating its efforts with those of General de Gaulle's Comité Français de la Libération Nationale. Eventually an agreement was reached under which all patriotic organizations working for the liberation of France were to join forces. Contact with London (where de Gaulle was based) was maintained through the Gaullist intelligence network.

Keeping in touch with the *maquisards* in Haute Savoie was no problem for us because we had only to slip across the frontier near Geneva. But we also maintained contact with other partisan organizations waging the common struggle against Fascism. Occasionally delegates would get through to Switzerland from the Italian and even from the Yugoslav partisans, showing quite astonishing skill in dealing with all the countless obstacles involved, and I would detail a member of my group to meet them. They were a useful source of information about what was going on in their areas.

From their reports as well as from the reports of other sources it emerged that Fascist Italy, Hitler's staunchest ally, was in the grip of a military and political crisis of unprecedented proportions. The spring of 1943 brought spreading discontent among the masses, increasingly powerful strike movements in industry, and a wave of anti-war demonstrations throughout the country. There was disunity even in the ranks of the Fascist party, with many members making no secret of the fact that they thought Italy should withdraw from the war. Mussolini's purges did no good; by then a powerful movement of opposition to his leadership had crystallized in the governing class, in the general staff, and in the various political parties.

Information coming in during that summer indicated that the days of the Fascist regime in Italy were numbered. Long reported that the feeling in Italian diplomatic circles was that Italy would be out of the war within three months.

It was likewise through Long's anti-Fascist contacts that I heard the Italian opposition had split into two camps: the Catholics followed the Vatican in wanting an alliance with the United States, their contacts with the US government being Cardinal Spellman and the US ambassador to the Vatican, Myron Taylor; the Liberals, the Socialists, and the Communists wanted to go in with England. All opposition groups were demanding that the king pull Italy out of the war and get rid of Mussolini immediately, threatening to organize a campaign of terrorism and assassination if he did not.

One of the sources Long had been in regular contact with for a long time told us about some more goings-on behind the scenes at the Vatican:

22 June 1943. To the director.
Via Long.
According to a letter that Vatican secretary of state Maglione has sent the Jesuits in Switzerland, Italy is already trying to create the kind of atmosphere that will put her in a better position than Germany in the peace negotiations to come. Italy is being supported in these efforts by the Vatican and by the British ambassador to the Vatican. Apparently even Mussolini thinks the war is lost and is prepared to cooperate with the king in setting up a new regime. Mussolini and the Vatican are looking into the possibility of a rapprochement with Poland, whom they would like to use as mediator. Mussolini saw the Polish ambassador to the Vatican at the end of May.

Dora.

Mussolini did indeed believe the war was lost. This emerges from his correspondence with Hitler, which was published shortly after the war. In his letter of 25 March 1943, for example, Il Duce, while assuring the Führer that Italy was prepared to 'pursue the war until the ultimate victory', added: 'It is my conviction that the destruction of Russia is an impossibility, even in the unlikely event of Japan's entering the war.'*

The Germans too realized that, with Italy incapable of conducting serious hostilities, their ally was no longer to be relied on. To meet this changed situation the German military leadership swiftly modified its strategic concept, as I learned in June:

7 June 1943. To the director.
From Werther.

**Les lettres secrètes échangées par Hitler et Mussolini*, Paris, 1946, pp. 184-5.

a) The Wehrmacht high command is significantly reducing the number of German troops stationed in Italy and has in effect abandoned its earlier standpoint whereby Italy was to constitute a bulwark against the Allied assault on Europe.

Having surrendered the western Mediterranean the, German military leadership is now concentrating its defence strategy on the Balkans. It is acting on the assumption that the Allies will land in Italy shortly and in the conviction that Russo-Anglo-American adhesion will require an assault on the Wehrmacht's Balkan positions once the Allies have conquered southern Italy.

b) The German high command is making preparations to merge the 2nd air fleet with the weakened German air force units currently in the Balkans.

c) Kesselring has been withdrawing the Luftwaffe from northern Sicily and southern Sardinia since 25 May.

Dora.

28 June 1943. To the director.

From Werther.

a) As a result of the heavy Allied air raids beginning on 14 June the Italian defences in western Sicily had collapsed completely by 15 June. Roads and railways have been damaged so extensively that the Italian mobile units concentrated near Calatafimi and Salemi can no longer be put into action. The Germans believe the chief aim of the Allied air bombardment is to soften up the west coast of Sicily for a landing.

b) Allied air action is clearly aimed at cutting off Sardinia, Sicily, and Calabria completely. German fighter units have been moved down to airfields in Apulia. At the request of the Germans Italy is building fortifications along the Strait of Otranto coast. This is being done because the Germans fear an Allied attack on north-west Greece, Corfu, and Albania. The Germans are having to use coercion to get the Italians to cooperate. The Wehrmacht high command has already given up Sicily, which interests it only in so far as, like the whole of Italy, it constitutes a strategic approach to the Balkans.

Dora.

For once the German generals were right; events in the Mediterranean unfolded almost exactly as they had supposed they would. The Italian fleet, virtually confined to harbour by the superior strength of the Allied navies, offered no resistance, thereby facilitating the Allied landing in Sicily.

The island was to play the role of a bridgehead for the conquest of Italy. The fighting there, which began on 10 July, was not over until 17 August. In other words two large armies consisting of thirteen British and American divisions took well over a month to clear the island of a far smaller quantity of Italian and German troops. Jon Kimche is to the point here: 'The Allied advances were proceeding with agonizing slowness. . . . The Germans were preparing to withdraw because they felt themselves too weak to halt the Allied advance—but the Allies would not advance.'* What is more, the Allies had launched the invasion at a time when the Red Army was belabouring the cream of the Wehrmacht in the Kursk salient, so that the German high command, unable to withdraw a single division from the Russian front to help out its desperate ally, was having on the contrary to pull its last reserves out of Europe and send them east.

I referred to the military situation in Italy in a telegram of 22 July:

> *. . . Both the time and place of the landing in Sicily took the Axis by surprise. The Germans reckon Italy will have fallen by the end of August. An attempt is being made to build fortifications on the Po, but not even the Germans are taking this seriously.*

Twelve days earlier, on 10 July, I had forwarded a report to the effect that Mussolini's government would be out within a fortnight at most. I always condensed as much as possible when encoding, so instead of putting 'within a fortnight' I put a date: 25.VII. The days went by, with the Allies already landed in Sicily, and still the Fascists were in power. The twenty-fifth of July arrived; that evening I went out myself to the villa on the outskirts of town with the latest batch of urgent telegrams already encoded for Edouard to send off, and on the way back I remember cursing myself for having made my 'prophecy' so precise. I got home—it was after midnight—switched on the radio, and there was the news I had been waiting for: the king had dismissed Mussolini, a new

*Jon Kimche, *Spying for Peace*, p. 110.

government had been formed under Marshal Badoglio, and Il Duce had immediately been put under arrest.

So my date turned out to have been right after all. And next morning, as I left the house, I was amused to see a large portrait of Mussolini sticking out of my neighbour's dustbin, my neighbour being the Italian consul—only recently an 'ardent' Fascist.

By getting rid of Mussolini the king and the upper middle class hoped to kill two birds with one stone: they thought they could prevent an outburst of popular anger in the country and at the same time secure an amnesty from the British and Americans. Their calculations went astray, however, as disturbances broke out in cities up and down the country.

Furthermore the presence of German troops in Italy was like a sword of Damocles above the heads of Badoglio and his government. The following telegram reflected the situation in Italy immediately after Mussolini's fall:

8 August 1943. To the director.

From Werther, 7 August.

a) Richthofen is still in Italy but in view of events and in consequence of a fresh directive from the Wehrmacht high command he has not yet replaced Kesselring as commander of the 2nd air fleet. It is possible Richthofen will return to southern Russia or that he will set up his headquarters in the Balkans.

b) The Wehrmacht high command has decided to maintain the present combat strength of the 2nd air fleet on the Italian airfields by means of reinforcements. Restoring the original combat strength of the 2nd air fleet is neither projected nor possible.

c) The Wehrmacht high command has allowed Laval to organize French regiments against the danger of Italy's defecting. One such regiment has been in existence since 20 July; a second is currently being organized. Rundstedt will have to use these regiments to replace the Italians in France.

d) The Wehrmacht high command informed Badoglio on 29 July that it reserved to itself every possible means of preventing the Allies from gaining a foothold in Italy or Italian-occupied areas.

e) Göring visited Italy on behalf of the Wehrmacht high command on 29 July and apparently met Badoglio.

Dora.

R

The Italian government, determined at all costs to stay in power, pursued secret negotiations with the Anglo-American military leadership, and on 3 September the armistice was concluded that called for Italy's unconditional surrender. Five days later the Allies broadcast the agreement over the radio. And on the same day, 8 September, the king, the government, and practically the entire military leadership, fearing their former ally's vengeance, fled to the south of the country and the protection of the Allied troops. By then the Allies had already landed on the mainland and were driving the Germans northwards.

Before the landing I heard from one of Lucy's sources that Taranto and the region around it had been completely evacuated by the Germans and that no serious resistance was to be expected there. I gave the report to Pakbo for coding—but that was not all he did with it. As he later confessed, he took a copy straight round to Mrs Wiskeman (I believe that was her name), the press attaché at the British embassy in Berne, who scrambled it with the embassy code and sent it off to London. A few days later the Allies took Taranto—a naval base—without striking a blow, and Mrs Wiskeman communicated to Pakbo her country's undying gratitude (I believe that was what he said).

Furious at Italy's betrayal, Hitler ordered the country occupied in order to halt the Anglo-American advance. The German mobile divisions, encountering no resistance to speak of from the Italian army, duly occupied the Apennine peninsula from the Alps to Naples. In the northern part of the country the Germans set up a Fascist puppet state called the Italian Social Republic and put Mussolini, who was freed by German paratroopers on 12 September, at its head.

The Anglo-American troops made extraordinarily slow progress. Despite the fact that the Allies had twice the amount of infantry, artillery, and tanks and several times the air power, the Germans managed to put up a successful defence. Jon Kimche again: 'The months rolled on, and the Allies crept up the peninsula with painful slowness.'*

Or as the Buro Ha's December report put it: the Italian working man could not and would not accept that the Anglo-American troops could not have moved faster had the Anglo-American

*Jon Kimche, *Spying for Peace,* pp. 110 f.

leadership wanted them to.* In December the front stabilized in central Italy.

In the Hungarian history of the war I have quoted a number of times already we read: 'The hesitancy and subsequent total suspension of Allied operations in Italy compelled Molotov, the people's commissar for foreign affairs, to ask US ambassador Harriman to communicate to his government the extreme puzzlement of the Soviet government, Soviet public opinion, and the Soviet military leadership at the non-progress of military operations in Italy. Despite clear numerical superiority the Allies had shown no sign of combat activity for a long time and had failed to keep their promises regarding the operations to be carried out in Italy. All this had made it possible for the German Fascist military leadership to throw further reinforcements across to the Soviet-German front.'†

The British and American governments, however, ignoring Molotov's message, pushed their Italian advance no further in 1943. It was already apparent then that leading circles in Britain and America favoured postponing a decision in Italy in order to weaken the Red Army. The Swiss group sent Central several reports to this effect.

Be that as it may, by the autumn of 1943 there was a yawning breach in the monolith of Fascism: Hitler had lost his chief allies. From then on Nazi Germany was fighting virtually on its own, not only on the eastern front but also in southern Europe. Defeat was already throwing its dark shadow over the Third Reich:

18 September 1943. To the director.

From Agnes.

Official circles in Berlin are for the first time beginning to acknowledge the possibility of the collapse of the eastern front. The reserves are exhausted. All commanders are complaining of the poor morale of their troops.

Dora.

*See Alphonse Matt, *Zwischen allen Fronten,* p. 205.

†*History of the Great Patriotic War of the Soviet Union, 1941-45* (Hungarian) vol. 3, p. 470.

CHAPTER 38

The Swiss join the hunt

The occupation of northern Italy by the Germans came as a shock to Switzerland. Anglo-American help was as yet a mere promise, and the little republic now had German troops on all four frontiers. Neutrality, independence, freedom, and peace all hung by a hair. And although the Swiss made every effort not to offend their insatiable northern neighbour—German munitions transports still sped through the country unhindered on their way to Italy, and Swiss industry continued to turn out war material for the Reich—responsible circles in the confederation were aware that, far from having diminished, the danger had greatly increased.

Colonel Masson, who was still in touch with Schellenberg, insisted that the plan for occupying Switzerland had been definitely abandoned. General Guisan, however, was convinced that in the summer of 1943, following Mussolini's fall, Switzerland was in desperate peril.* With the German leadership jittery after its defeats on the eastern and southern fronts, anything was possible. Any pretext might be taken to order the occupation of Switzerland, or the Germans might demand free passage for their troops to ensure the defence of Italy. The Swiss government would have refused, of course—and it would have been war. The Swiss army was on the alert, but the leaders of the country were under no illusion as to its ability to hold out for any length of time. There was nothing for it but to make one concession after another and so preserve the country's usefulness as far as the Nazis were concerned.

It was just about this time that the Swiss police and Swiss Counter-intelligence received orders to track down our organization. The Germans would appear to have put heavy pressure on Masson, possibly even threatening sanctions against Switzerland. On the other hand, however, no pressure may have been necessary. The West German war historian Wilhelm von Schramm suggests:

*See Jon Kimche, *Spying for Peace,* p. 113.

'In the autumn of 1943 it [i.e., the activity of our intelligence group] was becoming too much for the Swiss as well, particularly for the government, to which the federal police was subordinate. . . . The Russian successes were so enormous as to constitute a threat to central Europe. . . . It is not out of the question that the head of American Counter-intelligence, Allen W. Dulles, himself took steps in Berne. Before the invasion they [the Allies] could not tolerate central Europe falling into Soviet hands.'*

There is documentary evidence to the effect that the Swiss police began looking for us on 9 September, the day after Italy's surrender had been announced and German divisions started marching into Italy. This is interesting. It suggests strongly that events in Italy, constituting as they did a threat to Switzerland's neutrality, finally persuaded Masson to take the decision that Schellenberg and Himmler had been pressing for for so long.

The Swiss began by looking for our transmitters. Here the Germans may have given them the preliminary findings of their own monitoring activity: two transmitters in the Geneva area or in the city itself, one in Lausanne. A special radio-reconnaissance unit was set up by Swiss Counter-intelligence under the command of Lieutenant Maurice Treyer and equipped with three short-range monitoring devices mounted on lorries. Treyer posted his monitors at three points on the outskirts of Geneva with orders to listen in for us around the clock.

Between the static interference and the familiar call-signs of the Swiss army's transmitters they soon distinguished some alien Morse signals. The monitoring devices immediately gave them the wave-bands and approximate position of the illegal station concerned, and Lieutenant Treyer reported to his superiors that one transmitter had been picked up and that he was trying to pinpoint its location. The lorries began cruising slowly through the streets of Geneva, closing in on the spot from three directions.

As we know from Lieutenant Treyer's log book and from what he told Jim after the arrests, the Swiss first picked up Edouard and Maude's transmitter on 11 September. A fortnight later they already knew more or less where our two Geneva sets were: one in the neighbourhood of the route de Florissant, the other in the

*Wilhelm von Schramm, 'Die rot-weisse Kapelle', in the *Frankfurter Allgemeine Zeitung*, 13 December 1966.

densely-populated city centre, probably in the rue Henri-Mussard.

Meanwhile, knowing nothing of all this, Edouard, Maude, and Rosa worked on night after night. My reports during this period dealt not only with southern Europe but also with the theatre of operations in the far north, because what was happening there affected the northernmost sector of the eastern front:

19 September 1943. To the director.
From Werther.
The purpose of the German attack on Spitzbergen was to cover up the troop withdrawals from Norway. Practically all units that were not in the coastal bases between Namsos and Mosjøen, Ranfjord, Foldenfjord, and Satefjord have been pulled out. Coastal defence between Namsos and Tromsø has been shifted entirely to the island and fortified bases. Bases left in the evacuated area are at Namsos, Tosnø, Vikten, Brøten, on Røros Island, and in ten other places. These are garrisons and combat units with strengths of between 500 and 2,000 men. An exception is Narvik, with a division and several smaller units. The bases in the evacuated coastal region are being held by a total of 20,000 men. . . .

On the eastern front the advancing Red Army was driving the enemy from Soviet territory. Werther reported:

. . . As of 15 September Manstein's army group can be regarded as beaten. In the period since 15 August it has lost half its equipment and heavy guns and 40 per cent of its strength or a total of some 250,000 men. . . .

It was again through Werther that we learned what countermeasures the Germans were taking:

24 September 1943. To the director.
From Werther, 20 September.
The Wehrmacht high command has decided to pull its eastern-front supply organization back to and behind the 'eastern rampart'. This partially fortified line is the so-called tank-buster line planned in January. Deviating from the January plan, however, they are not going to pull their supply organization in the western Ukraine back to the Dnestr but intend to wait to see how enemy pressure develops in the eastern Dnepr salient and up

to the line Sarny-Korosten-Kiev-Cherkassy-Voznesensk-Dnepr mouth.

The plans forsee completion of the withdrawal to the approaches to the 'eastern rampart' by 1-5 November. These new decisions do not affect the plan to hold up the Russian advance by organizing resistance in improvised retreat and rear positions, e.g., at the Dnepr bridgeheads and in the Dnepr salient between Kremenchug and Krivoyrog.

Dora.

On 25 September Soviet troops retook Smolensk. Again it was Werther who was our source for the following:

. . . The Germans beat a hasty retreat from Smolensk after having destroyed the lines of communication in the hinterland north of the railway line to Vitebsk.

In the defensive fighting around Smolensk from 15 September on the 5th and 18th armoured divisions and the 8th-10th infantry divisions suffered heavy losses.

In giving up Smolensk the Germans have lost their strongest focus of resistance on the Soviet-German front since Orel. . . .

We were even busier than usual during this time, owing to the fact that so much material had piled up. All four operators were having to work every night. (Jim returned from his 'holiday' in the Ticino at the end of September and began sending again straightaway.) The transmitters were on the air for two, three, and even four hours at a time with only short pauses. Here are four of the last telegrams to go out of Geneva:

29 September 1943. To the director.

From Werther.

The Wehrmacht high command considers it possible that the Russian high command may very soon attack the Lake Ilmen-West Dvina and Kieve-Kremenchug lines in full force, piling on the tanks and mobile divisions, and that the attack may be pushed as far as the Gulf of Riga in the north and Odessa and the lower and middle Dnestr in the south before winter sets in; in the central sector the Russians will probably economize on troops and weapons. The Wehrmacht high command regards this as the most dangerous plan of all as far as the German army in its present condition and situation is concerned. The Wehrmacht high command has rejected the proposal put forward by Kleist and Küchler and is determined for political reasons not to rush things, not even after having lost Smolensk. Its feeling is that the longer the advanced German wings in the north-east and south-east hold out, the better the chance of braking the Russian advance in the middle sector. The Russians are inadequately informed as to the firepower of the German wings, and the less concern the Wehrmacht high command shows about what happens to its flanks, the higher the Russians will tend to rate their defensive strength.

Dora.

30 September 1943. To the director.

From Werther.

a) Following the transfer of German troops from Croatia to northern Italy, the German arms and ammunition dumps in the Ljubljana region, northern Dalmatia, and Croatia have fallen into the hands of Tito's partisans. This has turned the partisans into an effective army.

b) According to German estimates Tito's partisan army consists of 70,000 to 80,000 Croats plus an Italian force of 50,000 men. Since 9 September he has received significant reinforcements from the Zagreb government's police force. This government now controls only 20 per cent of the Croatian region.

Dora.

Werther further sent word at the end of September that the Wehrmacht high command no longer believed it could successfully defend the line Novosokolniki-Vitebsk-Orsha-Mogilev. The general staff had reported that the partisans put the Russians at an advantage in Byelorussia. At Vitebsk and Orsha the Germans were putting up only delaying resistance in order to gain time and postpone withdrawal of the front to the 'eastern rampart' until November. They reckoned that if they could manage to block the Russian attack on the Molodechno-Polotsk-Pskov railway line, this would make a Russian breach of the 'eastern rampart' between Minsk and Dvinsk that winter impossible or at best very difficult.

10 October 1943. To the director.
From Olga, 7 October.
a) Hitler recently moved his headquarters to Rovno.
b) Since 20 September the German troops in Volhynia have been proceeding with extreme brutality, burning whole villages to the ground with the aim of providing maximum security for Rovno, Dubno, and Lutsk, the present centres of German administration and economic organization in the Ukraine.

Dora.

11 October 1943. To the director.
From Werther, 8 October.
The Germans are reckoning with very big war-material losses in the Vitebsk region. They have only the road to Polotsk for moving out their heavy stuff.

Dora.

All this time our Morse signals were literally leading the Swiss monitoring crews to their prey. The circle was being drawn tighter and tighter. Treyer's lorries were already cruising in the vicinity of the houses where Edouard, Maude, and Rosa sat at their sets. The 'voices' of the quarry were coming through more clearly every day.

One day at the beginning of October my wife returned from a visit to Rosa and said the girl wanted to see me about something important. We met the next day in a small café outside Geneva. I found her in a terrible state of nerves, staring wildly at everyone who came in or went out of the door. She explained that a man had called at her flat saying he was from the electricity board and had come to check whether her lights were working, although she had not reported a fault. She was sure the man had done some snooping around in the flat. She had also noticed strangers strolling up and down the street and keeping an eye on the door of the house.

We know today that Rosa's building was being kept under observation by the Swiss police. Clearly the men were not German agents, because thanks to Hans Peters the Gestapo had no need of such measures; they were already being briefed on his gullible girlfriend's every move.

All we knew at the time was that her address had been discovered and that she must therefore stop transmitting immediately. Rosa must go into hiding, at least for a few days, and after that we would see what must be done.

We agreed she should go home to her parents for a while and that she should take the train to Basel on the Sunday. By then she was to have destroyed or handed over to me all papers, schedules, operating instructions, and anything else that might in the event of a police raid have served as incriminating evidence. I sent Edouard round to pick up her set, which he did in broad daylight, lugging the heavy suitcase past a row of unsuspecting Swiss plain-clothes men. He took it home and hit it in his shop.

The next day, 10 October, I told Central what steps I had taken to protect Rosa and throw the police off the scent.

The unexpected disappearance of one of the stations he had been monitoring did indeed confuse Lieutenant Treyer. The police, however, reassured him: they still had Rosa under twenty-four-hour observation. W.F. Flicke claims that German radio reconnaissance, which was continuing to monitor our dialogue with Central from just over the border, was aware of what had happened. He says they decoded my telegram of 10 October and knew that I had provisionally taken Rosa off the air and hidden her set. Peters received orders to stick to her like a leech and at all costs stop her leaving the city.

This is borne out by the fact that despite what we had agreed Rosa did not take the Basel train on Sunday but stayed on in Geneva. She simply locked up her flat and moved in with her boyfriend, Peters having evidently succeeded in persuading her that the journey was superfluous and promised to hide her from the police himself. The infatuated girl believed him—and deceived me for the second time in that she failed to tell me she was staying. She was undoubtedly afraid I would not let her go on working for the group if I discovered she was having an affair with a German hairdresser. She was right about that at least.

It happened differently with the Hamels. They noticed nothing suspicious. Edouard and Maude continued to take it in turns to send off the telegrams from the villa on the outskirts of town. Neither there nor in the vicinity of their flat and shop in the rue de Carouge (where the reserve sets were hidden) did they see any sign of prowling agents.

It looked to me as if they were not being watched and I let them carry on transmitting. We were taking a risk, of course. After what had happened to Rosa both Central and I realized that the police might well have placed Edouard under observation again as figuring on their list of suspicious persons. But we could not let caution—we were not then in a position to appreciate the real danger—rob us of our second and only other Geneva station. Jim was back from the Ticino, but for him to deal single-handed even with just the most important telegrams would have been a sheer physical impossibility. The only solution was for everyone who was in contact with the radio operators to take extra special care, and I told Edouard and Maude to do so too.

The safety of our last Geneva transmitter, however, already hung by a thread. In the report he later wrote for Central Jim mentioned a conversation he had had with Lieutenant Treyer at the police station during the pauses in his interrogation. Treyer had described how easy it had been to find the Hamels' set owing to the fact that the villa stood on its own. Much easier than in Rosa's case where, even when they had finally pin-pointed the house, they still did not know which of the many flats the transmitter was in. This is confirmed by the monitoring crews' log book.

Radio contact, the trump card of intelligence work, is also its Achilles' heel.

We knew this. We knew how vulnerable we were to monitoring and of course we did everything in our power to keep our radio link as flexible, as reliable, and as elusive as possible. The cipher specialist Marc Payot acknowledged in the appendix he wrote to the French edition of Otto Pünter's memoirs that 'the transmitters of Radó's network operated very carefully, changing their call-signs and transmitting times every night and their wave-bands several times a night.'*

That already made things difficult for the enemy monitors, but on top of that we were busy organizing a new station. We had the reserve sets; all we needed were reliable people to use them. Central were pressing us continually to recruit and train new radio operators and get them working for the group.

We started looking round for suitable people in the spring of 1943. We found two, a young man and a girl, both children of working-class families. I did some asking round about them, and

*Marc Payot's appendix to Otto Pünter, *Guerre secrète en pays neutre*, p. 266.

comrades whose opinion I trusted gave the girl a thoroughly positive recommendation: she was a determined, self-contained sort of person, not given to gossip, and a keen supporter of the struggle against Fascism. We met in June and she made a very favourable impression on me. Judging from the reports on the young man, he too was exactly what we were looking for. A discovery of Pakbo's, he was twenty-three years old, a fitter by trade, and an armourer in the Swiss army. His family owned a small house in Fribourg. His father was also a working man, and both of them had a lot of time for the Soviet Union.

Our two new members were enthusiastic at the prospect of being involved in intelligence operations directed against Hitler's Reich and had no thought for the serious consequences they would face if arrested. Their parents approved too, so that we had reason to be thoroughly pleased with our choice.

Both were to have trained under Jim. For a variety of reasons, however, we kept putting off the moment when they should start. We originally planned to begin showing them the ropes once the tempo of work dictated by the battle of Kursk slackened off a bit. Then Jim had to down tools and go off to the Ticino, and we agreed that he should take their training in hand as soon as he got back. But it was not to be.

On his return Jim found everything in his flat in order—or so he thought. He had deliberately left various notes and books lying around, and he found everything as he had left it.

From which Jim concluded—somewhat rashly as it turned out—that as far as he was concerned the coast was clear.

CHAPTER 39

The arrests in Geneva

On 6 October Jim reported to Central that he had spent some time in the Ticino as instructed, that he had taken precautions, and that as far as he knew he was not being watched. Relieved, the director gave permission for radio contact to be resumed, and I fixed a rendezvous with Jim in Geneva's Eaux-Vives Park.

More material than usual had piled up over the last few days because with Rosa not sending the Hamels had been unable to cope with it all. Now that Jim was back at work the situation would improve.

As we strolled together through the magnificent old park I handed Jim a sheet of telegrams to be dispatched. At first I did not mention how worried I was about Rosa being watched, nor did I tell him I had had the set removed from her flat. We'll get round the problem, I thought—what's the point of getting Jim all nervous? But when it came to working out how we were going to get the material to him—previously it had been Rosa who had travelled to Lausanne—we had to organize a new system. I had been thinking about this, weighing up various alternatives, and I had come to the conclusion that it would be best if Jim fetched the material himself. He would walk into the Hamels' shop just like any other customer and Edouard or Maude could slip him the reports for Central. And to avoid attracting attention by having him appear to patronize the shop too frequently, sometimes Edouard or Maude would travel to Lausanne. Jim agreed to this. We also agreed that he and I should continue to meet in the Eaux-Vives Park, which seemed to us eminently suited to the purpose.

On 14 October I set out for the rue de Carouge with a quantity of very important material. Normally my wife did this job, but we had been up until midnight encoding and she was not feeling too good. I had to see the Hamels about something anyway.

The material I had with me included another of Werther's reports from Berlin:

... The German high command estimates the Soviet troops attacking Vitebsk, Orsha, and Gorki at five army corps, including 2 armoured divisions, 5 armoured brigades, 3 or 4 mobile divisions, and 10 infantry and cavalry divisions. It is assumed that the main formation will attack along and to the south of the Smolensk-Vitebsk railway line. The decisive assault on Vitebsk is expected on the south-eastern perimeter of the city, where there are no continuous fortifications. When Smolensk was threatened fortifications were hurriedly thrown up at various points between the Smolensk-Vitebsk road and the Orsha-Vitebsk main railway line. The only well-fortified positions are in the Surash-Gorodok sector in the northern part of the city.

This information had to go off the same night, otherwise it would have lost its usefulness.

I knew Edouard and Maude would have had plenty to do out at the villa in the route de Florissant the previous night as well. Here are three of the telegrams I had sent round to them:

13 October 1943. To the director.

From Werther, 8 October.

a) The superiority of the Russian artillery on the Dnepr is already very considerable. In important sectors, e.g., around Kremenchug, the Russians have 150 to 160 guns to every 100 German pieces.

b) The Germans have found out that there are large Russian armoured and other units in the Gorodok-Nevel sector.

Dora.

13 October 1943. To the director.

From Werther, 10 October.

a) The Germans have established that significant Russian troop movements are taking place west of Mogilev and along the Mogilev-Mtislavl road as well as more to the south, near Chausy.

b) The Germans consider that an extension of the Russian bridgehead at Kanev would be dangerous. As it is the bridgehead allows the Russians to prepare an attack against the Kiev-Belaya Tserkov-Smela-Krivoyrog artery that the Wehrmacht high command wanted to use as its line of resistance west of the Dnepr.

Dora.

13 October 1943. To the director.

From Werther, 11 October.

a) In the Vitebsk, Gomel, and Kiev sectors as well as between Zaporozhye and Melitopol the Germans face crushing defeat at the hands of the advancing Russians unless the main body of the German forces bows to Russian superiority and retreats. The Wehrmacht high command has no alternative but to order fresh withdrawals. Apparently the surrender of Gomel was decided a long time back. The retreat from Vitebsk, Kiev, and in the southern sector of the front will be ordered shortly.

b) The Germans expect a further broadening of the Russian attack along the entire German defensive front west of the Dnepr and on the line Novosokolniki-Novorshev. Judging from the Russian preparations the Wehrmacht high command reckons the decisive Russian offensive will come on 15 October or soon afterwards. So powerful a concentration of Red Army troops has been observed in the Cherkassy-Kremenchug-Pologi-Tokmak region that there can no longer be any hope of defending the German transport line Belaya Tserkov-Zvetkovo-Smela-Snamenka-Kirovograd-Krivoyrog. The Wehrmacht high command also regards as lost the defensive sector between Zaporozhye and the Crimea.

To be continued.

Dora.

It was not be to continued—but I did not know that as I made my way across town to the rue de Carouge on the afternoon of 14 October, confident that the Hamels would have slept off their heavy night's work by now and that I would find them in.

Approaching number 26, I glanced up at the window where we had agreed a sign would be displayed when it was dangerous to come near the building. No sign was visible; all clear, then.

There were two ways in: through the shop and up the stairs to the flat on the first floor, or via the courtyard and the back entrance. I usually used the first. Today, however, the door of the shop was locked. Puzzled, I rang the bell. Then I walked on a bit, turned, and gave the first-floor windows a careful scrutiny. It looked very much as if the Hamels were not at home.

Seriously alarmed by now, I hurried to the nearby Place du Plain-Palais where there was a telephone kiosk and rang the

Hamels' number. No reply. Had they perhaps slept very late at the villa and not got back yet? My watch said just before four: time enough for them to have slept their fill. Maybe the transmitter was playing up and Edouard had had to stay on and repair it? But even so Maude would have been at home because she knew we would probably be bringing fresh material. As luck would have it, coming out of the telephone kiosk I bumped into a man I knew who lectured at the University. It was all I needed; desperately anxious and racking my brains as to what could have happened, I had to spend several agonizing minutes making polite conversation.

Back home again I told Helene that I had not been able to deliver the material and why. She was sure my fears were groundless and did her best to calm me down. But my premonition had been right: in the evening edition of the *Tribune de Genève* we read that the federal police had arrested 'a group of foreign agents' in Geneva on the night of 13-14 October. The brief account gave no details, but I did not doubt for a moment that they had got our radio operators.

That same evening I met a member of our group who had already made inquiries in the appropriate quarter and found out what had happened the night before. Edouard and Maude had been arrested, as I had feared, but that was not all: the police had picked up Rosa as well. The group was even worse hit than I had thought.

We learned later that the police had taken elaborate pains to catch Edouard and Maude in the act, which was of course extremely important from their point of view. The monitoring crews had already told them the night before that the signals were coming from 192 route de Florissant. A small army of plain-clothes policemen surrounded the house and kept it under observation from the deserted street as well as from the adjoining Alfred Bertrand Park, where the dense vegetation would have offered excellent cover for a getaway at night. The French frontier was only half a mile away, and they had thought of that too, equipping the force of some seventy men with tracker dogs. It was a major operation, masterminded by the chief of the federal political police, the Geneva police chief, and the chief of staff of the Gendarmerie—all the top brass.

On the evening of 13 October the Hamels were allowed to pass through the cordon and enter the villa. In the darkness they saw nothing to arouse their suspicions.

The transmitter started up shortly after midnight, according to schedule. Maude took first turn; as soon as she received Central's call-sign she started nimbly tapping out the coded telegrams. The monitors picked her up immediately. The cordon was drawn tighter round the house, making escape impossible, and after a further ten minutes the police made their move.

At approximately half past twelve the front door and then the door of the transmitting room were opened soundlessly by a practised hand. Edouard and Maude, absorbed in their work, heard nothing above the hammering of the Morse key. Suddenly the room was full of policemen brandishing revolvers. It happened so swiftly that Maude did not have time to lift her hand from the key, let alone give Central the emergency signal.

The police began their search—not that they had far to look. There was the set, valves switched on, and there on the table beside it were the telegrams sent and received, the transmitting schedule, and several pages of the code book. It was all the evidence they needed. A subsequent search of the Hamel's flat and shop in the rue de Carouge came up with a bonus: Rosa's set, which Edouard had taken home with him and hidden in a gramophone case.

That same night the police broke into Rosa's flat at 8 rue Henri-Mussard, but she was not there. They found her in the early hours of the morning—at Hans Peters'. They had known where to look. Both were arrested.

Rosa was taken to her flat in order that the police could search it in her presence. Much to their surprise they failed to find a transmitter there. But they did find other evidence—various radio parts, a number of pages from the code book, and Rosa's call-sign schedule—that Edouard had carelessly overlooked when he collected the set.

Peters was released fairly promptly. Throughout the investigation and even after she had been released herself poor Rosa persisted in believing that he had had nothing to do with her arrest. He was a Communist, he was on the run from the Nazis, she was going to marry him.... Her disappointment was terrible when Peters was finally exposed.

Those were the first arrests. We still lived in hope that there was a great deal Swiss Counter-intelligence did not know and that we

s

would be able to preserve the core of our organization intact.

As soon as I knew for certain that my radio operators had been arrested I telephoned Jim in Lausanne. It was imperative to warn him without delay because he had a rendezvous with Edouard in Lausanne on 17 October, Edouard having taken over Rosa's job of bringing Jim his material. It was not impossible that Swiss agents had been tailing Edouard on previous trips and that Jim would walk slap into their arms.

'Edouard's been taken seriously ill,' I told Jim over the phone. 'We called the doctor and he's had him admitted to hospital. No visitors allowed for the time being.' ('Illness' in our special lingo meant 'arrest' and 'hospital' meant 'prison'.) Jim said he understood and was very sorry to hear about it.

Later that day I travelled to Lausanne myself. At Jim's I wrote out a report for the director and instructed Jim for security reasons to send it off in his own code, since I did not know whether or not the police had found my code book when they picked up the Hamels.

Jim showed me a telegram he had received the night before. Moscow was inquiring anxiously why both the Geneva transmitters were failing to answer their call-signs. (Central knew I had wanted to start Rosa transmitting again on 16 October.) We agreed that Jim should let me have the director's answer through Helene, who would be calling on him.

From Lausanne I went on to Berne, told Pakbo what had happened, and gave him a safe address in Geneva through which we could keep in touch by post and also personally. I spent the journey back to Geneva thinking about how we must now take the devil's own care of Jim: his set was our one and only link with Moscow.

Jim's answer from Central was:

> *. . . You absolutely must keep in touch with Albert* [i.e., myself]. *Both of you are to be very very careful. Keep your reports brief and confine them to the state of the organization. Tell Albert we approve of the steps he has taken. The group had better stop work for a while. We shall be listening for you nightly on schedule.*

The case, which started out as a police affair but after about three months was transferred to military jurisdiction, was kept heavily under wraps. Nothing appeared in the Swiss press about it. Consequently for the first few days after the arrests we had no idea where our people were being held, where they were being taken for interrogation, whether the police had managed to get anything out of them, and what if anything the police had found in their searches—all of which it was vital that we should know. Somehow or other we had to establish contact as soon as possible. Anyway, as the head of the group it was my duty to get legal representation for the arrestees Edmond and Olga Hamel and Margarete Bolli—if we could not manage to organize a gaolbreak first. I must find a lawyer who would not simply take on the case from professional interest, or for the money, or because of its sensation-value, but who would plead it from the explicitly anti-Fascist standpoint.

After about a week I not only found out through a friend which prison our radio operators were being held in; I was even able to get messages to them. All three were being kept in solitary confinement in Geneva's Saint-Antoine Prison. They were taken for interrogation separately, only seeing one another at confrontations—when they were not allowed to exchange a word. The prison regulations were observed to the letter in their case, but we had a bit of luck: Edmond Hamel's warder was prepared to act as postman. Through him we were able to correspond. Unfortunately the system did not function for very long because the man soon got the sack. But by then I had already learned quite a lot.

The first thing Edmond told me was exactly what papers the police had found in their search. For the first time I realized the extent of the damage done: they had *everything* that had been hidden at the villa and in the Hamels' flat. I advised the comrades to lie wherever the police had no proof and on no account to admit to being members of Soviet Intelligence. But Edmond wrote back from prison that the police knew a great deal more about us than I had bargained for. At his last interrogation they had shown him a photograph of me and named me by name. They also knew that Dora was my codename. The police inspector had said he realized that I, Alexander Radó, was the head of the organization and that the prisoners were in contact with me, and he had promised to set them all free if they would admit it. None of them had given me away, Edmond wrote; they had all sworn up and down that they had never seen the man in the photo before.

I had confidence in them, and this was reinforced by the fact that for the moment the Swiss took no action against my wife and myself. But how long would it last? Would the three of them hold out? Supposing the interrogating officers had other proofs of our association and sprang them on the prisoners? If they had my photograph they must have found out something about me and possibly about other members of the group as well. Pakbo and Jim were threatened anyway because Rosa had been their contact and Swiss agents might have observed their meetings.

I came to the conclusion that either the Swiss had had their eye on me for a long time or—and this seemed more probable—they had drawn their information from the Gestapo and from people like Rameau-Zweig. There appeared to be nothing for it but to go underground. Still, I decided to wait for a bit, principally because it is incomparably more difficult to run an intelligence group when one is living outside the law. And in any case, before going underground I first had to satisfy myself that Pakbo and Jim were in the clear. I must also introduce them, because with things in such a mess they alone would be in a position successfully to protect the interests of the organization. And I must make arrangements to have our imprisoned comrades taken care of.

A friend of mine who knew a number of prominent Geneva lawyers was able to get that giant of Swiss jurisprudence, Hermann Dutoit, interested in the radio operators' case. By an extraordinary coincidence Dutoit had also been my legal adviser in various personal matters including the business of my residence permit, though of course he had no idea at this stage that I had anything to do with the Hamels.

Central approved my choice, and although the authorities would not at first allow any lawyer to see the prisoners and examine the evidence in the case, Dutoit agreed to take on their defence. He asked for a fat fee, too. Another thing we managed to do was to lay on some decent food for the comrades. Swiss prisons allow a certain amount of latitude in this respect, and once my contacts had got some money through to the prison authorities Edmond, Olga, and Margarete were able to have their meals sent in from a restaurant.

On 19 or 20 October, however, our improvised prison post brought some more bad news: Edmond had learned during the course of an interrogation session that the monitoring crews were after a third transmitter in the Lausanne area.

I informed Jim immediately and he got off a telegram to Central. On 25 October Moscow sent the following directive:

Cut your transmissions down to a minimum. For camouflage purposes we suggest you never spend more than twenty minutes on the air at any one time. [Then came various details regarding dates, times, and wave-bands, which had to be changed constantly.] *Observing the foregoing you can call us two or three times nightly. You can receive us without risk.*

Director.

PART 4

CHAPTER 40

I go underground

I was already being watched.

On the other side of the rue de Lausanne was a large park, and in the park, immediately opposite our house, was a little lodge where the park keepers often sat. The park keepers, however, would disappear from time to time, probably on tours of inspection, whereas the two men who now occupied the lodge sat there day and night and definitely had the look of policemen.

The lodge commanded an excellent view of the front door of our house. When I left the house on foot I noticed nothing suspicious, but as soon as I boarded the tram that stopped in front of the house a young man appeared on a motorbike and escorted the tram until I got off.

It happened several times and there could no longer be any doubt that the police had their eye on me. They must have copied my picture—probably the one Edmond had been confronted with by his interrogator—and distributed it to their men. As soon as the latter had orders to they would pounce.

I had to disappear. I had to shake them off and go into hiding. Above all I had to keep calm. The police had messed around with me more than once in my twenty-four years as an emigrant, and I knew that the one thing I must not do was let them see I was aware of being watched. I must keep calm, and I must keep my eyes peeled. This was one cat-and-mouse game the mouse had to win at all costs.

I racked my brains for a way of saving the organization from complete extinction, which to judge from this increased activity was what the police and the secret service were aiming at. Jim brought me a message from Central advising us to ask our friends for help. But who were these friends supposed to be? Jim and I wondered. Central could hardly be thinking of the Swiss Communist party because we were forbidden all contact with it. Jim thought they might mean the Allies or the Allies' embassies in

Berne, where Pakbo had useful connections through Salter. Perhaps we could try using the British diplomatic mission as a hide-out for a while. It would not be easy, but I hoped that in view of the seriousness of the situation the Allies would be prepared to help. In fact the British embassy would have been extremely suitable for our purposes because the Swiss authorities showed great respect for the British flag and turned a blind eye to the intelligence activities carried out under it.

There was another reason for trying the British.

According to Jim the Lausanne authorities were under the impression he worked for British Intelligence anyway. He had heard about this from the wife of the Rumanian minister of economic affairs, a lady who visited Lausanne occasionally and from whom Jim had elicited quite a bit of useful information. On this occasion she had smilingly confessed over a glass of wine that her friend, the wife of the Rumanian ambassador, harboured this suspicion and had apparently communicated it at a diplomatic reception to one Colonel Perron of Swiss Counter-intelligence. Perron's reply had been that he suspected as much himself, but that as long as this Englishman did not harm Swiss interests and did not collect Swiss military intelligence he saw no reason to interfere in any way with the representative of a friendly power.

That had been back in July and Jim had told Central about it immediately in response to a telegram from the director, who was then getting very worried about his Lausanne station as a result of the business of the phoney courier and various other alarming episodes.

So the British solution would have suited Jim as well—now our last remaining contact with Central.

At the end of October I radioed Moscow as follows:

... The situation is becoming less and less favourable to our continuing operations. To all appearances the Swiss police intend to smash our organization. I suggest we try and contact the British and continue our operations in a new form from there. Request instructions urgently repeat urgently.

Dora.

Central, however, rejected the idea. The director radioed back on 2 November:

. . . The suggestion that you go into hiding with the British and continue operations from there is completely unacceptable. You and your organization would forfeit your independence. We realize you are in a difficult situation and we are doing what we can to help. We are bringing in a well-known American attorney with good connections in Switzerland. He will certainly be able to help you and all who are in difficulties. Let us know immediately whether you can hold out or whether there is somewhere you could hide for two or three months.

Director

So I had Central's permission to go underground. But how? More brain racking—and there was precious little time available for it. Fortunately I found something quickly: a doctor who had helped us in a tricky situation before, when we had had to smuggle a passport across the frontier and back for an Italian comrade, came to the rescue again and offered to hide me in his flat.

There were other worries too. What was to become of my family? And what was to happen about Geopress, which although it did not make a vast profit at least kept us going?

We were not worried about our sons for the time being since we could leave them in the care of their grandmother. The elder was already eighteen and the younger thirteen; they had their ration cards, and I left my mother-in-law enough money to support the three of them. This sort of thing was nothing new to Helene's mother, who had not only raised her three daughters in poverty and unaided, but in First World War Berlin had sheltered Russian and German revolutionaries on the run. She was no stranger to conspiratorial work, and she not only agreed but positively insisted that her daughter and I should go underground as soon as possible.

Helene and I decided that she should first go into a clinic and that I should then make my disappearance alone, since our leaving the house together would have alarmed the police immediately. So we installed her in the clinic, and afterwards my mother-in-law took our youngest son off to a boarding-school in the mountains, as we had agreed.

Now it was my turn. The thing was to disappear from circulation without the police, who were watching my every step, realizing that I had gone—at least for a few days, if possible. I worked out a very simple plan that depended on our being able to divert the agents' attention successfully. This we managed to do with the aid of my elder son and our dog, a large Alsatian.

Several evenings in succession I took the dog for a walk round the house and through the park to get the men in the lodge used to the idea. On the evening of my escape, just as it was beginning to get dark, I left the house with the dog as usual and made my way to a nearby subway under the railway. It was November and a pretty cold evening, but I had deliberately come out without either hat or coat, wanting the men to think I was merely walking the dog for a few minutes.

In the subway my son was waiting with a bicycle. I gave him the dog, jumped into the saddle, and rode away into the gathering dusk. My son took the dog home as if nothing had happened. Either the police were not on their toes that evening or they genuinely thought it was me bringing the dog back. At any rate they kept watching the house for weeks afterwards before they finally noticed that their quarry had flown. I heard later of a report they made to their superiors to the effect that I had locked myself in and did not dare show my face outside.

Under cover of darkness and assisted by the blackout I made it to the doctor's flat in the old town. My hosts were expecting me and showed me to the room that was to be my home for the next two months.

One half of the job was done: I had shaken off my 'tail'. Now for the other, more difficult half—organizing an intelligence group with myself in hiding, the police after me, and only one transmitter at my disposal, which for good measure was already being monitored. It called for extreme circumspection and reliable people to act as contact men. It was a matter I needed to discuss personally with Jim. There was no changing the time and place of our rendezvous at this stage, in spite of the risk of our both being picked up, so on 8 November, having made a few alterations to my appearance, I emerged from the doctor's house, hailed a taxi, and had myself driven to the Eaux-Vives Park.

Jim had arrived a bit early; I saw his broad-shouldered figure waiting at the park entrance as my taxi drew to a stop. I paid the driver and got out. As I walked up to Jim I was struck by the fact that instead of looking at me he was looking over my shoulder at something behind me. Involuntarily I turned, but could see only the taxi I had just emerged from parked at the kerb.

'Albert, let's get out of here,' I heard Jim mutter. 'The taxi-driver just ran across to that telephone box as if he'd had a pack of hounds on his tail. It can't be a coincidence.'

I looked again and saw that the driver's seat was empty. We hurried into the park.

It could have been a coincidence, of course. There might have been a hundred reasons why the driver had to make an urgent phone call. In any other situation probably neither Jim nor I would have attached the slightest importance to the incident. But we knew the police had a photograph of me—maybe the taxi-driver had a copy of it, had recognized me, and was now ringing the police. (In fact our suspicions were not unjustified: the police had distributed two hundred copies of the photograph not only to their people but also to Geneva taxi-drivers, asking anyone who spotted me to report immediately.)

Discussion was impossible under the circumstances. We had to disappear unobserved as soon as we could. But before he went Jim handed me Central's last message and I told him in as few words as possible that I had gone into hiding, giving him the doctor's address and saying he should come and see me there if anything urgent arrived from Moscow; we would then discuss how we should carry on.

I knew the Eaux-Vives Park well. At the other end there was a restaurant backing onto a quiet side street. We entered the restaurant, passed through into the kitchen, and hurried out through the back door into the yard. The cooks barely had time to register surprise before the two strangers in raincoats had disappeared again. Once in the side street we separated and went off in different directions.

If we had left it another ten minutes I believe we would have been arrested.

That night Jim reported to Moscow:

...Albert is convinced his house is being watched. He has succeeded in going underground.

He will maintain contact with me through Sissy. When I receive an agreed telephone message I shall call on Albert at the flat where he is hiding.

Maria [alias Helene, my wife] *has gone into a clinic; the younger son is away at boarding-school; the elder son is at home with his grandmother.*

Edouard and Maude are still in close custody but otherwise are being treated decently. They have given nothing away.

I knew the police would now start making inquiries about my wife and find out which clinic she was in. Having tracked her down, they would then arrest her. There was nothing else for it: she must join me in hiding.

The wife of the doctor with whom I was living visited Helene in the clinic with a message that she should come to me immediately. Telling her doctor that she wanted to visit her children, Helene left the clinic and made her way to the address she had been given. Not, however, without first making an enormous detour through the city, switching from tram to taxi to shake off any pursuers. She had had plenty of experience of this sort of thing and knew what she was doing. She arrived at the doctor's flat safely, and for the next six weeks neither of us set foot outside the place.

The question now was to set up a new system of contacts between the members of the group. Previously the Hamels, Rosa, and Helene had couriered between myself and Jim, Pakbo, and Sissy, but they were of course now out of action. This and other urgent problems I talked over at length with Jim, who came to see me once or twice a week.

Jim took every precaution on his visits. For a start he always came after dark. Leaving the station he would stroll through the streets of the city for a while, pop into a café or a restaurant, and then take a taxi to the old town, dismissing the driver several blocks before the house where the doctor lived. Geneva was in blackout and it was a simple matter for him to slip into a courtyard and shake off anyone who seemed to be following him. Every now and then he would duck into a doorway and listen for footsteps, which in the deserted streets were audible from a long way off. He was not admitted to the doctor's flat until he had given the password.

Sissy visited me there too, and for the same reason. She had been told the address on the express condition that she reveal it to none of the other members of the group. Under the circumstances we could only survive as an operation by sticking rigidly to the rules of conspiratorial work.

Having gone over every possibility together we communicated our suggestions to Central. The reply was as follows:

... Your suggestions are in order. Instruct Sissy and Pakbo to continue working independently for the time being. The important material they should pass on through Jim.

Jim must find himself a new flat in another town immediately. The main thing is that the important and urgent reports get through without delay.

Director

The main thing indeed was to keep the stream of intelligence flowing. Pakbo sent in stuff regularly, but Sissy only got in touch with me twice. I suggested she make direct contact with Jim: the information would get through faster and she need not make superfluous calls at the doctor's flat. She would not listen to my suggestion, however, thinking that, with the situation as it was, it would be extremely dangerous to make a fresh contact, especially with a radio operator. Pakbo and Jim did manage to establish direct contact and we hoped that at least this line would function without myself. The only thing I could still do was condense the material as much as was anyhow possible and pass it on like that. But I was by no means sure that Jim would be able to send it as Central had drastically cut his transmitting schedule. As far as a new flat was concerned, he could not find anything for the time being. Not every flat is suitable for installing a transmitter. Besides, in wartime an alien needed police permission to change his place of residence, and if he wanted to move to another town he had to give a good reason.

An attempt to get the radio operators out of prison misfired. The police found out about it and the obliging warder was dismissed from the prison service. Edmond, Olga, and Margarete were transferred to another prison and the interrogations continued.

The details of the interrogations were revealed by the radio operators themselves on their subsequent provisional release and confirmed at the trial the Swiss authorities held after the war.

Margarete was the first to talk. For a month she had denied that she belonged to an illegal organization. They had shown her two photographs, one of Jim and one of myself, even using our names, but she had steadfastly denied knowing either of us. Around the middle of November, however, under pressure of the evidence collected by the agents who had been watching her—the interrogating officer described the exact circumstances of her meetings with myself, Jim, and Pakbo—she broke down and confessed. Being confronted with the full extent of the police's knowledge about her was too much for her youthful inexperience.

Margarete told the police practically everything about herself and all she knew about those members of the group with whom she had been in contact. She stressed that the group's activities had not been detrimental to Swiss interests but had been directed exclusively against Nazi Germany, maintaining that she had in fact been protecting the interests of her country. The only thing she kept back was that she was a member of Soviet Intelligence; she insisted, and continued to insist until February 1944, that she worked for Great Britain and the United States.

The Hamels showed great courage during interrogation. In spite of the weight of evidence against them they emphatically denied every accusation and refused to recognize my pictures, so that for months the police could get nothing of any importance out of them. Again it was fresh evidence that finally cornered them into an admission.

CHAPTER 41

Jim's arrest

As we busied ourselves with various precautionary measures and tried desperately to think of ways of keeping our crippled organization going, Lieutenant Treyer's monitoring crews continued their search for our third and last transmitter—Jim's set in Lausanne.

We know now exactly how they went about it.

I quote first from Treyer's reports to his superiors:

'In the course of our monitoring operation in Geneva, which ended on 14 October 1943 with the arrest of the operators of two illegal transmitters and the confiscation of their sets, we monitored a third transmitter with the identical characteristics.

'When we first picked up this transmitter's signals at 00.25 hours on 27 September 1943 they were barely audible, but on the basis of certain features we concluded with certainty that the station belonged to the same organization as the others. To make it harder to monitor the transmitter operated erratically, which is why it proved difficult to find.

'9 October 1943: We knew for certain that it was in Lausanne.

'20 October: We knew which quarter....

'25 October: ...which house....

'5 November: We were now in possession of all technical data, which supported the hypothesis advanced by the federal police on the basis of the first monitoring operations. Being in possession of this data, we ascertained the address at which the transmitter was situated: 2, chaussée de Longeraie, 4th floor, Foote residence.

'11 November: We ascertained the station with which Foote was in contact, a high-powered transmitter using the call-sign OWW. Measurements showed that it was in Russia.

'The texts of the monitored telegrams were handed over to the Swiss general staff's cipher department.'

Extracts from the detachment's log book complete the picture:

'18 October 1943: We have set up a monitoring station in

Lausanne to record the operations of US [this was how they referred to Jim's transmitter]. The mobile monitoring patrol is also in Lausanne and is collaborating with Inspector Pasche.

'5 November: US alternately transmits and receives. During transmissions the patrol carries out several close-range checks while the other patrol compares volume in the immediate vicinity of US. We have completed localization.

'14 November: OWW today sent US two telegrams, each of 283 digit-groups.

'19 November: The operation set up by the federal police in collaboration with the security police and the "Radio 7" detachment and its instruments [i.e., the arrest] has been postponed because US is not on the air.'

Jim noticed nothing of the impending danger because the police, not wanting to arrest him for the time being (we shall see why in a moment), took extra special care to diguise their operations.

Jim lived in a densely populated part of Lausanne and finding his transmitter was no easy matter. To pin down its exact location the police had to wait until Jim started transmitting and then go from house to house turning off the power. If the signals continued they tried the next house, and so on until they established that he was in no. 2, chaussée de Longeraie, an apartment house consisting of a large number of flats. The final phase of the operation was carried out with the aid of special receivers small enough to fit in a coat pocket. The house was checked floor by floor, and it was found that on the top floor, the fourth, outside the door at the end of the long corridor, the signals came through loudest and strongest. The search was over.

Jim of course had no idea that well-dressed men were wandering up and down the stairs pretending, whenever they bumped into one of the occupants, to have got the wrong house. He never saw them—for the simple reason that they only appeared when he, Jim, was tapping his Morse key with his usual lightning precision or listening to Moscow through his headphone and taking down the incoming digit-groups. Their paths never crossed, except that once, coming home, Jim had the feeling that someone was watching him from the door of the flat opposite. As he went down the corridor he distinctly heard the latch click behind him. But he put it down to his nerves, which had been strung pretty tight over the last few days, and dismissed the matter from his mind.

Following Moscow's strict instructions Jim was now mostly confining himself to receiving, though he did get off a report from time to time. On 16 November he visited me again at the doctor's flat, having seen Pakbo previously, and that night he radioed my telegrams to the director as well as, in his own name, the following:

17 November 1943. To the director.

Long and Salter have some information of great value to Central. I am doing all I can to get hold of parts and build a transmitter in case I should be arrested.

The Swiss appear to have missed this transmission as it does not figure in their log book for 17 November. Jim used a number of wave-bands and several different call-signs, switching arbitrarily from one to another, and this time Treyer evidently 'lost' him. Two or three days previously, however, Swiss Counter-intelligence had picked up a telegram of the director's that, had it got through unmonitored and its recommendation been carried out, would have put a real spanner in the works as far as the police were concerned. Addressing me and using my code, Central had recommended that, in view of the obvious danger, Jim go underground as soon as possible. Unfortunately the police had been in possession of my code since the raid on the villa and had no difficulty in deciphering the message. Jim's arrest was ordered immediately.

They originally planned to take him on the night of 18-19 November, but as we have seen he did not come on the air. The police needed to catch him in the act, so the raid was postponed.

But the next night it was on.

Jim told the story in the report he drew up for Central after the war:

'My last meeting with Dora was on 16 November at the doctor's house. He gave me a number of encoded telegrams and we agreed to meet again on the evening of 20 November.

'On the evening of 19 November I decided to call up Central (to make myself more difficult to monitor I had not been sending since 16 November) to ask if they had anything for Dora, since I was meeting him next day. They had a long telegram and I started taking it down.

'At 00.45 hours a group of fifteen policemen forced an entry into my flat. They opened the door with a crowbar and came in brandishing guns. In the seconds at my disposal I managed to burn the telegrams in the candle flame and put the set out of action with a blow of the hammer. Two technicians raced across to the set and tried to get it going but it was no longer usable. The police knew the OWW call-sign and five of my seven call-signs from having monitored them.'

The log book of the monitoring detachment contains the following entry concerning the raid:

'20 November 1943, 00.04 hours: US answers OWW and sends a telegram of 59 digit-groups. OWW confirms receipt and sends a message of 321 digit-groups.

'00.45 hours: Foote raided while operating. Forced to break off by the noise at the door, he ripped the leads and burned the telegrams.

'A good many transmitter components were found in a cleverly devised hiding-place in the wardrobe. Also found there was the typewriter case in which he had kept the set.'

The raid was led and the official report signed by police inspectors Knecht of Geneva and Pasche of Lausanne, a general-staff officer, and the officer commanding the monitoring detachment.

Back to Jim's report:

'I was taken to the police station, where inspectors Knecht and Pasche took charge of my case. The cipher expert Marc Payot was also called in to help. Pasche told me during interrogation that he had not wanted to arrest me yet because the police had been planning to expose as many members of the group as possible first. . . . But when Central sent me instructions through Dora to go underground the police had decided to pounce for fear of losing track of me.'

It was no skin off Colonel Masson's nose how long our Lausanne station continued to operate because it did not represent the slightest threat to the security of Switzerland. In practical terms, however, his involvement with the Germans obliged him to go after our group and wipe it out.

Moscow knew nothing of Jim's arrest and for some time went on trying to renew contact:

1 December 1943.

1. Were you able to communicate our message to Sissy and Pakbo? What is their situation?

2. Exercise particular care with regard to your contact with Central. Move the transmitter to another town as soon as possible. Send only the most urgent reports. We shall be listening carefully for your call as and when arranged. Best wishes.

Director.

But neither the message nor the wishes ever reached Jim or anyone else. Undeciphered, unanswered, they disappeared in the ether.

During his interrogation Jim learned certain details of what the police had already achieved in their drive to expose our organization. I quote from his 1945 report again:

'At my first interrogation I was asked whether I admitted having together with one Alexander Radó passed on political, military, and economic intelligence for the Soviet Union and operated against an unnamed power. The police knew a lot about us, if not everything.

'1. They knew that I had trained Rosa, Edouard, and Maude and claimed that it was I that had installed their sets.

'2. They knew (from Dora's telegram to Central) that I was to meet Pakbo, but they did not know who Pakbo was.

'3. They knew I was to train someone else but thought it was a man and were consequently looking for a man.

'4. They had learned from the last telegram that I had been instructed to go underground.

'5. They had also learned from the telegrams that Dora had established contact with the imprisoned Edouard.

'... At my third and last interrogation Inspector Pasche mentioned for the first time the names of Mrs Dübendorfer and others, but the names meant nothing to me because I did not know them. At the same time they mentioned someone from Berne whom they might be arresting. They may have meant Pakbo (I did not catch the name because again I did not know it; I only knew his codename).

'The police believed I had a second, special code with which I had communicated with the Wehrmacht high command officers, with Werther and the rest of them. They thought I received their reports by radio. They had found a German novel at my flat in which I had underlined certain words and they had assumed that this was my code book for deciphering the telegrams I received from Germany. They reckoned I was using three codes in all: one for talking to Central, another for Germany, and a third for France.

'During my interrogation it became obvious to me that: 1, the Swiss had been told about our organization by the Germans; 2, the Germans had given them the approximate positions of our transmitters (Edouard and Maude's one kilometre from the French frontier, Rosa's three kilometres, and mine ten kilometres); 3, the Swiss police had been given a photograph of me by the Germans but did not know my name, although they did know that I belonged to Dora's organization.

'Inspector Knecht told me that the Gestapo knew a great deal about our organization in Switzerland and that by arresting me the Swiss police had quite possibly saved my life.'

Knecht's claim was not without foundation. Accoce and Quet state in the book I have several times referred to that in examining the SD archives after the war they came across a plan to have Jim kidnapped and smuggled out of Switzerland. Secret agents had been entrusted with the operation and a date set—23 November! In other words Himmler missed him by a hair.

In March 1944 Jim's case was transferred from police to military jurisdiction, but Jim continued to deny that he was a member of our organization. He decided on his lawyer's advice to admit as much as could be proved against him. He admitted to having worked for a member state of the League of Nations and passed on intelligence to the detriment of Nazi Germany, but said that he had worked on his own in Switzerland, his group leader living abroad; he claimed he had had nothing whatever to do with me, the Hamels, Margarete Bolli, and all the rest of them.

Having signed a statement to this effect, Jim was not interrogated again before his release.

CHAPTER 42

Voluntary imprisonment

I was expecting Jim on 20 November as agreed, but he did not turn up. Knowing his reputation for punctuality, I immediately feared the worst. We had known that neither of us was safe now: the police might pounce at any moment.

It was a week before I learned for certain that he had been arrested. It at once became imperative that I find a fresh hiding-place. Of course, looking at the thing logically I realized that Helene and I would have been arrested that same evening if on one of his visits Jim had unwittingly led the police to the doctor's flat. But it is sometimes hard to know just what the opponent is up to. The rules of conspiratorial activity require one to allow for various possibilities. They say: when a comrade who knows where you are hiding is arrested, go and hide somewhere else.

Finding a new place to hide, however, was no easy matter. Even among the people you can trust, not many will be prepared to conceal in their home someone the police are looking for. But at the end of January 1944 we did find somewhere—not far from the doctor's place, with a friend of a member of our organization. We moved under cover of darkness, even dragging bedclothes and mattresses along with us. Our new hosts had a separate, top-floor flat with no neighbours, but it was extremely small. They gave us a room we could barely move about in; the floor space accommodated a collapsible bed and our two pairs of feet—that was about all.

Having no alternative, we installed ourselves as best we could. The only really unpleasant thing about it was having to sit for hours on end hardly able to move a muscle—during the day on account of the daily help who came to do the cleaning and shopping, and during the evening on account of the friends who trooped in for bridge. None of them knew of our presence, and we had to sit in utter silence lest we should give it away.

Looking back on the long months we spent in that tiny room, it amazes me how Helene and I ever found the patience to bear our voluntary imprisonment, and in particular the ordeal of immobility it imposed. Our hands and feet became increasingly stiff; we even thought after a while that we could feel the blood stiffening in our veins. Sometimes we felt like saying 'To hell with it!' and simply getting up and going out. We had both only just turned forty at the time: we needed movement, our bodies cried out for it. But no—the room was our cell, and there we had to sit.

I think it was perhaps the hardest period of my whole life, if we except the postwar years that were the lot I shared with many others as a result of false accusations made at a time when socialist justice was in abeyance.

The Swiss police had finally brought us to our knees, forcing us to break off contact with the remaining free members of our organization and virtually bury ourselves alive. But there was nothing else we could have done: they had agents looking for us all over the country. This was clear from the news I received from a friend who had connections with the police. He was the only person who knew where I was in hiding. He came to see me occasionally and kept me informed about the state of the organization. Together we racked our brains for a way of getting into radio contact with Moscow again.

That was my first concern—not the fact of my virtual imprisonment.

From the newspapers and the wireless I learned how things were developing on the Soviet front and in Europe. In January the Allies resumed operations against the German troops in Central Italy, having done nothing further since the autumn of 1943. Near Leningrad and in the Ukraine the Red Army continued its advance. In the Korsun-Shevchenkovski region large enemy army groups were encircled and destroyed. Soviet troops were driving the occupier out of the Crimea and Byelorussia; they were approaching the Rumanian border. The Red Army offensive was gaining steadily in momentum, but the enemy too, losing one position after another, was putting up a more and more dogged defence.

The intelligence material we had collected lay idle. A great deal had accumulated since the arrest of our radio operators, but how were we to pass it on, deprived as we were of all means of communication? It was a paradoxical situation: the intelligence-collecting potential of our organization was greater at the end of

1943 than it had ever been, but as an effective unit we were crippled.

I was no longer able to provide active leadership myself but my principal assistants, Sissy and Pakbo, were still at liberty and still receiving regular reports from their sources. All the group's sources and contacts were intact, including the most important line—Lucy and his comrades in Berlin.

So why, you might ask, did I so mercilessly rack my brains for ways and means? Ought I not simply to have given my people instructions to start collecting transmitter components, build a set, quickly train the pair we had selected, and carry on sending?

Unfortunately it was not as easy as that—not even in the relatively favourable conditions obtaining in unoccupied Switzerland. Assuming they had managed to get hold of the necessary parts and put together a set—where were they to accommodate it and, even more important, who was to train the newcomers? All our operators were in prison, and their acquired skills with them. Jim had not even been able to arrange a meeting with the two youngsters before his arrest. None of the rest of us knew the first thing about wireless technology.

Nevertheless I clung to the hope that after a time, once the police showed signs of taking the heat off, I should be able to get the organization rolling again.

Having learned nothing from the prisoners about me, the police redoubled their efforts to track down the leader of the group. Their agents continued to come up with nothing, so the authorities resorted to inhuman methods that bore a distinct resemblance to those of the Nazis.

In March my elder son, who had remained at the flat with his grandmother, was arrested by the Swiss police. All night long they interrogated and beat him in an attempt to make him tell them where his father and mother were hiding. If they had tortured him for a week there was nothing he could have told them, because he did not know. Next morning they sent him home.

That was only the beginning. The police, determined to lure us out of hiding by making us get in touch with our family, used every means in their power to drive the children and my mother-in-law to desperation. My younger son, a child of thirteen, was expelled from his school, the children and their grandmother had their ration cards taken away for two months, and finally they were even turned out of the flat.

But that was not all. Helene's poor old mother, who was of German nationality, was threatened with repatriation—tantamount to being handed over to the Nazis—and they tried to tell my elder son that he must go to the German embassy and get a transit visa in order that he could be packed off to Hungary, his father's country of birth. He would have had to travel through Germany and would undoubtedly have fallen into the hands of the Nazis too.

Things began to look very bad indeed for them and my wife suffered terribly as a result. It was all I could do to keep her from making an irreparable mistake. Great strength was required of both of us, for we had no right to let ourselves be arrested.

I do not know what would have become of our children and their grandmother if it had not been for the intervention of our friends. Pakbo and other comrades finally managed with the assistance of various influential personalities to put a stop to the persecution. They helped them to find another flat and saw to it that their ration cards were reissued and that my sons were readmitted to their schools. One of these 'friends in need' was in fact a relative as well, namely the world-famous conductor Hermann Scherchen, then head of the Swiss Broadcasting Company. His efforts on behalf of the children and my mother-in-law were decisive.

The police had no alternative but to give up. Their calculations had gone astray; we were not to be had by Gestapo methods.

What about our comrades in prison—how were they getting on? (Jim I have already told about.)

The record shows that practically all the prisoners behaved splendidly, doing everything they could to put the police on the wrong track. What the police wanted from them—proof that certain already exposed persons were members of our organization—they failed utterly to obtain.

The Hamels and Margarete Bolli were in the Bois-Mermet Prison in Lausanne, to which they had been transferred when the authorities learned of my intention to get them out of Saint-Antoine. At the end of November Jim was taken to Bois-Mermet too. They were kept in solitary confinement. The warders were even forbidden to answer their questions. Their lawyers were refused access to them. The only thing they were allowed to do was have one meal a day sent in from a restaurant at their own expense; they could also buy cigarettes and receive parcels and books from outside.

Edmond and Olga Hamel, who denied having had anything to do with intelligence work, bravely persisted in that denial right up until March 1944—nearly six months. They confessed only when driven hopelessly into a corner by fresh evidence that the police had collected in the meantime.

'Edouard's' story then was that he had been radio operator to a man called Albert, but only since the autumn of 1942; he said he had built two or three transmitters and worked for England against Hitler, but that he had in no way harmed his own country. 'Maude' confirmed this by saying that she had only started helping her husband in the summer of 1943, and that in the weeks before the arrest she had helped Albert with encoding work. Neither of them was prepared to identify me from the photograph. Even as late as March 1944 they were still hoping to put their interrogators off the scent by muddling everything up and telling only half the truth.

Following Jim's arrest Swiss radio reconnaissance, acting on the orders of the federal public prosecutor, the federal police chief, and the head of the Swiss army's counter-intelligence service, made an attempt to contact Moscow in his name. They knew Central's call sign, they had Jim's schedule, and they were also in possession of a great deal of information about our group. By means of this trick, and by keeping the fact that they had mopped up the Lausanne transmitter strictly secret, they hoped to gain even more information about us, in particular the identities behind the codenames, the whereabouts of our rendezvous points, and if possible the address where I was hiding.

Moscow, however, was not to be duped. Realizing immediately what was going on, the director pretended to have been taken in and proceeded to send pseudo-Jim instructions and advice, the idea being to lead the Swiss astray and at the same time try and find out more about the situation we were in.

The mistake the Swiss had made was to use my code, since they did not know Jim's code-key. It was weeks before they twigged that it was a case of the biter bit and broke off the attempt—leaving Central the winner, of course, because the director now knew for certain that Jim had been arrested, whereas the Swiss had only been wasting their time.

Counter-intelligence having failed in its attempt to swindle information out of Moscow, the police were given a freer hand and fresh arrests followed.

On 19 April 1944 they picked up Rachel Dübendorfer ('Sissy'), Paul Böttcher, and Christian Schneider ('Taylor'). Exactly a month later Rudolf Roessler ('Lucy') was arrested. They were all taken to Bois-Mermet and put in solitary confinement.

Masson himself clearly had no interest in arresting these additional members of our group since his promise to Schellenberg (assuming he did in fact make one) was already fulfilled: we had been out of touch with Moscow since November 1943, we were totally unable to pass on one iota of military intelligence, and what is more the Germans knew it—their monitors told them so. On the other hand they were still afraid that we would resume operations from somewhere else, and it was presumably for this reason that they insisted our group be wiped out completely. At any rate the head of Swiss Intelligence succumbed to their pressure, though he was at pains not to damage his own interests in so doing.

One of his interests was to preserve at all costs a secret that was of the utmost importance as far as the security of the Swiss Confederation was concerned—the secret of Rudolf Roessler and his extraordinarily effective Berlin group. It was undoubtedly not Masson's intention to throw into gaol the man through whom the Swiss general staff received regular intelligence from leading military circles in the German Reich. The federal police, however, knew nothing of Roessler's secret role. Our radio operators had never been in contact with Roessler; they had never even heard of him; they could no more give the police information about him than they could supply information about Sissy or Taylor, never having been in contact with them either. Not even Sissy knew anything about Lucy; we had once asked her to lift the veil of secrecy for our own benefit. So her arrest could mean nothing to Masson.

The only member of my group who knew Roessler personally was Taylor, alias Christian Schneider. If he wanted to, he could tell the police a lot. And he decided he wanted to. He confessed. He gave them everything, even down to Roessler's name. It was clearly more than Masson had bargained with, and he was now compelled to contribute to having Roessler arrested.

In view of his importance to them the military authorities could of course easily have had Roessler's arrest rescinded. But once his name had appeared in Taylor's statement in connection with a Soviet intelligence group, Masson feared—quite rightly—that the fact would come to the ears of the Germans, secret inquiry or no secret inquiry. And if Schellenberg's people once found out that the German emigrant Rudolf Roessler was 'Lucy', they would make short work of him, either killing him in Switzerland or kidnapping him and smuggling him out of the country—and Swiss Intelligence would have lost one of its most important sources. There was nothing for it but to get him out of harm's way before it was too late, and about the only place where it was virtually impossible for SD or Gestapo agents to touch him was in gaol.

Besides betraying his friend, then, Taylor also blabbed about his connection with Sissy and confessed to having worked for Soviet Intelligence, thus putting all the other prisoners in a difficult situation.

Against Sissy the police had concrete evidence on top of Taylor's statement. While searching her flat they had come across encoded radio messages made from telegrams and reports that I had written myself; Sissy had hung onto them in the hope of being able to forward them to Central as soon as an opportunity presented itself. But they did not find her code book because it was not in the flat at the time of her arrest. Nor did it turn up in subsequent searches. Mindful of the possibility of arrest, Sissy had kept her code book somewhere else.

Eventually all the prisoners were charged with having worked for Soviet Intelligence as members of the Radó group. The police had more than enough evidence to support the charge, and ultimately it was useless for my people to continue to try and deny it. These last arrests completely paralysed our organization and it now collapsed. Although Lucy's Berlin group remained intact and one of my principal assistants, namely Pakbo, was still at liberty and could, with Long, Salter, and others, have got things going again, we had lost our sets, we had lost our radio operators, and we had lost that *sine qua non* of intelligence communication, our code. Once your code is in enemy hands it is useless.

The Swiss police, to the immense satisfaction of the Germans, had accomplished our downfall.

In July 1944 I learned that Edmond and Olga Hamel and Margarete Bolli had been released from prison on bail—a common practice in many capitalist countries. They were further made to sign a declaration that they would not leave the territory of the Swiss Confederation before their case came up for trial.

I learned this from friends who came to see me in my own self-imposed prison—Pakbo, who had heard about Margarete from her mother, and another comrade who had spoken to the Hamels. My first reaction was one of surprise, but looking back on it afterwards I realized what the police hoped to achieve with their generous gesture.

One reason was undoubtedly that the political and military situation in Europe in the middle of 1944 had altered to the advantage of the League of Nations. The Soviet army was already approaching the frontiers of Nazi Germany. American and British troops had landed in Normandy, opening the long-promised second front, and two days later, on 4 June, the Allies had taken Rome. In these changed circumstances the Swiss government began to feel less unsure of itself and less afraid of its bullying neighbour—who had for his part become less concerned with threatening and occupying other countries than with saving his own skin. This of course had its effect on relations between the two countries' secret services. SD and Gestapo were no longer able to twist the Swiss round their little finger, as they had so successfully done in the past. From now on Masson could indulge in the luxury of ignoring Himmler's and Schellenberg's orders.

The other reason behind the release of our radio operators was of a quite different nature. It lay in a clever piece of calculation—one, incidentally, that constitutes an accepted part of international police practice. It was a favourite method with the Germans, and here were the Swiss apparently trying their luck with it too. They reckoned that if the radio operators were set at liberty the head of the organization would get in touch with them again either personally or through his agents. In this case it seemed particularly likely that he would do so because, as the Swiss knew, the three had not been replaced. The Hamels and Bolli were undoubtedly kept under close observation after their release; anyone getting in touch with them would most certainly have picked up a tail. This would have enabled the police to expose the remaining members of the group, and they might even have found their way to me.

When Pakbo visited me in August (it was the first time I had seen him since going underground; I had asked the comrade who visited me regularly to bring him along) we did indeed discuss together the question of whether we should contact the Hamels. We decided not to, however, realizing that it was a trap. I also forbade Pakbo to meet Margarete Bolli, particularly as he said the police had long suspected him, were keeping an eye on him, and would arrest him as soon as he offered them the slightest pretext.

Nearly nine months had gone by since the liquidation of our Lausanne station, and not once had we managed to make contact with Moscow. The situation seemed hopeless. It hardly made sense to go on collecting intelligence. It was time I made a decision.

I knew that my friends were leaving no stone unturned in their efforts to find a way of breaking the deadlock. I could do nothing myself as long as I was living underground. Clearly the only place from which I could resume contact with Central was abroad; only from across the frontier could I report to the director what had happened and ask for instructions—whether to wind up operations in Switzerland or reorganize on a different basis.

The only frontier in question was the French one, Austria and Italy being occupied by the Germans whereas the situation in France had changed completely by the autumn of 1944. American and British troops had landed in the south, the Allies were advancing in Normandy, and the August insurrection in Paris had driven the occupier from the capital. In Haute-Savoie, just across the frontier from Geneva, the partisans were rounding up German troops and taking them prisoner. I must go to the partisans.

But how were we to slip past the Swiss frontier posts? I spent hours discussing this seemingly insoluble problem with my Geneva comrades and Pakbo. Someone even suggested tunnelling under the electrified wire-entanglements. Another proposal was that we should flee to Campione, an Italian enclave in the Ticino that was in partisan hands, but that would have meant travelling right across Switzerland by rail, there having been practically no motor transport for some time because of the fuel shortage. Moreover the only approach to Campione was across the Lake of

Lugano, which was heavily patrolled by Swiss frontier police boats. We rejected both suggestions as being unrealistic. I was in favour of crossing the Swiss frontier into France with the aid of the *maquisards*, who knew the territory better than anyone else and would certainly not refuse us their help.

While Helene and I were chewing over this problem the comrades brought us some good news: the police had released Jim (though like the others he was not allowed to leave the country until his case was tried). That was on 8 September. I decided not to get in touch with Jim either, for the same reasons as had kept me away from the Hamels and Bolli.

The only sensible solution in the circumstances was to flee to France and try and make contact with Central's people there. That was my duty, and not even parental affection could be allowed to keep me from it. My wife too found it a terrible wrench to leave without seeing the children and her old mother again. But we had no choice in the matter. We placed our trust in our friends to stand by them and look after them in our stead, those friends having already proved their willingness to do so when the police had begun their harassment tactics.

CHAPTER 43

Flight from Switzerland

In the autumn of 1944 the Soviet troops, attacking along the whole length of the front, reached East Prussia, advanced through Poland, Czechoslovakia, and Hungary, and liberated Bucharest, Sophia, and Belgrade. Bulgaria and Rumania, acknowledging total defeat, turned their weapons against their former ally. In September the Finnish government broke off relations with Germany and concluded an armistice with the Soviet Union and Great Britain. In western Europe the Allies were similarly successful, driving the occupier out of most of France and Belgium and clearing the whole of central Italy.

Fascist Germany was on the verge of military and political collapse. Hitler's days were numbered.

Towards the middle of September I finally managed to make contact with the French partisans across the frontier in Haute-Savoie, who said they were willing to help. I gave their courier the address of the flat where I was in hiding, and soon afterwards they sent a major to see me, a young Frenchman who I was agreeably surprised to learn was a nephew of the celebrated Soviet academic Bach. The major and I meticulously worked out a plan of escape, knowing that the slightest mistake could lead to arrest.

Our plan was as follows:

On 16 September, a Saturday, the doctor in charge of the clinic to which my wife had been admitted at the time I went underground was to fetch us in his car. He would drive us to the railway tunnel through which a branch line led to Annemasse, virtually a suburb of Geneva but already on French soil and now in the hands of the Maquis. All train traffic between France and Switzerland had of course stopped with the occupation of France by the Germans. Every Saturday, however, a single locomotive came through the tunnel from Annemasse—which although in France belonged to the Swiss customs area, forming part of the so-called 'free zone'—with a truckload of churns of milk, the reason being that the

French farmers of the free zone had since Napoleon's day enjoyed the privilege of supplying the population of Geneva with milk and other victuals. A lot of empty milk churns collected in the course of a week, and these were sent back by the same train.

We were to enter the tunnel, where the major would be waiting for us. The train, on its way back from Geneva's Eaux-Vives station with a load of empties, would halt for a moment in the tunnel while we climbed aboard, the railwaymen being of course in league with the partisans.

The Saturday came. The doctor arrived punctually at the time agreed. Painfully, because in the months of enforced immobility we had almost forgotten how to walk, my wife and I dragged ourselves the few yards to the car, and the car drove off.

On the bridge above the tunnel we saw the policeman who patrolled the bridge area on his bicycle. We waited until he was out of sight, then leapt out of the car and half walked, half ran towards the dark tunnel entrance, stopping for breath a couple of times because we were even less used to moving fast.

In the seconds it took us to reach the tunnel I was seized by a curious feeling. This was my first time out after eleven months' enforced/voluntary imprisonment. It was a Saturday afternoon, the working week was over, there were a lot of people on the balconies of the houses around—and they all seemed to be watching us. Helene had the same impression. Afterwards she told me that, looking up at the houses with their rows of balconies, she had felt just as if she had been naked before all those people.

Everything seemed to be all right so far, however, and we plunged into the darkness of the tunnel, groping our way forward. Suddenly we became aware that we were being followed. Looking back, we saw a group of silhouettes coming down the tunnel after us. We quickened our pace. But then, our eyes growing used to the darkness, we recognized the figure of the major and heard him say reassuringly that these were his people.

Just at that moment the locomotive and its one truck clattered past us and out of the tunnel to halt at Eaux-Vives station a little way down the line. We heard the men loading the empty churns. In the event of the train's being escorted back by a Swiss frontier guard it had been arranged that the driver should give a whistle to let us know the escape was off.

After a little while the train came back; there was no whistle, and it entered the tunnel and stopped when the major waved. Helene and I climbed aboard the locomotive, followed by the five men who had come down the tunnel after us.

The driver set off again, heading for the frontier. He was clearly very worried. He told us he could not guarantee that the plan would succeed because when the train was not escorted by a soldier there was a check at the frontier. The major suggested driving straight through the check point without stopping, regardless of the consequences.

The driver promptly accelerated to full speed and swept past the guardhouse before the soldiers realized what was happening. They came rushing out and started shooting, but no one was hit, and we were soon out of range and then out of sight.

In Annemasse we were met by partisans who ushered us straight to a waiting car to take us to their headquarters at Annecy. As the last Swiss frontier posts disappeared behind us we knew we had made it: now neither Counter-intelligence nor the police could get us.

Not that all danger was past—far from it. In fact we were treated to a sample on the way to Annecy as the little car overturned on the narrow winding road and we were nearly pitched into a gorge. We were extremely fortunate to get away with a few scratches.

At last we reached Annecy, which was likewise in the hands of the Haute-Savoie *maquisards*. We received a hearty welcome and were put up in a villa on the shore of the magnificent lake. There we stayed for a while, for we both needed a rest and, strange as it may sound, we first had to learn to walk again. In order to put us back on the right side of the law they made Helene a first lieutenant and myself a lieutenant colonel of the partisan army, which was some 50,000 men strong in the region.

We were already feeling better after a few days and taking more of an interest in our surroundings. We learned that the Allied troops that had landed at Marseille were thrusting northward. Paris had been liberated by popular insurrection, but access to the capital was still barred by German road patrols.

While in Annecy we got to know two interesting people: Paul Langevin, the famous physicist and Nobel Prizewinner, and Jules Moch, who subsequently became a minister in the French government. Moch was an officer in the British Royal Navy and was in

Annecy on behalf of General de Gaulle. He had been sent to find out whether it was true that a soviet republic had been set up in Haute-Savoie. Rumours had got around because there were quite a few Communists in the local Maquis leadership. Moch's worries turned out to be superfluous, however; in Annemasse the Communists had been fighting shoulder to shoulder with the Catholics and no one had proclaimed a soviet republic.

Langevin on the other hand was there by pure chance. His field was nuclear physics, and the Germans had tried to make him work for them. The partisans had quickly stepped in, kidnapped him from the Nazis, and helped him escape to Switzerland. He had come back of his own accord.

Before we left Annecy the *maquisards* organized a farewell feast for us, with Langevin, Moch, my wife, and myself occupying the seats of honour.

Next morning we two and Langevin left for Lyon, where we were held up for several days. Only recently liberated by the Americans, Lyon lay in ruins. The streets were covered in plaster, broken glass, and whole doors blasted off their hinges. Of the city's twenty-five bridges only one was intact; all the rest had been blown up by the retreating Germans.

We shared a hotel with a number of French Communist trade-union leaders returning from exile or hiding. Like us they were making for Paris, but Paris was not an easy place to reach. No trains were running, and on the roads vehicles were at the mercy of French Fascists and German soldiers who had lost touch with their units.

Not even Lyon was safe. One evening we invited Comrade Hénaffe, secretary of the Paris trade unions, and his wife to come on a tour of the city with us. We were cruising through the streets when suddenly a group of Vichy government supporters opened fire on our car, wounding Madame Hénaffe.

To get to Paris we needed French papers; without them we might have been stopped on the way. But neither Helene nor I had even an identity card. Again our friends came to the rescue. Yves Farges, then city commissioner of Lyon and later general secretary of the World Council of Peace, issued us with a French passport that had us coming from Lorraine.

We joined a group of French Communist party leaders who had spent the war in hiding or fighting in the Maquis and were now in a hurry to return to Paris. They included several members of the Party's politburo as well as the writer couple, Louis Aragon and Elsa Triolet. Aragon I knew from the Inpress days before the war. In a long column of vehicles we set out for the capital. Each vehicle was fitted with a machine gun to deal with the remnants of the encircled and defeated German army that were still hanging out in the woods and forests. At every village and town we came to we were received and escorted by armed patrols of Communists and Catholics, the Catholics often with the parish priest at their head.

On 24 September 1944 our convoy finally entered Paris—a Paris by then completely cleared of Fascists.

Meanwhile what was happening to my colleagues back in Switzerland?

The last members of the group were released in September, namely Sissy, Taylor, and Lucy; Paul Böttcher had been let out of prison earlier—only to be interned in an aliens' camp since he was in effect an emigrant and had no residence permit for Switzerland.

But supposing we let Jim report on this period as he told it to Central in 1945:

'On 7 September 1944 I was informed that in view of the fact that Switzerland was no longer surrounded by German troops and German pressure on the country had diminished I could be set at liberty provided I put up two thousand francs' bail and undertook not to leave the country without permission. I did so and left prison the next day, taking the room in the Central-Bellevue Hotel, Lausanne, that the police had booked for me. In October my residence permit was returned and I was allowed to live in a private house in the canton of Vaud and move about the country freely.

'The day after my release I telephoned my lawyer ('Braun'), who said he had some news for me and could we meet? We met, and Braun told me that a good friend of his who had long been in touch with Dora was anxious to get in touch with me. We agreed that I should meet his comrade in Geneva, which I did; he informed me that Dora was still in Geneva but would be leaving with his wife for Paris in a few days. A couple of days later the same comrade arranged for me to meet Edouard and Maude, who told me certain details regarding their detention including what the police had found at their place. In interrogation they had both said they worked for the British and did not know their superior's name.

'At the end of September Braun rang me again and asked me to come to his chambers. There he told me that a woman called Dübendorfer wanted to see me. The name rang a bell immediately and I said I was prepared to meet her. Mrs Dübendorfer introduced herself as Sissy, told me she had been released on 14 September and said that Roessler, who had also been released, wished to talk to me. She said she had never met Lucy herself and would be seeing him for the first time in the Zurich café where the rendezvous had been arranged.

'It was my first and last meeting with Lucy. He explained that he had been passing the Swiss general staff intelligence about Germany for years. . . . I told Lucy I was leaving for Paris in a few days, whereupon he said he would give me one or two reports for Central. (I received these *via* Sissy and forwarded them after my arrival in Paris.) Sissy, Lucy, and I talked in the café for five hours. Sissy must really have been seeing Roessler for the first time because on arriving at the café she walked past all the tables several times before I indicated with a wave that we were expecting her. Moreover their conversation confirmed it. Lucy speaks no French and his English is poor so we talked in German.

'. . . Around this time one of Dora's people arranged for me to meet Pakbo, who said his sources were furnishing better material then ever before but how was he to pass it on? He had met Rosa several times since her release. Rosa told him that the police had been watching her for a long time (during interrogation she was shown Dora's photo and mine); the police knew exactly when she had met whom, including Pakbo, and they also knew she had been in Pakbo's flat in Berne. Pakbo was certain he was being watched too and that his telephone was still tapped but said he was not particularly bothered because as a journalist he was entitled to collect information and pass it on as he pleased; they could do nothing to him as long as he did not harm Swiss interests. Pakbo gave me a parcel of developed films with intelligence material on them, which I handed over to Central's man in Paris.

'I met Sissy several times more before leaving for Paris. She told me that all the intelligence material she had received from Lucy since there had been no means of contacting Central was in a safe belonging to a person who enjoyed diplomatic immunity in Switzerland. She asked me urgently to communicate this fact to Central. Sissy is convinced that the Gestapo had a hand in blowing the group and that Peters, Rosa's boyfriend, is a Gestapo agent. . . .

'I considered it my duty to proceed to Paris and there get in touch with Central. Although I had permission to leave Switzerland I was unable to obtain a visa for France as I could give no satisfactory reason for my journey. On the evening of 7 November I entered France with the aid of the Savoy partisans. On 9 November I arrived in Paris and not long afterwards met Radó.'

Nearly a year had passed since his arrest when Jim and I met again in Paris. He told me that he had already established contact with Central's representative in France. I had of course done so myself before this, namely at the end of October.

After an absence of more than eight years my wife and I found ourselves in Paris once more. The whim of fate had brought us back to the place where we had lived and worked after our emigration from Germany and whence we had departed again to help combat the dark forces of Fascism.

We emigrants had always had a soft spot for Paris. We loved the city for its history, its democratic traditions, and its inimitable *joie de vivre*. Now, however, a lot of that careless gaiety was gone. War and occupation had left their sombre mark, though the Parisians had managed to save the city itself from destruction.

We took a furnished room—for which, incidentally, we had to pay an astronomical sum. The events of the last few months had in conjunction with the autumnal cold played havoc with our health; Helene had a chronic case of bronchial catarrh and I was plagued with rheumatism.

We had very little trouble with papers and registration. The Hungarian consulate in Paris had preserved its diplomatic status because its leadership had dissociated themselves from the Horthy government in April 1944 and in any case Hungary was not at war with France. We were both given passports as Hungarian citizens, and with these we were able to obtain temporary residence permits.

A piece of ghastly news reached me in Paris: I learned that practically all my relations had been killed in Auschwitz, including my mother. It was not until ten years later that I learned my younger sister had got out of the camp alive.

Suddenly my wife could not bear to be without her sons and her old mother any longer. We had no news of them because there was still no postal service between Switzerland and France. It seemed an impossible project to have the family join us in Paris; France was still at war, and civilians, especially if they were aliens, could only travel with a special pass. But somehow Helene contrived to get hold of one. Armed with military papers, she drove down to Annecy (there were no trains yet) to consult our Maquis friends. The *maquisards* went across to Geneva and asked the authorities to issue permits for the boys and their grandmother to leave the country. It just so happened to be the middle of the Christmas holiday, but in spite of that fact (or was it because of it?) the whole thing was settled inside twenty-four hours and the necessary permits handed over. The net result of Helene's perseverance and the kindness of our friends in Paris, Annecy, and Geneva was that the beginning of 1945 saw the five of us reunited.

Epilogue

The Swiss authorities did in the end bring our group to trial.

One would have thought they would be satisfied with having put us completely out of action, that the case would then have been closed and the accused, if not decorated, at least publicly rehabilitated with a recognition that our activities had been prompted by conscience and had, objectively considered, done Switzerland nothing but good. But there were influential reactionary circles for whom it was important for a variety of reasons that we should be made to answer for activities they alleged to have been illegal.

One trial was held in October 1945; the other was held two years later—clearly as a sacrifice on the altar of the Cold War, then just beginning.

Charges of having conducted intelligence operations against Germany were brought against myself, Helene, Rachel Dübendorfer, Paul Böttcher, Rudolf Roessler, Christian Schneider, Alexander Foote, Margarete Bolli, and Edmond and Olga Hamel. The court martial passed sentences varying from three months' to three years' imprisonment, plus fines. Roessler was acquitted. As the leader of the group I was given three years, and was banned from Switzerland for fifteen.

As things turned out, however, none of us had to serve his term. The Hamels and Margarete Bolli, being Swiss citizens, received suspended sentences. Schneider had already served his few months—with interest! And the rest of us who received prison sentences—myself, Helene, Foote, Rachel Dübendorfer, and Böttcher—were no longer in the country (the latter two having fled to France in July 1945). We had been condemned *in absentia.*

Apart from our not having harmed Swiss interests, another reason for the relative leniency of the sentences was that our counsel referred openly to the fact that the Swiss federal police and Swiss Counter-intelligence had in the persons of Inspector Knecht and Colonel Masson been in close touch with the Gestapo. This charge on the part of the defence was never officially rebutted.

For a number of years after the war I had no means of finding out what had happened to my former colleagues. Since then, however, I have been able to discover a certain amount—more about some than about others.

'Edouard', 'Maude', and 'Rosa' are, as far as I am aware, alive and well in Switzerland, the country of their birth.

'Pakbo' headed the Social Democratic party's information office (known as INSA during the war) for a while; in 1947 he became president of the Association of Journalists Accredited to the Swiss Government; and in 1956 he was appointed press secretary to the Swiss Broadcasting Company, retiring in 1964 on grounds of age. He is now (1971) about seventy, still active, and he has been elected to serve as a magistrate.

I have not seen him for more than twenty-five years, but I did hear that he appeared on Swiss television in 1966 and talked about the work of our group and the part he played in it. The occasion was the publication of Accoce and Quet's sensationally entitled *La Guerre a été gagné en Suisse* ('The war was won in Switzerland'), to which Swiss television devoted a 'Roundtable' programme on 15 May 1966. Those who took part were—in addition to Pünter—Matt, then editor of the *Weltwoche,* Hausamann, the ex-chief of the 'Buro Ha', the war historian Wilhelm von Schramm, and a friend of Roessler's named Schnieper. Pünter also talked about the book, as he did in an interview that appeared in the Geneva newspaper *La Suisse* some eighteen months later and in which he fulminated against the French authors' 'phenomenal ignorance'.*

But Pünter had already spilled ink about us ten years before this in the lengthy appendix that accompanied the second edition (1957) of W.F. Flicke's *Agenten funken nach Moskau.* Curious that a self-styled 'socialist', who had worked for Soviet Intelligence for what he claimed to be ideological reasons, should have seen fit to appear in print between the same covers as a dyed-in-the-wool Nazi ex-counter-intelligence officer. Any comment on my part would seem to be superfluous. Nor do I propose to waste any words on Pünter's memoirs, which appeared in 1967 under the absurdly

**La Suisse,* 18 November 1967.

hepped-up title *Der Anschluss fand nicht statt: Bericht des Geheimagenten Pakbo* ('The *Anschluss* that wasn't: secret agent Pakbo reports').

Incidentally Drago Arsenijevič, whose book I have quoted before, rightly raises the question of why the Swiss police left Otto Pünter unmolested. According to this author Pünter admitted freely that he had been left in peace 'because he often did the police a favour'.*

Another survivor is Paul Böttcher, until recently deputy editor of the famous *Leipziger Volkszeitung*, the organ of the German Democratic Republic's Socialist Unity party.

Other members of our organization are no longer with us. 'Sissy', who had also become a citizen of the German Democratic Republic, ended her days in Berlin in 1973.

Arsenijevič reports that 'Jim' died on 1 April 1956. Having returned to England he opened the still-growing series of books about the Swiss group as early as 1949 with his *Handbook for Spies*. Marc Payot, the Swiss cipher expert and a man no one would describe as harbouring leftist sympathies, writes: 'Foote's book positively teems with inaccuracies and even untruths.'† Von Schramm's opinion is the same: 'His book is a first-person account and not a historical report. He wanted it to sell and so strove for a sensational effect.' Further: 'Foote was decidedly not the sort of source one could draw on unreservedly.'‡ And Gert Buchheit, in his history of the German secret service, writes: 'Foote's book is a mixture of reality and imagination.'**

But worse than all Foote's sensation-seeking was his political *volte-face* and his utter repudiation of the work he had done during the war. He sank back into the swamp of petty-bourgeois existence from which, fired by a momentous task, he had been able for a while to free himself. His character was marked by an inner contradiction that his betrayal finally sealed.

'Lucy', too, is dead. The man who had been one of Himmler's biggest headaches was buried on 12 December 1958 in Kriens, near Luzern, the place where he had spent so many of his emigrant years

*See Drago Arsenijevič, *Genève appelle Moscou*, pp. 181 ff.

†See his appendix to Otto Pünter, *Guerre secrète en pays neutre*, p. 259.

‡ Wilhelm von Schramm, *Verrat im Zweiten Weltkrieg*, pp. 25, 146.

**Gert Buchheit, *Der deutsche Geheimdienst*, p. 338.

doing, together with his Berlin friends, everything in his power to bring about the collapse of the National-Socialist war machine.

Rudolf Roessler's secret was probably buried with him, though there is a version according to which before his death he told the son of his Swiss friend Schnieper who the officers were who had passed him such exceptionally valuable information direct from the Wehrmacht high command. Roessler allegedly made it a condition of telling him that Schnieper's son should not publish the officers' names for another twenty years. He certainly had reason enough to fear for his friends' lives: the Nazis would undoubtedly have taken their revenge. Fate willed otherwise, however, and a year after Roessler's death the young man to whom he had entrusted his secret died in a car crash. One can only speculate as to whether the cause of death really was accidental. Roessler's secret, at any rate, remains unsolved to this day.

Although many Nazi war criminals paid for their misdeeds, the mildness of Walter Schellenberg's punishment was out of all proportion to his crimes against humanity. Schellenberg, as SD chief the author of so many despicable acts directed against other states, escaped the hanging he so richly deserved and succeeded in surviving his boss Himmler.

In 1945, with the days of the Hitler regime already numbered, Schellenberg managed to flee to Sweden, taking with him a large group of Scandinavian men and women whom the Germans had interned at various times. With these he purchased asylum. Later the British had him flown secretly to London. In the hope of purchasing a pardon Schellenberg promised to tell the British Intelligence Service everything they wished to know. He spent three years giving them a great deal of useful information, leaving London only once during that time. That was in January 1946, when he appeared as a witness at the Nuremberg War Crimes Trial. There he testified against a number of Nazi high-ups including his former SD colleague Kaltenbrunner, who was hanged. After the trial the British took him home with them again—allegedly for a cure, the doctors having diagnosed gallstones.

But Schellenberg did not entirely escape punishment, despite the British and Americans taking him under their wing. In the spring of 1949 he was summoned before a United States court martial. He got off lightly, though, receiving a four-year prison term with effect as from 1945. Four years—and he did not even have to serve them!

Accoce and Quet write: 'In view of his deteriorating health the British secured his release. Having no idea where to go, he looked up his one-time opposite number, Masson.... Masson was prepared to help him, but only in secret, because the Swiss authorities might have made a fuss about his doing so. He placed him in the care of his surgeon, Dr Lang, who hid the German somewhere near Romont, half way between Lausanne and Fribourg. The news filtered through after a few months and an order went out for the sick man to be deported immediately....'*

After his deportation Schellenberg settled in a comfortable villa on the shore of Lago Maggiore, just across the Swiss-Italian frontier. There he lived out his days on British money, the British having paid him well for initiating them in the secrets of the German Reich. He died in 1953.

Colonel Masson, the head of Swiss Intelligence, was in the end called to account for the game Schellenberg had induced him to play. The Swiss opened an investigation against him. He was never brought to trial, though; he was pensioned off in the autumn of 1945 and died in 1967.

The so-called 'Red Orchestra Detachment', founded by Himmler at the Fuhrer's insistence to combat the Soviet Union's European intelligence network, came to an inglorious end in August 1944 when the insurgents retook Paris and the detachment's entire staff fled the French capital in disarray. Fearing reprisals, the leaders turned themselves back into civilians and split up in search of asylum. Pannwitz himself apparently enjoys a comfortable petty-bourgeois existence in Stuttgart on a West German government pension, but a great many of his agents were caught and brought to justice.†

A word in conclusion about Helene and myself.

I now live and work in socialist Hungary, the goal for which I joined the Communist party more than half a century ago. In 1955, after a series of protracted and difficult ordeals and after more than

*Pierre Accoce and Pierre Quet, *La Guerre a été gagné en Suisse,* p. 307.

†See Giles Perrault, *L'Orchestre rouge,* pp. 521-43.

thirty-six years spent abroad, I was at last able to return home. Here I have been able to bring to fulfilment many of my academic ambitions in the fields of geography and cartography, ambitions I had dreamed of for decades. The socialist regime of the Hungarian People's Republic offers me as a scientist a solid and magnificent basis for my work. I am only sorry that my seventieth year already lies behind me.

After my ten-year absence I had only a further three with Helene in the new Hungary, to which, already seriously ill, she returned from Paris as soon as she received word of my release. She died on 1 September 1958, aged fifty-eight. Her ashes rest in Budapest, in a monument donated by the Hungarian People's Republic; carved on her gravestone are the words:

FOUNDER MEMBER OF THE GERMAN COMMUNIST PARTY